SCHRIFTENREIHE
MEDIENFORSCHUNG

BAND 81

Mark D. Cole | Christina Etteldorf | Carsten Ullrich

CROSS-BORDER DISSEMINATION OF ONLINE CONTENT

Current and Possible Future Regulation
of the Online Environment with a Focus
on the EU E-Commerce Directive

Landesanstalt für Medien NRW
Sabrina Nennstiel (Leiterin Kommunikation)
Dr. Meike Isenberg (Leiterin Forschung)
Zollhof 2, 40221 Düsseldorf

www.medienanstalt-nrw.de

The Deutsche Nationalbibliothek lists this publication in the
Deutsche Nationalbibliografie; detailed bibliographic data
are available on the Internet at http://dnb.d-nb.de

ISBN   978-3-8487-6501-0 (Print)
          978-3-7489-0643-8 (ePDF)

British Library Cataloguing-in-Publication Data
A catalogue record for this book is available from the British Library.

ISBN   978-3-8487-6501-0 (Print)
          978-3-7489-0643-8 (ePDF)

Library of Congress Cataloging-in-Publication Data
Cole, Mark / Etteldorf, Christina / Ullrich, Carsten
Cross-Border Dissemination of Online Content
Current and Possible Future Regulation of the Online Environment with a Focus on
the EU E-Commerce Directive
Mark D. Cole / Christina Etteldorf / Carsten Ullrich
280 pp.
Includes references.

ISBN   978-3-8487-6501-0 (Print)
          978-3-7489-0643-8 (ePDF)

Onlineversion
Nomos eLibrary

Volumes 1–48 published by VS-Verlag,
volumes 49–80 published by VISTAS Verlag.

Published by Nomos Verlagsgesellschaft, Baden-Baden, Germany 2020.
Printed and bound in Germany.

Preface

Europe ensures both – peace and freedom. Protecting this freedom at the same time means respecting rules based on European core values. It is up to us as independent regulators to enforce our standards of a free media order in Europe.

However, there are currently significant challenges in cross-border enforcement on the Internet. These include, in particular, the enormous duration of the legal procedures and the question of accountability for the cross-border dissemination of illegal and problematic online content. In addition, the uncertainty concerning the jurisdiction between national regulators and the increasing dominance of platforms such as Google, Facebook and Co. as well are part of this complex situation.

Given the obligation to protect fundamental European democratic values, even difficulties in the effective enforcement of rules do not justify not trying to do so. In a nutshell – inactivity is not an option.

In order to ensure a free media order, it is our duty now to define clear responsibilities of all players in this market and to agree on fast and effective procedures between Member States.

The study conducted by the Institute of European Media Law (EMR) on behalf of the State Media Authority NRW is a constructive framework for this – it provides a comprehensive analysis of the EU legal framework as well as the concrete indication of the need for a reform of the E-Commerce Directive.

I thank Prof. Dr. Mark D. Cole and his team for their excellent work and wish you, dear readers, an inspiring lecture.

Dr. Tobias Schmid
Director of the State Media Authority of North Rhine-Westphalia

Summary Table of Contents

Table of Contents

List of Abbreviations

AG	Advocate General
Art.	Article
AVMS	audiovisual media services
AVMSD	Audiovisual Media Services Directive
AVMS-RADAR	AudioVisual Media Services – Regulatory Authorities' Independence and Efficiency Review (study)
BeckOK	Beck Online Kommentar
BEREC	Body of European Regulators for Electronic Communication
B2B	business-to-business
B2C	business-to-consumer
CCHSO	Code of conduct on countering illegal hate speech online
CFR	Charter of Fundamental Rights of the EU
CJEU	Court of Justice of the EU
COD	Ordinary Legislative Procedure and former Co-decision procedure
COM	Communication
CPD	Code of Practice on Disinformation (EU)
C-	Case-
DCMA	Digital Millenium Copyright Act (US)
DG	Directorate-General
DOS	Denial of Service
DPA	Data Protection Authority
DSL	Digital Subscriber Line
DSM Directive	Directive on copyright and related rights in the Digital Single Market
DVBl.	Deutsches Verwaltungsblatt
DöV	Zeitschrift für Öffentliches Recht und Verwaltungswissenschaften
EC	European Community
ECD	e-Commerce Directive

ECHO	Report of the Commission on Ending Childhood Obesity
ECHR	European Convention on Human Rights
ECtHR	European Court of Human Rights
ECU	European Currency Unit
EDPB	European Data Protection Board
EDPL	European Data Protection Law Review
EDPS	European Data Protection Supervisor
EEA	European Economic Area
EEC	European Economic Community
EECC	European Electronic Communications Code
ELJ	European Law Journal
EJIL	European Journal of International Law
EMR	Institute of European Media Law/ Institut für Europäisches Medienrecht
EP	European Parliament
ERGA	European Regulators Group for Audiovisual Media Services
et seq.	et sequens (Latin) / and the following
EU	European Union
EuGRZ	Europäische Grundrechte-Zeitschrift
EuR	Zeitschrift für Europarecht
EuZW	Europäische Zeitschrift für Wirtschaftsrecht
FTC	US Federal Trade Commission
GDPR	General Data Protection Regulation
GewArch	Gewerbearchiv
GRUR	Gewerblicher Rechtsschutz und Urheberrecht
HLEG	High Level Expert Group
ICT	Information and Communications Technology
IMCO	Committee on the Internal Market and Consumer Protection
InfoSoc Directive	Directive on the harmonisation of certain aspects of copyright and related rights in the information society
IP	Intellectual Property
IPRED	Intellectual Property Enforcement Directive
IPRs	Intellectual Property Rights
ISDN	Integrated Services Digital Network
ISO	International Organization for Standardization

ISS	Information Society Services
ISSP	Information Society Service Provider
IT	Information Technology
JHA	Justice and Home Affairs
JIPITEC	Journal of Intellectual Property, Information Technology and Electronic Commerce Law
JuS	Juristische Schulung
K&R	Kommunikation & Recht
lit.	litera (Latin) / letter
LRTK	Lithuanian Radio and Television Commission
MMR	Multimedia und Recht
M&K	Zeitschrift für Medien & Kommunikationswissenschaft
NetzDG	Netzwerkdurchsetzungsgesetz
NJW	Neue Juristische Wochenschrift
NRA(s)	national regulatory authoritie(s)
OJEU	Official Journal of the European Union
OJ C	Official Journal – Information and Notices
OJ L	Official Journal - Legislation
para.	paragraph
P1ECHR	Protocol No. 1 to the ECHR
P2B	Platform-to-Business
SEC	Single European Code
Slg.	Sammlung der Rechtsprechung
SME	small and medium-sized enterprises
SSRN	Social Science Research Network
supra	ut supra / as above
subpara.	subparagraph
SWD	Commission Staff Working Document
TEC	Treaty establishing the European Community
TERREG	Regulation on preventing the dissemination of terrorist content online
TEU	Treaty on European Union
TFEU	Treaty on the Functioning of the European Union
TV	Television
TwFD	Television without Frontiers Directive
URL	Uniform Ressource Locator

UWG	Gesetz gegen den unlauteren Wettbewerb
VAT	value added tax
VoD	Video on Demand
VSP(s)	video-sharing platform(s)
WCT	WIPO Copyright Treaty
WIPO	World Intellectual Property Organization
WP	Working Paper
WTO	World Trade Organization
ZaöRV	Zeitschrift für ausländisches öffentliches Recht und Völkerrecht
ZAW	Zentralverband der deutschen Werbewirtschaft
ZöR	Zeitschrift für öffentliches Recht
ZPEU	Zeitschrift für das Privatrecht der Europäischen Union
ZUM	Zeitschrift für Urheber- und Medienrecht
5G	5th Generation

Executive Summary

English Version

Background of the Study

1. The dissemination of online content across borders is challenging the national and European Union (EU) legal frameworks for monitoring service providers and enforcing the law. Not only the vast amount of, and increasingly easy access to, illegal or harmful content via online service providers raises the question how efficient enforcement can be organised. It is also due to the uncertainty of who is responsible for the content and which party in the process of disseminating content from its production to the reception by the end-user has an active role and could be held liable, a strong call for reconsidering the applicable rules.

2. Phenomena such as easy access to illegal content, content inciting to hatred and terrorist propaganda, but also disinformation, are only examples for a problematic aspect of the possibility for users to create and disseminate content via intermediaries. While there is a strong foundation of both the EU and its Member States on a set of commonly accepted values, to which most prominently the fundamental rights belong, the protection of these values have functioned much better in the "offline world" and during the first phase of wide use of the Internet. With the ever-growing availability of user-generated audiovisual content, which is disseminated outside of more traditional channels that necessitated a provider with editorial responsibility, categories of online services in existing legal provisions are questioned.

3. In order to respond to the changing role of online service providers, namely "platforms", which are addressed in different ways in more recent EU legislation, it is not surprising that the EU has passed several corresponding legislative acts and supporting policy documents as part of the Digital Single Market strategy in the last couple of years. While major changes were introduced for platforms that host audiovisual content both by revising the Audiovisual Media Services Directive and creating the Directive on copyright in the Digital Single Market (DSM), the core piece of legislation for online service providers, the E-Commerce Directive (ECD), remains untouched until now although it dates back to the year 2000. The future Commission has signaled that it will

take up this challenge, and there are signs that it will propose some form of revision or replacing legislative Act (potentially named Digital Services Act).

Aim of the Study

4. Against this background, the present study gives a detailed overview of the overall legal framework which is, or can be, relevant for dealing with the dissemination of online content. It presents the relevant EU legislative acts including those new texts that include potential role models for a revision of the ECD. A special focus is laid on the question of liability for online content in light of the need to clarify what supervisory authorities can do in order to tackle illegal or harmful content and thereby safeguard fundamental values and principles also in the online context. The interpretation of the relevant sections of the ECD by the Court of Justice of the EU (CJEU) is included as well as discussions about whether liability exemptions for different types of information society services (ISS) have to be reconsidered as a result of duty of care standards. Finally, the study identifies areas that need to be resolved either by legislative action or forms of increased cooperation between Member States and competent authorities if an improved enforcement of legal standards in the online context shall be achieved.

Fundamental Rights, Freedoms and Values

5. The basis and framework for any solution are fundamental rights as laid down in the Charter of Fundamental Rights of the EU (CFR), the European Convention on Human Rights of the Council of Europe and national constitutional provisions. These rights feature prominently human dignity, which, according to the CFR, is "inviolable", i.e. needs to be considered as an overarching goal to be protected. They include also the protection of minors on their own behalf. On the other hand freedom of expression (of service users that create content as well as recipients of this content) and rights of the service providers that might be confronted with increased legal obligations are to be considered.

6. Fundamental freedoms are the building stones for the functioning of the single market in the EU. One aspect concerns the right of companies to choose where to establish themselves, thereby falling under the jurisdiction of a specific State. In principle, activities of such entities cannot be stopped by Member States when they cross their borders. This is laid down for goods and services in the Treaties. However,

Member States can impose limitations on the free movements when the measures are justified. If there is specific secondary law applicable, especially in form of harmonisation or coordination of Member State rules, then this question needs to be answered based on the specific legislative act's provisions.

7. In the context of discussing the adequate response to regulating online content dissemination, the fundamental values and goals of the EU are also relevant. These values do not only have theoretical relevance, but actually there is a specific procedure inserted in the Treaties to ensure that the Member States respect them. Where the EU has competence and the States are barred from applying their own rules, the values and goals necessitate that the EU itself acts in order to enable the States when applying these rules to achieve the values and goals. Consequently, the EU has passed numerous legislative acts that foster the functioning of the single market by harmonising Member States' laws and creating rules that establish a level approach in the States. This holds true also for the media and online sector, whilst regulation in these fields needs to consider that impacting the fundamental right of free speech or the shape of the media market needs to be cautious in respecting the Member States' reserved competences especially in light of their cultures and identities.

Relevant EU Legislative Acts for Online Services

8. The ECD is a horizontally applicable ruleset for ISS. It established a minimum harmonisation approach that focused on a closely circumscribed field of coordinated activities and a relatively strictly applied country-of-origin principle. At the time, the focus was on providing predictable and simple rules for the emerging Internet economy and guaranteeing the application of single market principles. Where derogations existed, they were closely defined and aligned with the exemptions provided by the EU Treaties. Other than the ECD from 2000, for the online sector recent revisions to existing laws or creation of new ones have brought significant changes, such as the AVMSD.

9. The AVMSD is the cornerstone for the distribution of (linear and non-linear) audiovisual content since its predecessor was created in 1989. It creates a single market legal framework allowing for the dissemination of audiovisual content across the EU. The foundational country-of-origin principle ensures that there is in principle only one control of the provider by the Member State under whose jurisdiction it operates; consequently the content flows freely. The agreement of minimum

21

conditions applying to all audiovisual media service providers in the Directive is aimed at assuring that only content legal in that sense is available. The possibility of derogating from the country-of-origin principle and the prohibition of circumvention enable the receiving Member States to react to content from non-domestic providers. The basic principles of the AVMSD have been maintained throughout, but it has been revised once every decade and adapted to new social and technological developments, particularly in the digital environment. The 2018 reform has strengthened the rules on hate speech, protection of minors and advertising regulation and responded to changes in the audiovisual media landscape by including video-sharing platform services in its scope.

10. The legal framework of data protection law is relevant in connection with the cross-border dissemination of online content not only because data processing is omnipresent in online services, but also because the EU rules for this field include technical aspects in the rules and, in some cases, take a transnational approach. The General Data Protection Regulation (GDPR) establishes the marketplace principle by linking its scope to the legitimate interests of the data subjects and thereby giving domestic authorities the possibility to address even non-EU providers in certain cases. The detailed rules on structure, competencies and powers of the supervisory authorities in the GDPR can also be used for consideration and evaluation of a new, more harmonising regulatory approach at EU level in a digital environment.

11. For intellectual property rights the first relevant Directives impacted the role of ISS, e.g. by introducing certain injunction possibilities against them, but left the ECD liability rules untouched at least in the wording of the Directive. The CJEU had to deal with defining the limits of what obligations could be imposed on providers in order to safeguard author's rights. Essentially, this led to an expansion of the obligations that the providers might be asked to comply with. The new DSM Directive of 2019 is noteworthy not only for the creation of a specific definition of "online content-sharing service provider", which refers to different criteria than existing comparable provisions in other EU legislative acts, but mainly for introducing a completely new category of obligations for such providers.

12. The Platform-to-Business Regulation has a wide scope of application, even though not in the relation to consumers. It is relevant because certain information obligations – creating increased transparency – are imposed on these platforms. In doing so, the question of passiveness of

such platforms regarding the content disseminated may have to be answered in a new way. The Proposal for a Regulation on tackling terrorist content online – although the outcome of the legislative procedure is not yet clear – is specifically aimed at hosting service providers and introduces the obligation for certain proactive (or: specific) measures which clarify what an expeditious removal of content is, but it also relies explicitly on a duty of care standard. Even though the position of the European Parliament essentially lowered the strictness of measures that the Commission has proposed, the responsibility of these platforms for user-generated content (of this specific type) will change with the Regulation if it is adopted.

13. The "hard" EU legal instruments as displayed above are supplemented by "soft" EU coordination, support and supplementary measures, which nevertheless are highly important and can represent (potentially) a first step towards new rules. With increased relevance in the area of online content, the EU has addressed above all the areas of protection of minors, human dignity, hate speech and disinformation online. By issuing recommendations, setting up High Level Groups and developing and publishing codes of conduct and best practices, a framework is created here – with the active participation of stakeholders – which is regularly legally non-binding but promotes the effectiveness of achieving the objectives pursued and promotes the establishment of minimum standards. Furthermore, the principles and best practices found in this framework, which often also involve non-EU, in particular US-American, stakeholders, make it possible to identify necessary and possible legislative measures.

Significance of the E-Commerce Directive and Challenges in Its Application

14. The ECD has no explicit extraterritorial scope. Member States are free to regulate activities of ISS providers established outside the EU as the country-of-origin principle only relates to providers established in the EU. Although the definition of ISS providers has been clarified and refined by the CJEU, the emergence of new online-platform business models, namely in the so-called sharing economy, challenges the boundaries of the application of the ECD. This is especially the case concerning the protections for intermediary service providers, defined in Art. 12–15. The premise of wide-reaching protections for passive hosts as long as they do not have any actual knowledge of illegal content or activity has been consistently questioned and reinterpreted by

courts. This is a reflection of the dramatic change in the online intermediary ecosystem over the last 15 years. The rise of Web 2.0 interactivity has meant that most intermediaries have moved away from being simple hosts. They are now interactive content management platforms where the exploitation of user data and network effects are at the centre of the business model. The increasing diversity of business models questions the rather simplistic categorisation of today's platforms as "hosting providers".

15. The unabated occurrence and rise of illegal content and activity promulgated through these platforms have thrown doubts on whether liability protections that were conceived in a different technological and socio-economic context still can be valid today. The problem of the current liability framework for intermediaries lies first with the condition of neutrality. Secondly, determining actual knowledge has remained problematic, especially in the absence of any more formalised notice requirements and with the unclarity of the protection for "Good Samaritan" efforts by intermediaries. Thirdly, case law has also exposed the technological tension between Art. 14 and 15 ECD, which on the one hand allow for specific infringement prevention injunctions but prohibit general monitoring obligations on the other.

16. New solutions to these problems see a move away from liability immunities to formulating explicit responsibilities for these new online platforms. In its case law the CJEU has tried to come up with some concepts such as that of the diligent economic operator. One answer would see the creation of duties of care being imposed on online platforms in the fight against illegal content. Duties of care could take account of the increasingly active role of platforms in the management and dissemination of third-party content. Specific preventive duties, following a risk-based approach, would be tied to clearly defined reactive obligations of notice and takedown and transparency reporting.

17. Liability and more generally provisions creating responsibility obligations for providers are laid down in new legislative acts of the EU for new actors. In the revised AVMSD, video-sharing platform providers are now within the scope of application, but the obligations imposed on them are subject to leaving untouched the liability exemptions of the ECD. However, the obligations imposed on these service providers actually necessitate apprehending a much more active role as the platform has to help ensuring that its users comply with applicable rules. Having to undertake ex-ante risk assessments and depending on the outcome concerning the potential for harm, the provider has to imple-

ment preventive measures without which the platform is assumed to fall short of its obligations.

18. Although limited to the context of intellectual property rights, the DSM Directive departs from the mere referral to the liability provisions of the ECD and introduces a significant obligation for online content-sharing service provider, which seems to be a consequence of the CJEU jurisprudence on the right of communication to the public. It creates an exception to the safe-harbour exemptions for host service providers under the ECD and requires an active role of the platform providers to obtain authorisation for the dissemination of copyrighted content or – in the absence of such – the prevention of availability of the content. Irrespective of clauses limiting the liability for certain platforms and making it conditional, this is a clear change in approach to the role of platforms in EU legislation. It could also lead to different types of liability of one provider for the same content if it violates not only copyright but also other rights.

19. Beyond the copyright context there is a number of other legislative acts of the EU that impact the liability rules of the ECD by creating increased duty-of-care expectations or other obligations vis-à-vis certain online service providers, namely certain types of platforms. These are expected to comply with professional due-diligence requirements if consumer protection requires this. Even though the platforms concerned are not mainly dealing with dissemination of online content, it is a strong indicator of how generally the liability exemptions of the ECD are being limited by other sectorial legislation. This holds especially true for the currently debated Proposal for a Regulation on tackling terrorist content online: as it appears now, at least certain types of increased obligations to monitor will be introduced if a platform has been repeatedly used for dissemination of such illegal content.

Conclusions

20. Based on these findings, some conclusions on the way forward can be drawn. The difficulties in applying a ruleset designed two decades ago for a completely different Internet environment have become obvious. The actors have changed and the role of platforms in dissemination of online content has become dominant. First legislative steps reflecting this new setup have been enacted, whereas there are clear differences in the way they relate to the liability exemptions under the ECD. Not only have new categories of ISS been introduced, for some of them specific obligations are now expected. Partly these new rules rely on

co-regulatory approaches and involve the reliance on technical solutions to prove compliance. Other legislative solutions even in form of Regulations strike a balance between harmonising standards and more importantly institutional cooperation between competent Member States' bodies while allowing to respect differing traditions in the States when applying the rules.

21. In order to avoid a further fragmentation of the rules applicable to different types of online service providers and having to introduce new categories of service providers depending on the further development of the online sector, the EU has the possibility to replace the existing cross-sectorial approach in form of the ECD by a new horizontally applicable act concerning all types of "information society services". In that case it will not only be necessary to identify whether content disseminators need to be treated in a specific manner as they have – due to their contribution to using the freedom of expression of users, but also because of the potential for serious and permanent harm in case of illegal content due to its fast and wide spreading – a different role in the online environment than a platform for selling goods; it will also be necessary to agree on new criteria to define providers. A different avenue could be to amend the existing ECD in a way that it clarifies the conditions under which liability exemptions do not apply and what type of providers are included in the scope.

22. Should no legislative clarification be achieved in the near future, competent authorities will have to apply existing rules also to cross-border dissemination of content in a more proactive manner even if it may not seem clear from the outset whether, for example, a targeted provider may be able to claim a liability exemption. In light of the need for an efficient protection of fundamental rights and values also in the online context, inactivity is no option. Based on the obligation to protect fundamental rights, typically provided for in national constitutional provisions, and public interest goals – which are also the underlying values of the EU –, even difficulties in achieving an effective enforcement of rules do not justify refraining from attempting at it. This holds especially true if – as is the case for online content dissemination – there is a policy conclusion that action is necessary.

23. In light of the difficulties of enforcement not least due to uncertainties about the role of service providers and the cross-border dimension, regulation should attempt at including the concerned industry in the enforcement process as much as possible. Increasingly, EU legislative instruments introduce themselves, or suggest Member States to rely

on, co-regulation approaches in order to first address the parties concerned by obligations in the regulation to be active themselves, secondly to be able to rely on the development of industry standards and thirdly to allow a regulatory approach that has a less infringing nature on fundamental rights. Typically, such co-regulatory approaches involve the creation of Codes of Conduct. Here, and more generally speaking, it is necessary to point out that co-regulation necessitates the possibility of action by regulatory authorities if compliance is not achieved via the industry approach as well as an involvement in the process of creating such "rules".

24. Two main challenges remain to be resolved, a substantive and a procedural question concerning which body is in charge of enforcing rules. The ECD, as well as the AVMSD, rely on the country-of-origin principle that assigns monitoring and supervision duties to the Member State that has jurisdiction over the provider, normally via an establishment. However, this principle does not apply unlimited: both rulesets foresee exceptional derogations from the principle in case of potential damage to overriding public interest goals due to a lack of enforcement in the origin state. In that case, the marketplace of the service can be trigger for a regulatory action. The conditions for such subsidiary competence as well as the procedures introduced in both Directives are very strict and entail lengthy timelines, as it was regarded necessary to shield the country-of-origin principle. The nature of online content typically being available until removed calls for solutions with which more speedily access to illegal and harmful content can be stopped. It is conceivable to maintain the country-of-origin principle but allowing for a marketplace intervention where necessary by either simplifying the procedures or explicitly defining the cases in which regulatory bodies not belonging to the home country can take action.

25. The second challenge concerns the institutional setup. There need to be clear assignments of competencies to bodies in charge of monitoring and supervising online service providers. Beyond law enforcement agencies that are in charge of investigating and prosecuting criminal charges, regulatory authorities need to be able to assume the role of dealing with illegal content. Because of the danger of damaging freedom of expression if there is a direct state influence in this process, independent regulators are best placed to take over this role. Accordingly, in most Member States of the EU regulators that traditionally dealt with audiovisual content in the linear dissemination of content also have been given competence for the online dissemination. Regula-

tory bodies should have clearly assigned tasks that include their role in co-regulation as well as being sufficiently equipped, e.g. with sanctioning powers. Moreover, in order to make cross-border monitoring efficient, some form of cooperation between national regulatory authorities in the EU is necessary. Within such cooperation "community standards" could be developed concerning an agreement on what is to be regarded as illegal and harmful and what type of action should regularly be taken by the national competent authority. The cooperation mechanisms should allow for rapid response in case they are triggered.

Deutsche Fassung

Hintergrund der Studie

1. Die grenzüberschreitende Verbreitung von Online-Inhalten stellt den nationalen und den Rechtsrahmen der Europäischen Union (EU) zur Überwachung von und Rechtsdurchsetzung gegenüber Diensteanbietern vor große Herausforderungen. Nicht nur die Vielzahl an und der immer einfachere Zugang zu illegalen oder schädigenden Inhalten über Online-Dienstleister stellen die Frage, wie eine effiziente Rechtsdurchsetzung organisiert werden kann. Auch die Unsicherheit darüber, wer für einen Inhalt verantwortlich ist und welche Beteiligten bei der Verbreitung von Inhalten von ihrer Produktion bis hin zum Empfang beim Endnutzer eine aktive Rolle spielen und daher haftbar gemacht werden können, hat dazu geführt, dass Forderungen nach einer Überprüfung des geltenden anwendbaren Rechtsrahmens lauter geworden sind.

2. Phänomene wie der einfache Zugang zu illegalen oder zu Hass aufstachelnden Inhalten, terroristische Propaganda, aber auch Desinformation sind nur Beispiele für Probleme, die aus der Möglichkeit für Nutzer, Inhalte über Intermediäre zu erstellen und zu verbreiten, resultieren. Sowohl die EU als auch ihre Mitgliedstaaten sind auf ein starkes Fundament aus allgemein anerkannten Werten gestützt, zu denen vor allem die Grundrechte gehören. Der Schutz dieser Werte in der „Offline-Welt" und in der ersten Phase der breiten Nutzung des Internets hat viel besser funktioniert. Mit der ständig wachsenden Verfügbarkeit von nutzergenerierten audiovisuellen Inhalten, die außerhalb der traditionelleren Kanäle verbreitet werden, welche einen Anbieter mit redaktioneller Verantwortung erforderten, wird die Kategorisierung von Online-Diensten in den bestehenden Rechtsvorschriften in Frage gestellt.

3. Um der sich wandelnden Rolle der Online-Dienstleister, namentlich der „Plattformen", die in unterschiedlicher Weise von neueren EU-Rechtsvorschriften adressiert werden, gerecht zu werden, ist es nicht verwunderlich, dass die EU in den letzten Jahren mehrere entsprechende Rechtsakte verabschiedet und ergänzende Strategiepapiere als Teil ihrer Strategie für einen Digitalen Binnenmarkt veröffentlicht hat. Während für Plattformen, die audiovisuelle Inhalte hosten, sowohl durch die Überarbeitung der Richtlinie über audiovisuelle Mediendienste (AVMD-RL) als auch durch die Schaffung der Richtlinie über das Urheberrecht im digitalen Binnenmarkt (DSM-RL) als Kernelemente des gesetzgeberischen Rahmens für Online-Dienstleister wesent-

liche Änderungen vorgenommen wurden, bleibt die E-Commerce-Richtlinie (ECRL) bis heute unberührt, obwohl sie bereits aus dem Jahr 2000 stammt. Die künftige Kommission hat signalisiert, dass sie sich dieser Herausforderung stellen wird, und es gibt Anzeichen dafür, dass sie in bestimmter Form eine Überarbeitung oder Ersetzung der ECRL (möglicherweise „Digital Services Act" genannt) vorschlagen wird.

Ziel der Studie

4. Vor diesem Hintergrund gibt die vorliegende Studie einen detaillierten Überblick über den allgemeinen Rechtsrahmen, der für den Umgang mit der Verbreitung von Online-Inhalten relevant ist oder sein kann. Sie stellt die einschlägigen EU-Rechtsakte vor, einschließlich neuerer Texte, die potenziell als Vorbilder bei einer Überarbeitung der ECRL dienen können. Ein besonderer Schwerpunkt liegt auf der Frage nach der Verantwortlichkeit für Online-Inhalte, da geklärt werden muss, welche Maßnahmen die Aufsichtsbehörden ergreifen können, um illegale oder schädigende Inhalte zu bekämpfen und damit grundsätzliche Werte und Prinzipien auch im Online-Kontext zu schützen. Dabei wird die Auslegung der relevanten Abschnitte der ECRL durch den Europäischen Gerichtshof (EuGH) ebenso einbezogen wie Diskussionen darüber, ob die bestehenden Haftungsbefreiungen für verschiedene Arten von Diensten der Informationsgesellschaft als Ergebnis eines „duty of care" (Sorgfalts)-Standards überdacht werden müssen. Schließlich identifiziert die Studie Bereiche, die entweder durch gesetzgeberische Maßnahmen oder durch Formen der verstärkten Zusammenarbeit zwischen den Mitgliedstaaten und den zuständigen Behörden Lösungen zugeführt werden müssen, wenn eine bessere Durchsetzung der Rechtsnormen im Online-Kontext erreicht werden soll.

Grundrechte, Grundfreiheiten und Werte

5. Grundlage und Rahmen für jedwede angestrebte Lösung sind die Grundrechte, wie sie in der Charta der Grundrechte der EU (GRC), der Europäischen Menschenrechtskonvention des Europarates und den nationalen Verfassungsbestimmungen manifestiert sind. Dazu zählt vor allem die Menschenwürde, die nach der GRC „unantastbar" ist und damit als tragendes und zu schützendes Prinzip zu berücksichtigen ist. Die Rechte umfassen auch den Schutz Minderjähriger auch als eigene Rechtsposition dieser Gruppe. Andererseits sind die Meinungsfreiheit

(von Dienstenutzern, die Inhalte erstellen, sowie von Empfängern dieser Inhalte) und die Rechte der Diensteanbieter selbst, die mit erhöhten rechtlichen Verpflichtungen konfrontiert sein könnten, zu berücksichtigen.

6. Die Grundfreiheiten sind die Bausteine für das Funktionieren des Binnenmarkts in der EU. Ein Aspekt betrifft dabei das Recht der Unternehmen, selbst zu wählen, wo sie sich niederlassen und dadurch in die Zuständigkeit eines bestimmten Staates fallen. Einen anderen Aspekt betrifft die Regel, dass Unternehmen grundsätzlich nicht an der Ausführung grenzüberschreitender Tätigkeiten durch die Mitgliedstaaten gehindert werden können. Dies ist für den Handel mit Waren und das Anbieten von Dienstleistungen in den Verträgen festgelegt. Die Mitgliedstaaten können jedoch den freien Verkehr einschränken, wenn die jeweils ergriffenen Maßnahmen gerechtfertigt sind. Wenn spezifisches Sekundärrecht anwendbar ist, insbesondere die entsprechenden Vorschriften der Mitgliedstaaten auf EU-Ebene koordiniert oder harmonisiert worden sind, dann muss diese Frage auf der Grundlage der Bestimmungen des spezifischen Rechtsakts beantwortet werden.

7. Relevant auch im Zusammenhang mit der Diskussion über angemessene Reaktionen auf die Regulierung der Verbreitung von Online-Inhalten sind die grundlegenden Werte und Ziele der EU. Diese Werte haben nicht nur theoretische Relevanz, sondern die Verträge enthalten ein spezifisches Verfahren, das ihre Einhaltung durch die Mitgliedstaaten sicherstellt. Wenn die EU über Kompetenzen verfügt und die Mitgliedstaaten daher an der Anwendung ihrer eigenen Regeln gehindert sind, erfordern es diese Werte und Ziele, dass die EU selbst so handelt, dass es den Staaten bei der Anwendung dieser Regeln möglich ist, die Ziele und Werte zu erreichen. Entsprechend hat die EU zahlreiche Rechtsakte erlassen, die das Funktionieren des Binnenmarkts fördern, indem sie die Rechtsvorschriften der Mitgliedstaaten harmonisieren und damit einen einheitlichen Ansatz in den Staaten festlegen. Dies gilt auch für den Medien- und Onlinesektor, wobei die Regulierung in diesen Bereichen berücksichtigen muss, dass bei Auswirkungen auf das Grundrecht auf freie Meinungsäußerung und bei der Gestaltung des Medienmarktes vor dem Hintergrund der Kompetenzverteilung insbesondere im Bereich der Kultur und nationalen Identität Zurückhaltung geboten ist.

Relevante Rechtsakte der EU für Online-Dienste

8. Die ECRL ist ein horizontal anwendbares Regelungsinstrument für Dienste der Informationsgesellschaft. Sie etablierte einen Mindestharmonisierungsansatz, der sich auf einen eng begrenzten Bereich koordinierter Tätigkeiten und ein relativ streng angewandtes Herkunftslandprinzip konzentrierte. Bei Schaffung der Richtlinie lag der Schwerpunkt auf der Bereitstellung vorhersehbarer und einfacher Regeln für die aufstrebende Internetwirtschaft und der Gewährleistung der Anwendung der Binnenmarktgrundsätze. Soweit Ausnahmeregelungen bestanden, wurden sie eng und entlang der in den EU-Verträgen vorgesehenen Ausnahmen definiert. Anders als die ECRL von 2000, haben die jüngsten Überarbeitungen bestehender oder die Schaffung neuer Gesetze für den Online-Bereich erhebliche Änderungen mit sich gebracht, wie beispielsweise die AVMD-RL zeigt.

9. Die AVMD-RL ist der Eckpfeiler für die Verbreitung von (linearen und non-linearen) audiovisuellen Inhalten seit der Vorgänger-Richtlinie aus dem Jahr 1989. Sie etabliert einen Rechtsrahmen für den Binnenmarkt, der die Verbreitung audiovisueller Inhalte in der gesamten EU ermöglicht. Das fundamentale Herkunftslandprinzip stellt dabei sicher, dass eine Kontrolle von Anbietern grundsätzlich nur durch den Mitgliedstaat erfolgt, unter dessen Hoheitsgewalt der Anbieter tätig ist, wodurch Inhalte frei verbreitet werden können. Die Vereinbarung von Mindestbedingungen, die für alle Anbieter audiovisueller Mediendienste im Rahmen der Richtlinie gelten, zielt darauf ab, sicherzustellen, dass nur in diesem Sinne legale Inhalte verfügbar sind. Die Möglichkeit, vom Herkunftslandprinzip abzuweichen und das Umgehungsverbot ermöglichen es den Empfangsmitgliedstaaten, auf Inhalte von ausländischen Anbietern zu reagieren. Die Grundprinzipien der AVMD-RL wurden beibehalten, aber die Richtlinie einmal pro Jahrzehnt überarbeitet und an neue gesellschaftliche und technologische Entwicklungen, insbesondere im digitalen Umfeld, angepasst. Die Reform von 2018 hat dabei die Regeln für die Aufstachelung zu Hass, über den Jugendschutz und die Werbevorschriften verschärft und auf Veränderungen in der audiovisuellen Medienlandschaft reagiert, indem sie Video-Sharing-Plattform-Dienste in den Anwendungsbereich einbezogen hat.

10. Der Rechtsrahmen des Datenschutzrechts ist demgegenüber im Zusammenhang mit der grenzüberschreitenden Verbreitung von Online-Inhalten nicht nur deshalb relevant, weil Datenverarbeitungsprozesse in Online-Diensten allgegenwärtig sind, sondern auch, weil die

EU-Vorschriften für diesen Bereich auch technische Aspekte beinhalten und in einigen Fällen einen transnationalen Ansatz verfolgen. Die Datenschutz-Grundverordnung (DS-GVO) legt das Marktortprinzip fest, indem sie in Bezug auf ihren Anwendungsbereich an die berechtigten Interessen der von der Datenverarbeitung Betroffenen anknüpft und damit den nationalen Behörden die Möglichkeit eröffnet, in bestimmten Fällen sogar Nicht-EU-Anbieter zu adressieren. Die detaillierten Regeln für Struktur, Kompetenzen und Befugnisse der Aufsichtsbehörden in der DS-GVO können zudem zur Betrachtung und Bewertung eines neuartigen, stärker harmonisierenden Regulierungsansatzes auf EU-Ebene in einem digitalen Umfeld als Vergleich herangezogen werden.

11. Für die Rechte am geistigen Eigentum wirkten sich die ersten einschlägigen Richtlinien auf die Rolle der Dienste der Informationsgesellschaft aus, z.B. durch die Einführung bestimmter Möglichkeiten für Unterlassungsverfügungen, ließen aber die Haftungsregeln der ECRL zumindest ihrem Wortlaut nach unberührt. Der EuGH hatte sich mit der Festlegung der Grenzen zu befassen, welche Verpflichtungen den Anbietern auferlegt werden können, um die Urheberrechte zu wahren. Dies führte im Wesentlichen zu einer Ausweitung der Verpflichtungen, die von den Anbietern eingefordert werden können. Die neue DSM-RL von 2019 ist vor diesem Hintergrund nicht nur in Bezug auf die Schaffung einer spezifischen Definition des Begriffs „Diensteanbieter für das Teilen von Online-Inhalten" bemerkenswert, die sich auf andere Kriterien als bestehende vergleichbare Bestimmungen in anderen EU-Rechtsakten bezieht, sondern vor allem wegen der Einführung einer völlig neuen Kategorie von Verpflichtungen für solche Anbieter.

12. Die Verordnung zur Förderung von Fairness und Transparenz für gewerbliche Nutzer von Online-Vermittlungsdiensten (auch P2B-Verordnung genannt) hat einen breiten Anwendungsbereich, wenn auch nicht in Bezug auf Verbraucher. Sie ist relevant, weil den dort regulierten Plattformen bestimmte Informationspflichten – die zu mehr Transparenz führen – auferlegt werden. Dabei muss die Frage der Passivität solcher Plattformen gegenüber den über sie verbreiteten Inhalten möglicherweise auf neue Art beantwortet werden. Der Vorschlag für eine Verordnung zur Verhinderung der Verbreitung terroristischer Online-Inhalte – obwohl das Ergebnis des Gesetzgebungsverfahrens noch nicht klar ist – richtet sich speziell an Hosting-Diensteanbieter und führt die Verpflichtung zu bestimmten proaktiven (oder: spezifi-

schen) Maßnahmen ein. Sie stellt klar, was eine unverzügliche Entfernung von Inhalten ist und bezieht sich auch ausdrücklich auf einen „duty of care"(Sorgfaltspflicht)-Standard. Auch wenn der Standpunkt des Parlaments im Wesentlichen die von der Kommission vorgeschlagenen strengeren Maßnahmen verringert hat, wird sich die Verantwortung dieser Plattformen für nutzergenerierte Inhalte (dieser speziellen Art) mit der Verordnung ändern, wenn sie angenommen wird.

13. Diese zuvor dargestellten „harten" Rechtsinstrumente der EU werden ergänzt durch „weiche" Koordinations-, Unterstützungs- und Ergänzungsmaßnahmen der EU, die nichtsdestotrotz von großer Bedeutung sind und einen (potenziell) ersten Schritt zur Schaffung neuer Regeln darstellen können. Mit zunehmender Relevanz im Bereich der Online-Inhalte, hat sich die EU vor allem mit den Bereichen Jugendschutz, Menschenwürde, Hassreden und Desinformation im Internet befasst. Durch die Verabschiedung von Empfehlungen, die Einrichtung von hochrangigen Expertengruppen und die Entwicklung und Veröffentlichung von Verhaltenskodizes und „Best Practices" wird hier – in der Regel unter aktiver Beteiligung der jeweils betroffenen Interessenvertreter – ein Rahmen geschaffen, der regelmäßig rechtlich nicht bindend ist, aber die Wirksamkeit der Erreichung der verfolgten Ziele fördert und die Festlegung von Mindeststandards vorantreibt. Darüber hinaus ermöglichen die in diesem Rahmen gefundenen Grundsätze und Best Practices, die oft auch Nicht-EU-, insbesondere US-amerikanische Interessenvertreter, einbeziehen, das Ermitteln notwendiger und möglicher gesetzgeberischer Maßnahmen.

Bedeutung der E-Commerce-Richtlinie und Herausforderungen bei ihrer Anwendung

14. Die ECRL hat nicht explizit einen extraterritorialen Anwendungsbereich. Den Mitgliedstaaten steht es frei, die Tätigkeiten von Diensten der Informationsgesellschaft mit Sitz außerhalb der EU zu regeln, da sich das Herkunftslandprinzip nur auf Anbieter mit Sitz in der EU bezieht. Obwohl die Definition der Anbieter von Diensten der Informationsgesellschaft vom EuGH geklärt und verfeinert wurde, stellt die Entstehung neuer Geschäftsmodelle für Online-Plattformen, namentlich in der sogenannten Sharing-Economy, die Beurteilung der Grenzen des Anwendungsbereichs vor Herausforderungen. Dies gilt insbesondere für die Haftungsprivilegierung der in den Artikeln 12-15 definierten Intermediäre. Die Prämisse eines weitreichenden Schutzes für passive Hosts, solange sie keine tatsächliche Kenntnis von illegalen In-

halten oder Aktivitäten haben, wurde von den Gerichten wiederholt hinterfragt und neu interpretiert. Dies zeichnet ein Spiegelbild der dramatischen Veränderung innerhalb des ökonomischen Umfelds der Intermediäre in den letzten 15 Jahren. Der Anstieg der Web 2.0-Interaktivität hat dazu geführt, dass die meisten Vermittler sich von einer reinen Hosting-Tätigkeit entfernt haben. Sie sind heute interaktive Content Management-Plattformen, bei denen die Nutzung von Benutzerdaten und Netzwerkeffekten im Mittelpunkt des Geschäftsmodells stehen. Die zunehmende Vielfalt der Geschäftsmodelle stellt die eher vereinfachte Kategorisierung der heutigen Plattformen als „Hosting Provider" in Frage.

15. Das unverminderte Aufkommen und die Zunahme illegaler Inhalte und Aktivitäten, die über diese Plattformen stattfinden, haben Zweifel daran geweckt, ob Haftungserleichterungen, die in einem anderen technologischen und sozioökonomischen Kontext konzipiert wurden, auch heute noch gültig sein können. Das Problem des aktuellen Haftungsrahmens für Intermediäre liegt zunächst in der Annahme der Neutralität. Zweitens ist die Feststellung der tatsächlichen Kenntnis nach wie vor problematisch, insbesondere angesichts fehlender formalisierter Benachrichtigungspflichten und der Unklarheit über den Schutz für „Good Samaritans"-Anstrengungen durch die Intermediäre. Drittens hat die Rechtsprechung auch die technologische Spannung zwischen den Artikeln 14 und 15 ECRL offenbart, die einerseits spezifische Unterlassungsansprüche zur Verhütung von Verstößen zulassen, andererseits aber allgemeine Überwachungsverpflichtungen verbieten.

16. Neue Lösungswege für die dargestellten Problematiken tendieren weg von Haftungsbefreiungen und hin zur Formulierung expliziter Verantwortlichkeiten für diese neuen Online-Plattformen. In seiner Rechtsprechung hat der EuGH versucht, einige Konzepte wie das des „sorgfältigen Wirtschaftsteilnehmers" (due diligent economic operator) zu entwerfen. Ein Lösungsansatz wäre die Schaffung von Sorgfaltspflichten, die Online-Plattformen im Kampf gegen illegale Inhalte auferlegt würden. Sorgfaltspflichten könnten der zunehmend aktiv(er)en Rolle der Plattformen bei der Verwaltung und Verbreitung von Inhalten Dritter Rechnung tragen. Spezifische präventive Pflichten, die einem risikobasierten Ansatz folgen, wären an klar definierte reaktive Verpflichtungen im Bereich des notice-and-take-down-Prinzips und der Transparenz-Berichtspflichten gebunden.

17. Die Haftung und allgemeiner formuliert Normen, die Verantwortlichkeiten für die Anbieter begründen, sind in neuen Rechtsakten der EU

für neue Akteure festgelegt. In der überarbeiteten AVMD-RL sind Anbieter von Video-Sharing-Plattformen nunmehr vom Anwendungsbereich erfasst, aber die ihnen danach auferlegten Verpflichtungen berühren nicht die nach der ECRL bestehenden Haftungsfreistellungen. Die den Dienstleistern auferlegten Verpflichtungen erfordern jedoch eine wesentlich aktivere Rolle, da die Plattform dazu beitragen muss, dass ihre Nutzer die geltenden Regeln einhalten. Der Anbieter muss ex ante-Risikobewertungen durchführen und je nach Ergebnis der Bewertung des Schadenspotenzials vorbeugende Maßnahmen ergreifen, ohne deren Ergreifen zu vermuten ist, dass die Plattform ihren Verpflichtungen nicht nachkommt.

18. Obwohl sie sich auf den Bereich der Rechte an geistigem Eigentum beschränkt, weicht die DSM-RL von der bloßen Verweisung auf die Haftungsbestimmungen der ECRL ab und führt eine signifikante Verpflichtung für Diensteanbieter für das Teilen von Online-Inhalten ein, die Folge der Rechtsprechung des EuGH über das Recht auf öffentliche Zugänglichmachung zu sein scheint. Sie schafft eine Ausnahme von den „safe harbour"-Befreiungen für Hosting-Diensteanbieter im Rahmen der ECRL und erfordert eine aktive Rolle der Plattformanbieter, um die Zustimmung des Berechtigten für die Verbreitung urheberrechtlich geschützter Inhalte zu erhalten oder – bei Fehlen einer solchen – dabei, die Verfügbarkeit der Inhalte für die Öffentlichkeit zu verhindern. Ungeachtet der Klauseln, die die Haftung für bestimmte Plattformen einschränken und sie an Bedingungen knüpfen, ist dies ein deutlicher Wandel im Ansatz der Beurteilung der Rolle der Plattformen im EU-Recht. Dies könnte auch zu unterschiedlichen Arten der Haftung eines Anbieters für denselben Inhalt führen, wenn dieser nicht nur das Urheberrecht, sondern auch andere Rechte verletzt.

19. Über den urheberrechtlichen Kontext hinaus gibt es eine Reihe weiterer Rechtsakte der EU, die sich auf die Haftungsregeln der ECRL auswirken, indem sie erhöhte Sorgfaltspflichten oder andere Verpflichtungen gegenüber bestimmten Online-Dienstleistern, namentlich verschiedenen Arten von Plattformen, schaffen. Von diesen wird erwartet, dass sie den Anforderungen der professionellen Sorgfaltspflichten entsprechen, wenn der Verbraucherschutz dies erfordert. Auch wenn sich die betroffenen Plattformen nicht schwerpunktmäßig mit der Verbreitung von Online-Inhalten befassen, ist dies ein starker Indikator dafür, in was für einer allgemeinen Form die Haftungsbefreiungen der ECRL durch andere sektorale Rechtsvorschriften eingeschränkt werden. Dies gilt insbesondere für den derzeit diskutierten Vorschlag

für eine Verordnung zur Verhinderung der Verbreitung terroristischer Online-Inhalte: Nach derzeitigem Stand werden zumindest bestimmte Arten von erhöhten Überwachungspflichten eingeführt, wenn eine Plattform wiederholt für die Verbreitung solcher illegaler Inhalte genutzt wurde.

Schlussfolgerungen

20. Basierend auf diesen Erkenntnissen können einige Schlussfolgerungen für das weitere Vorgehen gezogen werden. Die Schwierigkeiten bei der Anwendung eines Regelwerks, das vor zwei Jahrzehnten für eine völlig andere Internet-Umgebung entwickelt wurde, sind offensichtlich geworden. Die Akteure haben sich verändert und die Rolle der Plattformen bei der Verbreitung von Online-Inhalten ist dominant geworden. Erste gesetzgeberische Schritte, die diesem Strukturwandel Rechnung tragen, wurden eingeleitet, wobei es deutliche Unterschiede in Bezug auf das Verhältnis zu den Haftungserleichterungen der ECRL gibt. Es wurden nicht nur neue Kategorien von Diensten der Informationsgesellschaft eingeführt, sondern für einige von ihnen gelten nunmehr konkrete Verpflichtungen. Teilweise basieren diese neuen Regeln auf Ko-Regulierungsansätzen und beziehen sich auf technische Lösungen, die die Einhaltung von Vorgaben sicherstellen sollen. Andere legislative Lösungen, auch in Form von Verordnungen, schaffen ein Gleichgewicht zwischen der Harmonisierung der Normen und vor allem der institutionellen Zusammenarbeit zwischen den zuständigen Organen der Mitgliedstaaten, wobei sie es ermöglichen, bei der Anwendung der Regeln auch die unterschiedlichen Traditionen in den Staaten zu respektieren.

21. Um es zu vermeiden, die Fragmentierung der Vorschriften für verschiedene Arten von Online-Dienstleistern zu verstärken und neue Kategorien von Dienstleistern abhängig von der weiteren Entwicklung des Online-Bereichs einführen zu müssen, sollte die EU bestrebt sein, entweder den bestehenden sektorübergreifenden Ansatz in Form der ECRL durch einen neuen horizontal anwendbaren Rechtsakt für alle Arten von „Diensten der Informationsgesellschaft" zu ersetzen. In diesem Fall muss nicht nur festgestellt werden, ob die Verbreiter von Inhalten – nicht nur wegen ihres Beitrags zur Ausübung der Meinungsfreiheit durch ihre Nutzer, sondern auch wegen des Potenzials für schwere und dauerhafte Schäden bei illegalen Inhalten aufgrund ihrer schnellen und flächendeckenden Verbreitung – in einer bestimmten Art und Weise behandelt werden müssen, da sie eine andere Rolle im

Online-Umfeld haben als eine Plattform beispielsweise im Bereich des Verkaufs von Waren, sondern es muss sich auch auf neue Kriterien zur Definition von Anbietern geeinigt werden. Ein anderer Weg könnte darin bestehen, die bestehende ECRL so zu ändern, dass klargestellt wird, unter welchen Bedingungen Haftungsbefreiungen nicht gelten und welche Arten von Anbietern in den Anwendungsbereich einbezogen werden.

22. Sollte in naher Zukunft keine rechtliche Klarstellung erfolgen, müssen die zuständigen Behörden die bestehenden Regeln auch für die grenzüberschreitende Verbreitung von Inhalten proaktiver anwenden, auch wenn es vielleicht nicht von vornherein klar erscheint, ob beispielsweise ein adressierter Anbieter eine Haftungsfreistellung in Anspruch nehmen kann. Angesichts der Notwendigkeit eines effizienten Schutzes der Grundrechte und -werte auch im Online-Kontext ist Inaktivität keine Option. Ausgehend von der Verpflichtung zum Schutz der Grundrechte, die typischerweise in den nationalen Verfassungsbestimmungen vorgesehen ist, und den Zielen von öffentlichem Interesse – die auch den Werten der EU zugrundliegen – rechtfertigen es selbst Schwierigkeiten bei der effektiven Durchsetzung von Regeln nicht, den entsprechenden Versuch nicht zu unternehmen. Dies gilt insbesondere dann, wenn - wie bei der Verbreitung von Online-Inhalten - eine politische Schlussfolgerung gezogen wird, dass Maßnahmen erforderlich sind.

23. Angesichts der Schwierigkeiten bei der Rechtsdurchsetzung, die nicht zuletzt aus Unsicherheiten über die Rolle der Dienstleister und die grenzüberschreitende Dimension resultieren, sollte die Regulierung versuchen, die betroffene Branche so weit wie möglich in den Durchsetzungsprozess einzubeziehen. Zunehmend führen die EU-Rechtssetzungsakte selbst Ko-Regulierungsansätze ein oder empfehlen den Mitgliedstaaten solche Ansätze zu ergreifen, um erstens die von den Verpflichtungen der Regelwerke betroffenen Parteien zu einer aktiven Beteiligung zu bewegen, zweitens auf die Entwicklung von Industriestandards vertrauen zu können und drittens einen Regulierungsansatz zu ermöglichen, der weniger eingriffsintensiv in Bezug auf die Grundrechte ist. Typischerweise beinhalten solche Ko-Regulierungsansätze die Erstellung von Verhaltenskodizes. Hier und generell ist darauf hinzuweisen, dass die Ko-Regulierung die Möglichkeit von Maßnahmen der Regulierungsbehörden notwendigerweise vorsehen muss, wenn die Einhaltung der Regeln nicht über den Branchenansatz

erreicht wird, sowie eine Beteiligung am Prozess der Erstellung solcher „Regeln".

24. Zwei wesentliche Herausforderungen sind noch zu lösen, eine inhaltliche und eine verfahrenstechnische, welche die Frage betreffen, welche Stelle für die Durchsetzung der Vorschriften zuständig ist. Sowohl die ECRL als auch die AVMD-RL stützen sich auf das Herkunftslandprinzip, das dem Staat, der für den Anbieter zuständig ist, Überwachungs- und Kontrollaufgaben zuweist, in der Regel anknüpfend an die Niederlassung des Anbieters. Dieser Grundsatz gilt jedoch nicht uneingeschränkt: beide Regelwerke sehen Ausnahmeregelungen vom Grundsatz vor, wenn aufgrund mangelnder Durchsetzung im Herkunftsstaat übergeordnete Ziele des öffentlichen Interesses möglicherweise beschädigt werden. In diesem Fall kann der Marktort des jeweiligen Dienstes Auslöser für eine regulatorische Maßnahme sein. Die Bedingungen für diese subsidiäre Zuständigkeit sowie die in beiden Richtlinien eingeführten Verfahren sind sehr streng und mit langen Fristen verbunden, da es als notwendig erachtet wurde, das Herkunftslandprinzip zu schützen. Die Natur der Online-Inhalte, die regelmäßig bis zu ihrer Entfernung verfügbar sind, erfordert Lösungen, mit denen der Zugriff auf illegale und schädliche Inhalte schneller unterbunden werden kann. Es ist denkbar, das Herkunftslandprinzip beizubehalten, aber gegebenenfalls eine Anknüpfung an den Marktort zu ermöglichen, indem entweder die Verfahren vereinfacht oder die Fälle, in denen andere als die Regulierungsbehörden des Herkunftslandes tätig werden können, ausdrücklich definiert werden.

25. Die zweite Herausforderung betrifft den institutionellen Aufbau. Es bedarf einer klaren Zuweisung von Kompetenzen an Stellen, die für die Überwachung und Aufsicht von Online-Dienstleistern zuständig sind. Neben den Strafverfolgungsbehörden, die für die Ermittlung und Verfolgung von Straftaten zuständig sind, müssen die Regulierungsbehörden in der Lage sein, diese Rolle bezüglich des Umgangs mit illegalen Inhalten zu übernehmen. Wegen der Gefahr, die Meinungsfreiheit zu beeinträchtigen, wenn es in diesem Prozess einen direkten staatlichen Einfluss gibt, sind unabhängige Regulierungsbehörden am besten vorbereitet, diese Aufgabe zu übernehmen. Dementsprechend wurde in den meisten Mitgliedstaaten der EU jenen Regulierungsbehörden, die sich traditionell mit audiovisuellen Inhalten bei der linearen Verbreitung von Inhalten beschäftigt haben, auch die Kompetenz für die Online-Verbreitung von Inhalten eingeräumt. Die Regulierungsbehörden sollten klar zugewiesene Aufgaben haben, die

auch ihre Rolle bei der Ko-Regulierung umfassen und mit ausreichenden Mitteln ausgestattet sein, etwa mit Sanktionsbefugnissen. Um die grenzüberschreitende Überwachung effizient zu gestalten, bedarf es zudem einer noch auszugestaltenden Zusammenarbeit zwischen den nationalen Regulierungsbehörden in der EU. Im Rahmen einer solchen Zusammenarbeit könnten „Gemeinschaftsnormen" entwickelt werden, die eine Vereinbarung darüber enthalten, was als illegal und schädlich anzusehen ist und welche Art von Maßnahmen regelmäßig von den zuständigen nationalen Behörden zu ergreifen sind. Die Kooperationsmechanismen sollten im Bedarfsfall eine schnelle Reaktion ermöglichen.

1. Background of the Study

1.1. *Online Dissemination of Content*

The Internet can be regarded as mass medium. As such a mass medium, it contains a huge variety of different content, addressed to different audiences by different distributors. With this, the Internet has also become an integral part of other mass media as well as the media supporting industries, namely the advertising sector.[1] More traditional media providers such as broadcasters or the press remain to be content providers in the digital environment but can make use of the infrastructures of other distribution channels in order to make their content accessible to a wider audience. While at the beginning of the "Internet age" they still mainly used the services of Internet access providers or website hosting providers, for example to provide their own blogs or media libraries, and therefore remained distributors themselves, today they increasingly resort to new distributors such as platforms and other intermediaries that distribute third-party content on the basis of their own offerings. The initial advantage is obvious: content can be made available to a larger and also new audience if it is made available on large platforms with large numbers of users. Content producers therefore compete for the attention of users not only with other content providers but also with intermediaries and comparable providers. These users, however, are to a large extent no longer just recipients as they were 20 years ago. Rather, individual users can also slip into the role of content providers using the Internet, for example if they maintain their own blog or distribute content via third parties such as video-sharing platforms or social networks. All that a user needs is basically an Internet-enabled terminal device and a means of access, e.g. by wireless points. So the roles in the media and content dissemination landscape have certainly changed dramatically in the last years.

The Internet with its multitude of possibilities and communication spaces offers room for a variety of different offers. Content is distributed everywhere and is ubiquitously available, e.g. when using VSPs, social networks, blogs, forums, portals or other platforms. Such content can be found via search engines or the search function of platforms; it is often free

---

1 *Ohiagu*, in: Kiabara Journal of Humanities 16(2), 2011, p. 225, 225 et seq.

– at least without payment – and accessible to everyone, including minors, and it can be visual, audio or audiovisual in nature. The type of content is diverse, ranging from current news, general or thematic information, entertainment and education to purely promotional content. A major change that came with the Internet is the constant availability of information, one of the reasons why the "digital age" was originally referred to as the "information age".[2]

One of the more problematic sides of the large amount of information that is provided via the Internet is the false information that is disseminated and which is currently the subject of much legal debate under the heading "online disinformation" in light of the possibilities of influencing public opinion building.[3] Other examples are the strong rise of incitement to hatred, hate speech and other defamatory content, one reason for its increase seemingly being the inherent anonymity of the Internet.[4] Further negative phenomena are terrorist propaganda, which can be disseminated not only in closed networks but also via open platforms such as YouTube or Facebook, copyright piracy, child abuse material[5], and incitement to violence and crime. While some of that content regularly fulfils criminal law provisions, there are other types of content that are only of concern to a certain group of addressees. This refers especially to minors that need a specific protection against content that can be detrimental to their development, such as pornography or depictions of violence. Despite its unsuitability for this group of addressees, such content is nevertheless regularly accessible to everyone via online intermediaries.

These observations apply worldwide. Internet information exchange in principal knows no national borders, and, in particular, there is no need

---

2 Cf., for example, *Kirtiklis*, in: Lingua Posnaniensis 59(1), p. 65, 65 et seq. It was also the terminology used in EU law, e.g. when online services were defined as "information society services" or "harmonisation […] for information society" (title of Directive 2001/29/EC).

3 Cf. on the term and the risks of online disinformation, e.g., Report of the independent High level Group on fake news and online disinformation, A multi-dimensional approach to disinformation, available at https://ec.europa.eu/digital-single-m arket/en/news/final-report-high-level-expert-group-fake-news-and-online-disinforma tion.

4 Cf. on this, e.g., *Banks*, in: International Review of Law, Computers & Technology 24(3), 2010, pp. 233, 233 et seq.

5 In 2015 alone, the UK Internet Watch Foundation identified 68,092 unique URLs containing child sexual abuse content, hosted anywhere in the world; cf. IWF's 2015 Annual Report, available at https://www.iwf.org.uk/about-iwf/news/post/444-iwf-announce-record-reports-of-child-sexual-abuse-online.

for a domestic point of contact to address content to the target audience at that specific location.

Legal rules can offer protection against such problematic content. There are actually rules prohibiting certain types of content. Protective mechanisms can be derived from fundamental rights (on this, cf. Chapter 2.1), in particular concerning the protection of personal rights or intellectual property. Additionally, rules on copyright law, criminal law, audiovisual media services law or data protection law also establish rules of conduct that also apply to the online sector (on this, cf. Chapter 2.4.). Nonetheless, while there is a strong foundation of both the EU and its Member States on a set of commonly accepted values to which most prominently these fundamental rights belong, the protection of these values have functioned much better in the "offline world" and during the first phase of wide use of the Internet. However, whether and how content may be disseminated is still relatively easy to answer when considering these rules, but the real question and difficulty is how and against whom rights and claims can be enforced.

1.2. The Role of Platforms in the Online Dissemination of Content

Against whom rights may be enforced depends on who can be held responsible in which form for the distribution or accessibility of content. In this regard, a distinction has always been made between different providers or categories of providers. In the early days of the Internet, however, the players and the conditions under which they operated were different than they are today. There were already search engines at the beginning of the 1990s[6], but it was not until 1999 that the Google search engine was launched, which did not reach today's relevance for many years after.[7] There were also certain distributors, such as Internet access providers or website providers, which around the turn of the millennium could be divided into the categories of hosting, granting only access or even being mere caching services. This categorisation was picked up in legal texts, namely in the E-Commerce Directive (ECD)[8] (on this, cf. Chapter 3.).

---

6 *Schwartz*, in: Journal of the American Society for Information Science 49(11), 1998, pp. 973, 973 et seq.
7 Cf. the history of the company available at https://about.google/our-story/.
8 Directive 2000/31/EC of the European Parliament and of the Council of 8 June 2000 on certain legal aspects of information society services, in particular

However, this division began[9] to collapse after a few years and at the latest with the emergence and increasing significance of what is commonly referred to as platforms or "intermediaries". From the outset it is clear that there is much more heterogeneity in the categories of service providers than in the early days of the Internet, which can already be seen in the differing choice of terminology with which they are addressed. These types of providers no longer solely host or cache foreign content or give access to it; they need to rather be seen as complex platforms with a multitude of functions.[10]

In the Internet and digital economy, platforms are understood to be intermediaries that bundle media content, market it on digital markets and have an organisation and exclusion technology that enable the creation of a digital end consumer market.[11] Platforms are therefore intermediaries between media or content providers and recipients, i.e. part of the value chain. Due to the changing conditions in the digital environment, however, the term is not suitable for a conclusive definition, as shown by the lack of a detailed description of the organisational structure. Nevertheless, the platforms share some key characteristics, in particular the ability to create and shape new markets based on collecting, processing and editing large amounts of data. By operating in multisided markets, albeit with varying degrees of control over direct interactions between groups of users, they benefit from "network effects". Platforms rely on information and communication technologies to reach their users, and they play a key role in digital value creation.[12] Initially, the business model of platforms was generally[13] not geared towards providing own content but rather towards

---

electronic commerce, in the Internal Market (Directive on electronic commerce), OJ L 178, 17.7.2000, pp. 1–16.

9 For example, Facebook was launched in 2004 and YouTube in 2005, although their reach was of course not as high as it is today.

10 On the changing role of online platforms cf. also *De Streel/Buiten/Peitz*, Liability of Online Hosting Platforms, p. 23.

11 *Sjurts* (ed.), Gabler Lexikon Medienwirtschaft, p. 474.

12 Communication from the Commission to the European Parliament, the Council, the European Economic and Social Committee and the Committee of Regions, Online Platforms and the Digital Single Market Opportunities and Challenges for Europe, COM/2016/0288 final, available at https://eur-lex.europa.eu/legal-cont ent/EN/TXT/?qid=1466514160026&uri=CELEX:52016DC0288.

13 Facebook, for example, recently presented its initiative "Facebook News", where it will publish its own news in cooperation with several publishers and newspapers; cf. ZEIT ONLINE, 25.10.2019, available at https://www.zeit.de/digital/2019-10/facebook-news-tab-app-zeitungen-verlage-soziales-netzwerk.

collecting third-party content or having it collected and assembled by users. They therefore provide an attractive infrastructure. In order to attract (more) end users, however, the platforms in today's markets must regularly offer something in addition to the mere bundling of content in order to be able to distinguish themselves from competitors. Therefore, editorial measures are also regularly carried out on the platform, for example by categorising media content, integrating algorithms for preference systems, creating playlists or specifying search parameters based on individual user data they collect. Even from this limited selection of editorial measures it can be seen that it is regularly the platforms which decide about the content that is displayed, how it is displayed and to whom. This process is often not transparent for third parties.

This changing role of platforms leads to the conclusion that with the ever-growing availability of user-generated audiovisual content, which is disseminated outside of more traditional channels that necessitated a provider with editorial responsibility, existing categories of online services need to be questioned.

1.3. The Role of Supervisory Authorities in the Online Dissemination of Content

There is no general supervision of content disseminated via the Internet. Insofar this type of dissemination of audiovisual content is significantly different than it was and is the case for broadcasted content. Supervision of online disseminated content by definition would be much more challenging if it would be attempted in a comparable way, given the diversity of the content, addressees of monitoring efforts and the regulatory areas concerned as well as the cross-border character of such dissemination. Rather, there are several regulatory frameworks that address the online dissemination of content partially. This applies, for example, to audiovisual media services with the Audiovisual Media Services Directive (AVMSD)[14] of the

---

14 Directive 2010/13/EU of the European Parliament and of the Council of 10 March 2010 on the coordination of certain provisions laid down by law, regulation or administrative action in Member States concerning the provision of audiovisual media services (Audiovisual Media Services Directive), OJ L 95, 15.4.2010, pp. 1–24, as amended by Directive (EU) 2018/1808 of the European Parliament and of the Council of 14 November 2018 amending Directive 2010/13/EU on the coordination of certain provisions laid down by law, regulation or administrative action in Member States concerning the provision of

EU or copyright questions with Directive 2001/29/EC on the harmonisation of certain aspects of copyright and related rights in the information society (InfoSoc Directive)[15] and in future with the national transpositions of Directive (EU) 2019/790 on copyright and related rights in the Digital Single Market and amending Directives 96/9/EC and 2001/29/EC (DSM Directive)[16]. These are only two examples for rulesets that have an impact in the shape that they have been transposed by the Member States of the European Union (EU).

While copyright law pursues an approach of enforcing rights through private individuals in the form of asserting claims, it is supervisory authorities under the umbrella of the AVMSD that monitor compliance with the rules and regularly have a set of possible sanctions at their disposal which enables them to also enforce the implementation of the requirements (e.g. with regard to the protection of minors or protection against incitement to hatred) vis-à-vis providers. However, as far as online content is concerned, AVMSD only applies to the extent that the respective providers and services are within the scope of the Directive, i.e. audiovisual media services (linear and non-linear), commercial communication and, in future, video-sharing platforms (VSPs). Platforms therefore do not per se fall within the scope of AVMSD but only if their "essential functionality [...] is devoted to providing programmes, user-generated videos, or both, to the general public [...]" (Art. 1 para. 1 lit. aa AVMSD). This is problematic insofar as the supervisory authorities are dependent on the cooperation of the platforms (the distributors) in the performance of their tasks, either because there is no separate content creator or because they have no access to this content creator for certain reasons (e.g. because the original creator cannot be determined or there is no way of establishing a contact). Therefore, it would be a viable option if authorities could get access through other rules. The ECD, which is applicable to information society services, could be an obvious path, but with its aforementioned categorisation it provides for liability privileges of these types of service providers which can as a result also exclude the liability of platform providers (cf. Chapter 3.3.).

---

audiovisual media services (Audiovisual Media Services Directive) in view of changing market realities, OJ L 303, 28.11.2018, pp. 69–92.

15 Directive 2001/29/EC of the European Parliament and of the Council of 22 May 2001 on the harmonisation of certain aspects of copyright and related rights in the information society, OJ L 167, 22.6.2001, pp. 10–19.

16 Directive (EU) 2019/790 of the European Parliament and of the Council of 17 April 2019 on copyright and related rights in the Digital Single Market and amending Directives 96/9/EC and 2001/29/EC, OJ L 130, 17.5.2019, pp. 92–125.

It is not only the scope of application of the relevant Directives that limits the powers of supervisory authorities; it is also the territoriality of each service, since the AVMSD, and in principle also the ECD, prescribes the application of the country-of-origin principle relying for the question of jurisdiction on the Member State where a provider is established. Access to non-domestic providers of services is therefore not easily possible within the AVMSD or ECD framework. This poses a particular problem in the online context, as the offers do not require a local connection point in a sovereign territory in order to address their offers to the local public. Therefore, in this case the respective authorities are dependent on the cooperation of regulatory authorities in other countries, which is partly regulated in the Directive but with relatively complicated and lengthy procedures.

There is also a factual and regulatory problem, both in the audiovisual media sector and other areas where supervision is foreseen (including at national level) and in criminal law: providers are often not identifiable or reachable, either because they do not comply with existing (national or European) information obligations or because such obligations do not exist. In this case, the possibility of procedural access to the higher-level Internet access providers would be relevant. This, however, is not necessarily an easy alternative answer considering possible conflicts with freedom of expression. Such supervisory powers are therefore regulated in a very diverse manner in the EU Member States and globally.[17]

As a result of these framework conditions, supervisory authorities are often unable to perform the task assigned to them by law or are unable to do so effectively, whether due to deficits in the area of the legal framework or practical hurdles. This means in conclusion that the dissemination of online content across borders is challenging the national and EU legal frameworks for monitoring service providers and enforcing the law. Not only the vast amount of, and increasingly easy access to, illegal or harmful content via online service providers raises the question how efficient enforcement can be organised. Also there is, due to the uncertainty of who is re-

---

17 Cf. for non-EU area, for example, the new Russian Law No. 608767-7 amending the Federal Law on Communications and the Federal Law on Information, Information Technologies and Protection of Information with a view to ensuring the safe and stable functioning of the Internet on the territory of the Russian Federation (available at http://publication.pravo.gov.ru/Document/View/000120190501 0025) which entered into force on 1 November 2019 and provides, inter alia, for the possibility of the Russian media regulatory authority blocking Internet sites via contact points the internet service provider are obliged to establish.

sponsible for the content and which party in the process of disseminating content from its production to the reception by the end-user has an active role and could be held liable, a strong call for reconsidering the applicable rules.

1.4. The EU Digital Single Market Context

On 5 May 2015, the Commission presented its strategy for the creation of a Digital Single Market[18], which addressed the fact that

> *"[t]he global economy is rapidly becoming digital. Information and Communications Technology (ICT) is no longer a specific sector but the foundation of all modern innovative economic systems. The Internet and digital technologies are transforming the lives we lead, the way we work – as individuals, in business, and in our communities as they become more integrated across all sectors of our economy and society."[19]*

The main objectives of this strategy were to create better access to online goods for consumers and businesses, to ensure that citizens and businesses can take full advantage of the opportunities of digitalisation and to design the legal environment for digital networks and services. The reform of data protection law was already in full swing with the proposal for the General Data Protection Regulation (GDPR)[20] and was planned to be supplemented by a draft Regulation on Privacy and Electronic Communications.

On the basis of these objectives, the strategy of the Commission included an overall package for a Digital Single Market which resulted in numerous initiatives, the revision of many existing legal acts and the adoption of new rules. Amongst these were the modernisation of rules on copyright (DSM Directive) and audiovisual media services (AVMSD) in the light of

---

18 Communication from the Commission to the European Parliament, the Council, the European Economic and Social Committee and the Committee of Regions, A Digital Single Market Strategy for Europe, COM(2015)192 final, available at https://eur-lex.europa.eu/legal-content/EN/TXT/?uri=celex%3A52015DC0192.

19 Ibid., point 1.

20 Regulation (EU) 2016/679 of the European Parliament and of the Council of 27 April 2016 on the protection of natural persons with regard to the processing of personal data and on the free movement of such data, and repealing Directive 95/46/EC (General Data Protection Regulation), OJ L 119, 4.5.2016, pp. 1–88.

digitisation as well as new telecom rules[21] and many additional measures that will be presented in this study in more detail.

The creation of better access to online goods included also "new rules on e-commerce"[22] establishing in particular new rules on geo-blocking[23] and on purchasing digital content and services[24]. The strategy recognised that "[o]nline platforms (e.g. search engines, social media, e-commerce platforms, app stores, price comparison websites) are playing an ever more central role in social and economic life: they enable consumers to find online information and businesses to exploit the advantages of e-commerce". It, however, did not include the proposal for a reform of the ECD specifically but mentioned rather aspects of competition law in the online context by outlining that some platforms have evolved to become players competing in many sectors of the economy. It further held that the way they use their market power raises a number of issues that warrant further analysis beyond the application of competition law in specific cases.

Furthermore, the Commission revealed plans to combat illegal content on the Internet. It did so by first underlining that the principles of (limited) liability enshrined in the ECD have underpinned the development of the Internet in Europe. However, it was considered that, "when illegal content is identified, whether it be information related to illegal activities such as terrorism/child pornography or information that infringes the property rights of others (e.g. copyright), intermediaries should take effective action to remove it" and that "the disabling of access to and the removal of illegal

---

21 The so-called connectivity package (see for details and sources https://ec.europa.e u/digital-single-market/en/policies/improving-connectivity-and-access) included a new rule book for providers of internet access and communication services with the European Electronic Communications Code, common EU broadband targets for 2025, a plan to foster European industrial leadership in 5th generation (5G) wireless technology and a voucher scheme for public authorities who want to offer free Wi-Fi access to their citizens (WiFi4EU).

22 Cf. on this part of the policy https://ec.europa.eu/digital-single-market/en/new-eu-rules-e-commerce.

23 A new regulation on EU level (Regulation (EU) 2018/302 of the European Parliament and of the Council of 28 February 2018 on addressing unjustified geoblocking and other forms of discrimination based on customers' nationality, place of residence or place of establishment within the internal market and amending Regulations (EC) No 2006/2004 and (EU) 2017/2394 and Directive 2009/22/EC, OJ L 60I , 2.3.2018, pp. 1–15) ensure that online sellers must treat all EU consumers equally regardless of where they choose to shop from.

24 Directive (EU) 2019/770 of the European Parliament and of the Council of 20 May 2019 on certain aspects concerning contracts for the supply of digital content and digital services, OJ L 136, 22.5.2019, pp. 1–27.

content by providers of hosting services can be slow and complicated"[25]. Possibly a full reform of the ECD was nonetheless not tackled because of the factor that "[i]t is not always easy to define the limits on what intermediaries can do with the content that they transmit, store or host before losing the possibility to benefit from the exemptions from liability set out in the e-Commerce Directive"[26]. It should be noted that this observation may be a factor to be considered in the context of a reform but hardly serves as explanation not to attempt a reform if such reform is regarded to be necessary.

The Commission did announce a comprehensive analysis of the role of platforms, which was carried out with its Communication on Online Platforms and the Digital Single Market Opportunities and Challenges for Europe.[27] In this Communication, the Commission announced its intention to create a level playing field for comparable digital services, to ensure responsible behaviour of online platforms to protect core values, to address transparency and fairness for maintaining user trust and safeguarding innovation and to foster open and non-discriminatory markets in a data-driven economy. Regarding the existing intermediary liability regime, the Commission opted for a sectorial, problem-driven approach to regulation which, in addition to the new rules of the AVMSD and the DSM Directive, covered coordinated EU-wide self-regulatory efforts by online platforms. This in turn has led to numerous initiatives, in particular on illegal online content, hate speech and disinformation (cf. Chapter 2.5), which are being developed with the participation of industry.

1.5. Structure of the Study

The aim of this study is to analyse the current legal framework for the dissemination of online content and to identify problems arising from it as well as identifying possible paths for the future. Particular attention will therefore be paid to the provisions of the ECD, which will be analysed in this study in order to identify whether the application of these rules and its scope are still up-to-date. In a second step, this background analysis will make it possible to highlight those areas which need to be adapted by

---

25 COM(2015)192 final, supra (fn. 18), point 3.3.2.
26 Ibid.
27 COM/2016/0288 final, supra (fn. 12).

changing the legal framework, as well as the possible adaptation of administrative procedures under existing law.

For that purpose, it is necessary to initially set the scene by presenting an overview of the overall applicable legal framework in the online context (Chapter 2).[28] Not only the ECD is of relevance here but also a differentiated set of other rules on European level. As the most important principles that also impact the creation of any regular legislative act, fundamental rights are crucial (Chapter 2.1). They provide the "legal framework for the legal framework". In the EU specifically the fundamental freedoms (Chapter 2.2) are in particular relevant in the cross-border environment as they shape the European (Digital) Single Market. A general framework, which both the Member States and the EU have to observe in the Union legal framework, has also a priority significance at EU primary law level (Chapter 2.3): the objectives and values of the EU, which are of decisive importance in a value-based approach to legislation and regulation, and the division of competences between the EU and its Member States need to be taken into consideration. Primary law principles are incorporated into the secondary law of the EU, which takes on many different forms in the context of the online dissemination of content (Chapter 2.4). There is not only a single legal framework that plays a role in the digital environment. Instead there are a variety of Directives that address various aspects of relevance such as copyright, advertising or criminal content. For each of them the main provisions and elements of regulation that are potentially relevant in the context of online content dissemination and for the competences of national regulatory authorities will be addressed. This chapter concludes with an overview of non-binding sources of rules that recently have played an important role for addressing problems with online content dissemination (Chapter 2.5).

As the main applicable legislative act taking a horizontal approach to the online environment, it is the ECD which is in the focus of this study. In Chapter 3, the ECD is analysed in detail by putting a focus on its scope of application, the country-of-origin principle that the ECD follows and the intermediary liability regime. With regard to the latter, it is crucial to present the categories of Information Society Services (ISS) in the ECD, on one hand, and to draw on the relevant jurisprudence of the Court of Justice of the European Union (CJEU), on the other hand, in order to then raise the question which challenges result with regard to illegal online con-

---

28 The authors would like to thank Ass. iur. *Jan Henrich* for his preparatory contributions to some parts of this chapter of the study.

tent. The aim is to identify whether there is a duty of care-standard which online platforms have to fulfil. The chapter ends with the analysis of sector-specific liability provisions and their comparison with the provisions of the ECD as well as the examination of the compatibility of these regulatory regimes with each other. The question of continued relevance of these rules or whether they are outdated will also be discussed in this context.

Based on these findings, Chapter 4 deals with the future regulatory framework for online content. It summarises the lessons learnt in the application of the existing legal framework before considering possible avenues, in particular regarding a possible revision of the applicable legal acts, namely the ECD, in light of online content dissemination realities of today.

The study was completed in November 2019 and reflects developments until that point; subsequent changes for the preparation of the publication version were limited to formal aspects. The above reprinted executive summaries of the main findings of the study were already published in the context of the conference "safeguarding freedom - securing justice" organised by the Media Authorities in cooperation with the State Media Authority NRW and the Institute of European Media Law on 12 November 2019 in Brussels.

2. The Relevant EU Legal Framework for Online Content Dissemination

In order to start with the presentation of the existing legal framework for the dissemination of online content, which is also the starting point for enforcement measures, a number of provisions[29] and legal acts in the areas of fundamental rights as well as in primary and secondary law of the European Union needs to be considered. However, as the study focuses on regulatory issues at the EU level in order to identify possible improvements, the framework of international law will not be presented here.[30] In the online context, coordination, support and supplementary measures of the EU also play a role, particularly in the context of the direct involvement of third-country service providers.

2.1. Fundamental Rights

Fundamental rights[31] as the highest legal assets within democratic states, both in their (subjective) expression as defensive rights of natural and legal persons and partly as (objective) guarantees, must be safeguarded as the basis of every legal framework and in every legislative and regulatory activity. In some cases, they can oblige the states bound to them to (certain) actions in order to counteract (also actively regulating) existing circumstances that cannot be reconciled with fundamental and human rights and to eliminate existing impairments.

The online dissemination of content has a number of links to fundamental and human rights, which mirror the participation of different stakeholders with different interests. This includes above all the users who access the services of online service providers. They are the primary recipi-

---

29 The provisions in particular relevant in the context of this study are listed or reprinted in the Online Annex, available at www.nomos-shop.de/44382.

30 Cf. on international aspects *Ukrow*, Zuständigkeit der Landesmedien-anstalten/KJM für ausländische Anbieter; and *Cappello (ed.)*, Media law enforcement without frontiers, IRIS Special 2018-2.

31 Fundamental rights relevant in the context of this study are listed in the Online Annex, available at www.nomos-shop.de/44382, I.

ents who consume the content, and in some cases they are also active participants in the online content of third parties appearing as actors or as real persons. In both cases, human dignity and the protection of minors have key importance that needs to be taken into account by online content providers in order to comply with fundamental rights. These high-ranking values regularly run in parallel with the public interests that guide, and must guide, state activities. With regard to the latter group of users, personal rights aspects are also to take into account, namely in form of data protection and the protection of private life. While they can refer to their right to information as recipients, on the other hand, the users themselves are increasingly becoming content creators who disseminate their own contributions via intermediaries and thus can rely on the right to freedom of expression. The way in which they create and disseminate content as well as the extent to which they allow specific content to be disseminated, has an impact on how to categorise the providers. In particular, apart from being able to rely "only" on the freedom of expression they can likely also rely on the freedom of the media, which can have relevance, as within the framework of media freedom other criteria might be applied in light of the role of the media as a public watchdog. It is precisely this freedom of the media as well as the right to property, particularly with regard to intellectual property, that content creators regularly invoke when their content is disseminated via their own platforms or those of intermediaries. They have an interest in their content also being protected online. Finally, intermediaries who offer their services out of economic interest are protected by fundamental rights in terms of their freedom to conduct a business and their right to property.

To what extent and when these fundamental rights oblige the EU at Union law level and the states at national level to take active action will be examined below.

2.1.1. Fundamental Rights Sources: EU Charter, European Convention on Human Rights and National Constitutional Law

Although provided for in the Treaty on European Union (TEU)[32], the Union has not yet acceded to the European Convention on Human Rights (ECHR)[33]. Nevertheless, the ECHR has an important impact on the EU in two respects: On the one hand, the Member States as Convention States are bound to the ECHR as a source of international law, also in the implementation of Union law, which at the same time means that the Member States are guarantors of measures taken by the Union. On the other hand, even after the adoption of the Charter of Fundamental Rights of the European Union (CFR)[34], the ECHR is still one of the most relevant legal references within Union law.[35] The CJEU recognises in its decisions that "the principles on which the European Convention for the Protection of Human Rights and Fundamental Freedoms is based must be taken into consideration in community law"[36], and it states that "fundamental rights form an integral part of the general principles of the law, the observance of which is ensured by the Court. In safeguarding those rights, the Court has to look to the constitutional traditions common to the Member States, so that measures which are incompatible with the fundamental rights recognized by the constitutions of those States may not find acceptance in the Community"[37]. This means that the CJEU therefore incorporates both the norms of the ECHR and the case law of the European Court of Human Rights (ECtHR) into its decisions, in particular within the framework of the justification of infringements of fundamental rights guaranteed in the CFR.[38] This applies in particular due to the equality clause contained in Art. 52 para. 3 CFR, which states that, insofar as the CFR contains rights

---

32 Consolidated version of the Treaty on European Union, OJ C 326, 26.10.2012, pp. 13–390.
33 The European Convention on Human Rights, as amended by Protocols Nos. 11 and 14, supplemented by Protocols Nos. 1, 4, 6, 7, 12, 13 and 16, available at https://www.echr.coe.int/Documents/Convention_ENG.pdf.
34 Charter of Fundamental Rights of the European Union, OJ C 326, 26.10.2012, pp. 391–407.
35 *Kingreen*, in: Calliess/Ruffert, Art. 6 TEU para. 20 et seq.
36 CJEU, judgement of 15.5.1986, C-222/84, *Marguerite Johnston v Chief Constable of the Royal Ulster Constabulary*, para. 18.
37 CJEU, judgement of 13.7.1989, C-5/88, *Hubert Wachauf v Bundesamt für Ernährung und Forstwirtschaft*, para. 17.
38 CJEU, judgement of 26.6.1997, C-368/95, *Vereinigte Familiapress Zeitungsverlags- und vertriebs GmbH v Heinrich Bauer Verlag*, para. 26.

which correspond to rights guaranteed by ECHR, the meaning and scope of those rights shall be the same as those laid down by the said Convention. However, Art. 52 para. 3 also states that "[t]his provision shall not prevent Union law providing more extensive protection", which, in principle, could lead to divergences in jurisprudence. On the other hand, the ECtHR also assumes that an equivalent level of protection of fundamental rights is guaranteed in the Union[39], so that the application of different standards is rather unlikely.[40]

With regard to the relationship between the ECHR and the CFR, on the one hand, and national constitutional law, on the other, which should not be the subject of consideration of the present report, it must be said that these three levels of protection of fundamental rights, in principle, complement each other cumulatively.[41] This also corresponds to Art. 53 CFR on the level of protection of the CFR, which states that "nothing in this Charter shall be interpreted as restricting or adversely affecting human rights and fundamental freedoms as recognized inter alia by the Member States' constitutions".

On the part of Union law, however, the fundamental primacy of Union law, which is expressed in Art. 51 para. 1 CFR, must also be observed. The fundamental primacy of the fundamental rights of the Union over those of the national constitutions results from the transfer of sovereign rights to the Union, which is not changed by the regulation of Art. 53 CFR.[42] Therefore, it is settled jurisprudence of the CJEU that rules of national law, even of a constitutional order, cannot be allowed to undermine the effectiveness of EU law on the territory of that State.[43] Although the CJEU is guided by the constitutional traditions common to the Member States and the principles derived from the ECHR when interpreting the CFR and developing jurisdictional principles[44], conflicts are nevertheless conceivable. Such conflicts would then have to be resolved in favour of Union law, but this does not mean that far-reaching constitutional protection per se would be superseded.[45]

---

39 ECtHR, judgement of 30.6.2005, no. 45036/98.
40 *Kingreen*, in: Calliess/Ruffert, Art. 6 TEU para. 23.
41 *Ladenburger/Vondung*, in: Stern/Sachs, Art. 51 para. 39 et seq.
42 *Everling*, in: EuZW 8/2003, p. 225.
43 CJEU, judgement of 26.2.2013, C-399/11, *Stefano Melloni v Ministerio Fiscal*, para. 59 with further references.
44 *Everling*, in: EuZW 8/2003, p. 225.
45 *Ladenburger/Vondung*, in: Stern/Sachs, Art. 51 para. 39, 40.

This applies in particular to positive state protection obligations which can arise from the constitutions of the Member States – also against the background of Art. 51 para. 1 sentence 2 CFR. This is indicated in particular by considerations that can be drawn from the CJEU's case law on fundamental freedom. In the *Commission/France* case[46] the CJEU clarified not only that the prohibition rules derived from fundamental freedoms prohibit measures which are attributable to a Member State and which themselves create restrictions on trade between the Member States; it stated also that these rules can apply where a Member State abstains from adopting the measures required in order to deal with obstacles to the fundamental freedoms (in this case the free movement of goods) which are not caused by the State.[47] The fundamental freedoms may be affected, in the same way as they may be affected by an act of a Member State, by a Member State's failure to act, or its failure to take sufficient measures to remove obstacles to a fundamental freedom caused, in particular, by acts of private individuals within its territory which are directed against the activity protected by the fundamental freedom. Thus, the fundamental freedoms may oblige Member States not only to remedy certain infringements but also to take all necessary and appropriate measures, taking into account the frequency and seriousness of such infringements, for example by private individuals, to ensure that those fundamental freedoms are respected in their territory, unless they can prove that their action would have consequences for public policy which they could not overcome by their means. However, the Member States have a considerable margin of appreciation with regard to the concrete measures to be taken, which cannot be imposed by the Union[48] – probably outside of cases where there is no other appropriate solution.

---

46 CJEU, judgement of 9.12.1997, C-265/95, *Commission of the European Communities v French Republic*. Cf. on this already *Ukrow*, Zur Zuständigkeit der Landesmedienanstalten/KJM für ausländische Anbieter.

47 CJEU, ibid., para. 30.

48 Ibid., para. 33 et seq.

2.1.2. Relevant Fundamental Rights

2.1.2.1. Human Dignity

Human dignity is inviolable. It must be respected and protected. This overriding principle and fundament of all other fundamental rights can be found in Art. 1 CFR. Although the ECHR does not explicitly mention human dignity, the ECtHR assumes that the principle of respect for human dignity underlies all Convention guarantees[49] and that "[t]he very essence of the Convention is respect for human dignity and human freedom"[50]. Human dignity is both a fundamental right with subjective guarantee content and a principle under objective law.

The institutions, bodies, offices and agencies of the Union are bound by fundamental rights within the meaning of Art. 51 para. 1 CFR, in compliance with the principle of subsidiarity, as well as the Member States when they implement Union law. Private individuals, on the contrary, are not covered by the scope.[51] However, it has always been difficult to concretise the content of human dignity or even to find a definition.[52] Rather, in practice, it is treated by the CJEU[53] and the ECtHR as a kind of general clause or basic standard, which can be applied where a more sector-specific fundamental right is not applicable.[54] Without going into the historical development and its further development in the jurisprudence of the European courts in greater depth, it can be stated here that at least the minimum core of human dignity consists in the fact that every human being possesses an intrinsic worth, merely by being human, which should be recognised and respected by others. Recognising the intrinsic worth of the individual requires that the state should be seen to exist for the sake of the individual human being, and not vice versa.[55]

---

49 ECtHR, judgement of 11.7.2002, no. 28957/95, para. 90.
50 ECtHR, judgement of 29.4.2002, no. 2346/02, para. 65.
51 Cf. *Classen*, EuR 39(3), 2004, pp. 416, 429 et seq.; *Jaensch*, Die unmittelbare Drittwirkung der Grundfreiheiten, pp. 186 et seq.; for developments towards a horizontal impact of fundamental freedoms see *Schepel*, in: ELJ 18(2), 2012, p. 177, 192 et seq.
52 Cf. for an overview on the different approaches *von Schwichow*, Die Menschenwürde in der EMRK, pp. 13 et seq.
53 Cf., e.g., CJEU, judgement of 9.10.2001, C-377/98, *Kingdom of the Netherlands v European Parliament and Council of the European Union*, para. 70.
54 *Höfling/Kempny*, in: Stern/Sachs, Art. 1 para. 9.
55 In this regard *McCrudden*, in: EJIL 19(4), 2008, p. 655, 655 et seq.

As the wording of Art. 1 CFR unequivocally shows, human dignity is inviolable and thus not subject to any restrictions or justification.[56] On the other hand, the protection of human dignity can be a suitable objective within the framework of the restriction of fundamental freedoms. With regard to human dignity and the restriction of the freedom to provide services, the CJEU explained this in its *Omega*[57] ruling:

> *"There can therefore be no doubt that the objective of protecting human dignity is compatible with Community law, it being immaterial in that respect that, in Germany, the principle of respect for human dignity has a particular status as an independent fundamental right. Since both the Community and its Member States are required to respect fundamental rights, the protection of those rights is a legitimate interest which, in principle, justifies a restriction of the obligations imposed by Community law, even under a fundamental freedom guaranteed by the Treaty such as the freedom to provide services."[58]*

Especially the latter decision of the CJEU shows that it is not excluded that the assessment of human dignity as a protection objective in connection with the restriction of fundamental freedoms is based on a national understanding of this fundamental right[59] and not on an understanding under Union law.[60]

In the area of online content, there are many conceivable possibilities for violating human dignity. This applies in particular to audiovisual content that contains pornography or depictions of violence.[61] It also applies in the field of non-fictional depictions of violence, in which the effect of violence on the body of a person against his will can make him "an object" and therefore could come into conflict with human dignity. Examples include execution videos of terrorist organisations or so-called "snuff videos", for which the Internet is the most common means of dissemination. In fic-

---

56 *Höfling/Kempny*, in: Stern/Sachs, Art. 1 para. 27.
57 CJEU, judgement of 14.10.2004, C-36/02, *Omega Spielhallen- und Automatenaufstellungs-GmbH v Oberbürgermeisterin der Bundesstadt Bonn*. This case was about a prohibition of an installation known as a "laserdrome", normally used for the practice of "laser sport" in which the players shoot each other playfully with laser guns.
58 Ibid., para. 34, 35.
59 The so-called "laserdromes" were not prohibited in other Member States which was one of the arguments of the claimant.
60 In this regard also *McCrudden*, in: EJIL 19(4), 2008, p. 655, 710.
61 Cf. on the (also media-political) discussion already *Schulz*, in: M&K 48(3), 2000, p. 354, 354 et seq.

tional media content, on the other hand, in which all the actors voluntarily agree to the actions depicted, it will regularly not be possible to affirm a violation of human dignity through the production or publication of the content, even if these depictions are particularly obscene or glorify violence. In the latter cases, however, the human dignity of the viewer may be violated if the identification with the portrayed person violates his dignity, whereby the portrayal cannot escape him (because it may surprise him due to a lack of appropriate labelling).[62] Moreover, in principle, situations are also conceivable in the field of fictional content that must be subsumed under human dignity because, for example, the subjects acting in the video are not at all in a position – whether due to mental, physical or age-related incapacity to consent – to grasp what is portrayed and its effects in their entirety and thus cannot effectively consent to the production and/or publication of the content.[63]

2.1.2.2. Rights of the Child and Protection of Minors

The rights of children play a special role in the CFR. In accordance with the United Nations Convention on the Rights of the Child[64], Art. 24 CFR considers children to be independent holders of fundamental rights. This separate establishment in separate provisions outside of Art. 6 CFR shows that the CFR does not regard children as a union with their parents but rather treats them as independent rights holders.[65] Art. 24 para. 1 CFR guarantees that children shall have the right to such protection and care as it is necessary for their well-being (as a subjective right of participation and protection vis-à-vis the EU institutions and the Member States) and that they may express their views freely. Moreover, such views shall be taken into consideration on matters which concern them in accordance with their age and maturity. According to Art. 24 para. 2 CFR, in all actions relating to children, whether taken by public authorities or private institutions, the child's best interests must be a primary consideration.

---

62 *Schulz*, in: M&K 48(3), 2000, p. 354, 366.
63 Cf. extensively on this *Dörr/Cole*, Big Brother und die Menschenwürde, p. 82; *Dörr/Cole*, in: K&R 8/2000, p. 369, 377; *Cole*, in: HK-RStV, § 3 and § 41.
64 Convention on the Rights of the Child, New York, 20.11.1989, available at https:/ /treaties.un.org/Pages/ViewDetails.aspx?src=TREATY&mtdsg_no=IV-11&chapter =4&lang=en.
65 Cf. on this *Steindorff-Classen*, in: EuR 46(1), 2011, p. 19, 31.

As a value decision in favour of the welfare of the child, Art. 24 primarily contains an objective legal component as well as a connecting factor for the target-oriented restriction of other fundamental rights and a requirement for the welfare-oriented interpretation of other laws – including those on a national level.[66] Art. 24 therefore rather contains guidance for the interpretation of secondary law[67], while the CJEU is very cautious in deriving individual protective rights arising from it[68]. "Protection" within the meaning of Art. 24 para. 1 sentence 1 CFR means that children (which also includes youth) are to be protected from anything that could endanger their well-being, i.e., that could impair their health, safety, physical, mental or moral development.[69] This provision can, therefore, be invoked as a connecting factor where fundamental rights of third parties are affected by rules designed to protect the development of minors. Art. 24 para. 1 sentence 2 CFR has, in addition to Art. 11 CFR, less significance against a background of fundamental rights, since children also fall within the personal scope of protection of freedom of expression. Therefore, Art. 24 para. 1 sentence 2 CFR underlines at this point only once more that children are to be seen as independent personalities by emphasising their right to free speech.[70]

Although Art. 24 CFR is based on the United Nations Convention on the Rights of the Child, the provision, unlike Art. 17 of the Convention, contains no specific rules on the protection of minors from harmful media or in the media environment. Thus, the protection of minors in the media has so far played no role in the fundamental case law of the CJEU. It is rather – a small number of – judgements on the AVMSD and partly also on the ECD that have dealt with this issue. Protection of minors in the media continues to be an objective that follows to a large extent[71] from national constitutional law and is therefore essentially left to the discretion of the Member States in its implementation.[72]

---

66 *Ennuschat*, in: Stern/Sachs, Art. 24, para. 6.
67 Cf. on this CJEU, judgement of 6.12.2012, joint cases C-356/11 and C-357/11, *O and S v Maahanmuuttovirasto and Maahanmuuttovirasto v L.*
68 Cf., e.g., CJEU, judgement of 8.11.2012, C-40/11, *Yoshikazu Iida v Stadt Ulm.*
69 *Ennuschat*, in: Stern/Sachs, Art. 24, para. 8, 9.
70 In this regard also *Ennuschat*, in: Stern/Sachs, Art. 24, para. 13.
71 Although there are now links at secondary law level (e.g. Art. 6a AVMSD).
72 Cf. on national case law regarding the protection of minors in the media *Cappello* (ed.), The protection of minors in a converged media environment, IRIS plus 2015-1, pp. 53 et seq.

Although the protection of minors is not expressly regulated in the ECHR, the ECtHR repeatedly emphasises in its judgments the special need for protection of minors. In the context of this study, two judgments of the ECtHR are particularly relevant, since they are related to media or digital content. The *Söderman case* concerned the attempted covert filming of a 14-year-old girl by her stepfather while she was naked and her complaint that the Swedish legal system, which at the time did not prohibit filming without someone's consent, had not protected her against the violation of her personal integrity. In its judgment, the ECtHR assumed an infringement of Art. 8 ECHR pointing out that "the circumstances were aggravated by the fact that the applicant was a minor"[73]. While in this case the ECtHR did not also have to deal with the publication of the video material (this had not happened), the case *K.U. v. Finland* took place in the online environment. This case concerned a personal ad with sexual content that had been posted on a dating website on the Internet on behalf of a twelve-year-old boy. Neither the Finnish legislation in force at that time nor the police, nor the Finnish courts were able to oblige the Internet service provider to identify the person who placed the advertisement. In particular, the Internet service provider refused to identify the responsible person because this would constitute a breach of his duty of confidentiality. In this case the ECtHR held an infringement of Art. 8 ECHR too and highlighted the notion of private life, given the potential threat to the boy's physical and mental welfare at his vulnerable age.[74] The Court considered that the posting of the Internet advertisement about the applicant had been a criminal act that had resulted in a minor having been a target for paedophiles. It recalled that such conduct called for a criminal-law response and that effective deterrence had to be reinforced through adequate investigation and prosecution. Moreover, children and other vulnerable individuals were entitled to protection by the state from such grave interferences with their private life. According to the ECtHR, the Finnish Government could not argue that there had been no opportunity to put in place a system to protect children from being targeted by paedophiles via the Internet because it had been well-known that the Internet, precisely because of its anonymous character, could be used for criminal purposes. The widespread problem of child sexual abuse had also become well-known. Moreover, according to the ECtHR, the legislature should have provided a framework for reconciling the confidentiality of Internet services with the

---

73   ECtHR, judgement of 12.11.2013, no. 5786/08, para. 86.
74   ECtHR, judgement of 2.12.2008, no. 2872/02, para. 41.

prevention of disorder or crime, and the protection of the rights and freedoms of others.[75] Two other decisions are also noteworthy in this regard. In the first, the ECtHR stated that there was no unlawful restriction of freedom of expression when the Member States took measures against the (admonished) exhibition of Internet child pornography.[76] In the second, the ECtHR ruled that the national provisions with regard to fines and applicable procedures for the protection of minors must comply with the principle of proportionality[77].

2.1.2.3. Respect for Private and Family Life

The CFR, unlike many national constitutions and the ECHR, explicitly guarantees the right to the protection of personal data. In the context of the genesis of Art. 8 CFR the provisions of the Data Protection Directive[78] at that time were reproduced, which were taken over essentially also in the now valid General Data Protection Regulation (GDPR). According to this, everyone has the right to the protection of personal data concerning him or her (para. 1) as well as the right of access to data which has been collected concerning him or her, and the right to have it rectified (para. 2). Furthermore, Art. 8 para. 2 CFR lays down some important principles to take into account while processing personal data: personal data must be processed fairly for specified purposes and on the basis of the consent of the person concerned or some other legitimate basis laid down by law. Finally, according to Art. 8 para. 3, compliance with these rules shall be subject to control by an independent authority.

This results in a mainly subjective-legal component, according to which the individual has a right to the protection of his or her personal data in compliance with the requirements specified in Art. 8 CFR. Provisions,

---

75 ECtHR, judgement of 2.12.2008, no. 2872/02, para. 43 et seq.

76 ECtHR, judgement of 10.5.2011, no. 1685/10. The case concerned an artist (applicant) who exhibited her work "the Virgin-Whore Church" in an art gallery in Helsinki opened to the public. The work included hundreds of photographs of teenage girls or otherwise very young women in sexual poses and acts. The pictures had been downloaded from free Internet pages and some of them were extremely violent or degrading.

77 ECtHR, judgement of 21.7.2011, nos. 32181/04 and 35122/05.

78 Directive 95/46/EC of the European Parliament and of the Council of 24 October 1995 on the protection of individuals with regard to the processing of personal data and on the free movement of such data, OJ L 281, 23.11.1995, pp. 31–50.

inasmuch as they govern the processing of personal data liable to infringe fundamental freedoms, in particular the right to respect for private life, must necessarily be interpreted in the light of the fundamental rights guaranteed by the Charter.[79] The addressees of this fundamental right are the institutions and bodies of the EU and the Member States when implementing Union law (Art. 51 para. 1 CFR). Against the background of the increased importance of data protection, especially in the relationship between private individuals, the direct third-party effect of the fundamental right is also discussed.[80] The CJEU takes this matter into account insofar as it transfers the principles following from Art. 8 CFR to the interpretation of the data protection rules of the EU.[81] The justification of infringements takes place – beside the special limitation clause of Art. 8 para. 2 sentence 1 CFR, stating that personal data are to be processed only in good faith for fixed purposes and on the basis of a legally fixed basis – according to the horizontally applicable test of Art. 52 para. 1 CFR (see already above).[82]

The processing of (personal) data is omnipresent on the Internet – whether this takes place via the content itself (through processing of data of persons portrayed in the respective content) or is part of offer structures on the Internet (cookies, personalised advertising, data and address trading, etc.).[83] Both content providers[84] and distributors must therefore comply with data protection rules that result from the interests of those affected and are protected by fundamental rights. These specifications are comprehensively codified at the level of EU secondary law with the GDPR, which also provides for a differentiated sanction framework, which is used by the national authorities set up under the law of the Member States. In addition, thereby a further element of Art. 8 CFR is addressed, which was a

---

79 CJEU, judgement of 6.10. 2015, C-362/14, *Maximillian Schrems v Data Protection Commissioner*, para. 38; cf. also judgements of 20.5.2003, joint cases C-465/00, C-138/01 and C-139/01, *Rechnungshof v Österreichischer Rundfunk and Others and Christa Neukomm and Joseph Lauermann v Österreichischer Rundfunk*, para. 68; of 14.5.2014, C-131/12, *Google Spain SL and Google Inc. v Agencia Española de Protección de Datos (AEPD) and Mario Costeja González*, para. 68; of 11.12.2014, C-212/13, *František Ryneš v Úřad pro ochranu osobních údajů*, para. 29.

80 Cf. on this *Streinz/Michl*, EuZW 2011, p. 384, 385.

81 CJEU, *Google Spain v AEPD*, supra (fn. 79), para. 68

82 CJEU, judgement of 9.11.2010, joint cases C-92/09 and C-93/09, *Volker und Markus Schecke GbR (C-92/09) and Hartmut Eifert (C-93/09) v Land Hessen*, para. 53.

83 Cf. on this in detail para. 2.4.3.2.

84 On the special characteristics of journalistic services against the background of media privileges, cf. in more detail at para. 2.4.3.1.

previously unusual specific laying down of separate data protection rights in a fundamental rights catalogue and therefore deserves to be mentioned also in the context of this study.

The CJEU underlined "that the question of compliance has to be subject to control by an independent authority, as follows from primary law of the EU and, in particular, from Art. 8 para. 3 CFR and Art 16 para. 2 TFEU."[85]. It is necessary for the competent supervisory authorities to be independent so as to enable them to carry out their tasks without external interference. Such independence shall preclude, inter alia, any direct or indirect instruction or any other form of external influence which might guide their decisions and call into question the fulfilment of their tasks by the said authorities.[86] With this provision, therefore, an organisational regulation is anchored constitutionally, which is more closely designed in the provisions of Art. 51 et seq. GDPR and implemented accordingly by the Member States.

Regarding the ECHR, Art. 8 para. 1 sets out the precise rights which are to be guaranteed to an individual by the state – the right to respect for private life, family life, home and correspondence. According to the ECtHR, private life is a broad concept that is incapable of an exhaustive definition.[87] The ECHR, however, also subsumes the protection of data under this term if they have a connection to private life.[88] For example, the ECHR has recently clarified, in the context of the monitoring of employees at their workplace, that, even if the private use of company means of communication is prohibited, the employer does not have the right to monitor the use of the means of communication unrestrictedly and at his discretion.[89] Art. 8 ECHR is also primarily a right of defence against state interference. However, the ECtHR also recognises that the obligations included in Art. 8 may involve the adoption of measures designed to secure respect for private life even in the sphere of the relations of individuals between themselves.[90] Corresponding to Art. 51 para. 1 CFR, Art. 8 para. 2 ECHR states that the rights guaranteed by Art. 8 para. 1 ECHR are not absolute and that it may be acceptable for public authorities to interfere under certain circumstances. Only interferences which are in accordance with

---

85 CJEU, judgement of 8.4.2014, C-288/12, *European Commission v Hungary*, para. 47.
86 Ibid., para. 51.
87 ECtHR, judgement of 25.3.1993, no. 13134/87, para. 36.
88 ECtHR, judgement of 29.4.2013, no. 24029/07.
89 ECtHR, judgement of 5.9.2017, no. 61496/08.
90 ECtHR, judgement of 12.11.2013, no. 5786/08, para. 78.

law and necessary in a democratic society in pursuit of one or more of the legitimate aims listed in Art. 8 para. 2 CFR will be considered to be an acceptable limitation by the state of an individual's rights. However, the ECtHR leaves to the Convention States a margin of appreciation. This margin is given both to the domestic legislator and to the (judicial) bodies that are called upon to interpret and apply the laws in force. The scope of this margin of appreciation will differ according to the context, and it has been held, for example, to be particularly wide in areas such as child protection. Here, the Court has recognised that there is diversity in approaches to childcare and state intervention into the family among Convention States. Accordingly, it allows States a measure of discretion when examining such cases under the ECHR.[91]

2.1.2.4. Freedom of Expression and the Media

Art. 10 ECHR guarantees that everyone has the right to freedom of expression, which includes the freedom to hold an opinion and to receive and impart information. However, the ECHR does not guarantee these freedoms indefinitely but accepts that free speech is also associated with duties and responsibilities. In this respect, Art. 10 para. 2 allows limitations if they are prescribed by law and are necessary in a democratic society, in the interests of national security, territorial integrity or public safety, for the prevention of disorder or crime, for the protection of health or morals, for the protection of the reputation or rights of others, for preventing the disclosure of information received in confidence or for maintaining the authority and impartiality of the judiciary. Both at the level of the scope of protection and at the level of justification, the ECHR contains relatively abstract and broadly defined rules which can only be (or become) defined by the case-law of the ECtHR. Accordingly, the ECtHR also promotes a broad understanding of Art. 10 ECHR, which covers all communication behaviour irrespective of whether it is an individual expression of opinion or the mass media dissemination of information. Differentiation between different media manifestations, which is also influenced by the significance of the respective means of communication for the public opinion-

---

91 ECtHR, judgement of 27.11.1992, no. 13441/87; cf. on this in detail *Kilkelly*, Human rights handbook No. 1. This margin of appreciation applies also in the field of the protection of individual's data; cf. ECtHR, judgement of 5.9.2017, no. 61496/08, para. 112.

building, does not initially take place at the level of the scope of protection but rather at the level of justification of restrictions and the degree of state duty to protect to be guaranteed. Online content is, therefore, generally covered by this broad scope, including content that is insulting or shocking in nature.[92] Interventions in this comprehensively understood area of protection are conceivable in many ways and range from preventing or making more difficult the reception/accessibility of such services or individual contents to merely labelling them. Thus, the deletion of a comment representing "hate speech"[93] intervenes in the freedom of expression or freedom of the media just as much as a blocking obligation with regard to a news platform against an access provider.

At the level of justification, however, which initially demands an urgent social need for the use of the barriers under Art. 10 para. 2 ECHR, which must be asserted by the state appropriately, carefully and in good faith and presented convincingly[94], differentiation takes place. For example, the signatory states have a certain margin of appreciation when assessing the necessity of restrictions[95], but this is particularly limited in the case of interference in the freedom of the press and freedom of broadcasting (as partial manifestations of the fundamental right under Art. 10 ECHR).[96] This applies insofar as the respective media act with the aim of informing the public about socially relevant topics[97], thus fulfilling the task of a public watchdog[98]. It also applies outside the area of the "professional press" in the sense of an alignment of the scope of protection to situations typically threatening fundamental rights, provided that non-journalistic persons and lay journalists are in a situation comparable to that of the press with regard to their publication activities.[99] Publicly accessible media archives

---

92 ECtHR, judgement of 8.11.2012, no. 43481/09.
93 Cf. on hate speech for example ECtHR, judgement of 9.2.2012, no. 1813/07; of 16.7.2009, no. 15615/07.
94 ECtHR, in: EuGRZ 1995, p. 20.
95 *Daiber*, in: Meyer-Ladewig/Nettesheim/von Raumer, Art. 10 para. 33 with further references.
96 Cf. on this ECtHR, judgements of 7.6.2012, no. 38433/09; of 10.5.2011, no. 48009/08.
97 ECtHR, judgement of 6.1.2015, no. 70287/11; of 17.7.2001, no. 39288/98: "The Court considers that these principles also apply to the publication of books in general or written texts other than the periodical press".
98 ECtHR, judgement of 20.5.1999, no. 21980/93.
99 On the question whether a differentiation between classical journalists and other publicists within the personal scope of protection is compatible with Art. 10 ECHR, cf. ECtHR, judgement of 4.11.2014, no. 30162/10.

also play an increasingly important role in this context.[100] The particular relevance of the media to the formation of public opinion and their importance for a functioning democracy not only comes to bear within the framework of limited national margins of appreciation but also within the framework of the consideration to be carried out in the event of infringements of the fundamental rights of third parties.

In addition to issues of the protection of minors and of public safety and order, especially in the area of criminal law content, this applies above all to the impairment of the right to privacy (Art. 8 ECHR) of persons affected by a report or portrayed in media content. Due to the diversity of possible causes, a differentiated case law of the ECHR has developed over the years, from which numerous factors can be derived that play a role in the weighting of conflicting rights.[101] These include factors such as contributing to a debate of general interest, the role, function and past public behaviour of the person concerned, the nature of the activity being reported on, the way information is obtained, the truth of the content, and its form and impact. At least similar criteria are used by the ECtHR in conflicts with other rights of third parties, which may have a different direction of protection than the general right to privacy. This applies in particular to collisions between freedom of the media and copyright law, which, according to the ECtHR, are not fully protected even at the level of the ECHR.[102] Intellectual property may be restricted where freedom of expression, as an essential basis of a democratic society, requires it in the context of a debate of public interest. Human dignity, however, is not open to balancing of conflicting rights.[103]

The central provision of guarantees under media law, and thus of relevance in connection with the regulation of (online) content at Union level, is Art. 11 para. 1 CFR which states that every person has the right to freedom of expression, including the freedom to receive and pass on information and ideas without interference by public authorities and regardless of national borders. Art. 11 para. 2 CFR also stipulates that freedom and pluralism of the media shall be respected. Here too, the term "media" covers traditional media such as the press, radio and films as well as any other

---

100 ECtHR, judgement of 19.10.2017, no. 71233/13.
101 Cf. on this and the following instead of many: ECtHR, judgement of 7.2.2012, no. 39954/08.
102 ECtHR, judgement of 10.1.2013, no. 36769/08.
103 See, however, on tendencies of weighing human dignity against other rights in the case law of the CJEU: *Schwarzburg*, Die Menschenwürde im Recht der Europäischen Union, pp. 267 et seq.

form of mass communication that already exists or will only emerge in the future, provided that it is addressed to the general public.[104] Art. 11 CFR has been conceived in close accordance with or, as far as the scope of protection is concerned, in direct adoption of Art. 10 ECHR. Only the limitation rule of Art. 10 para. 2 ECHR has not been adopted, because the CFR as a whole contains a horizontally applicable standard limitation rule in Art. 52 para. 1 CFR.[105] In contrast to the ECHR, Art. 11 CFR explicitly mentions freedom of the media and its plurality, whereby the special importance of the media for freedom of expression is expressed on the one hand, but freedom of the media is also emphasised on the other hand from the context of a uniform fundamental right to communication.[106] In contrast to a comprehensive and differentiated case law of the ECtHR, the case law of the CJEU is less pronounced with regard to freedom of communication. This is also due to the fact that traditional restrictions to the freedom of communication tend to fall within the sphere of responsibility of the Member States in view of the EU's limited powers.[107] However, the case-law of the ECtHR on Art. 10 ECHR can be relied on to a large extent here, which also results from the corresponding explanations of the preamble to Art. 11 CFR.[108] This applies at least to Art. 11 CFR in its form as a right of defence. The CJEU makes increasing use of the possible recourse to the principles of the ECHR and their development by the ECtHR and refers in its rulings to the corresponding relevant case-law including the limitations contained therein.[109]

2.1.2.5. Freedom to Conduct a Business

Freedom to conduct a business is enshrined in Art. 15 CFR in the section on civil liberties. The ECHR, on the other hand, does not contain an inde-

---

104 *Von Coelln*, in: Stern/Sachs, Art. 11 para. 30.
105 *Löffler*, Presserecht, § 1 para. 88; *Von Coelln*, in: Stern/Sachs, Art. 11 para. 7 et seq.
106 *Löffler*, Presserecht, § 1 para. 89, 90 with further references also to the debate as to whether Art. 11 para. 2 CFR is to be accorded a legally independent meaning by highlighting the wording of this provision.
107 *Löffler*, Presserecht, § 1 para. 46, 86.
108 Explanations relating to the Charter of Fundamental Rights, OJ C 303/17, available at http://eur-lex.europa.eu/legal-content/EN/TXT/HTML/?uri=CELEX:32007X1214(01)&from=DE.
109 Cf. already CJEU, *Familiapress v Heinrich Bauer Verlag*, supra (fn. 38).

pendent regulation on freedom to conduct a business. However, partial elements of this freedom are also protected in the ECHR via individual fundamental rights. For example, freedom of expression from Art. 10 ECHR, the right to a fair trial from Art. 6 ECHR, freedom of property from Art. 1 of the First Additional Protocol to the ECHR and the right to respect for private life from Art. 8 ECHR are to be mentioned in this regard.[110]

Art. 15 CFR states that everyone has the right to engage in work and to pursue a freely chosen or accepted occupation; it states also that every citizen of the Union has the freedom to seek employment, to work, to exercise the right of establishment and to provide services in any Member State. However, this is not to be understood as a subjective position in the sense of a right to the creation of a – as appropriate as possible – job. According to the systematic position in Part 2 of the CFR, it is a purely fundamental right of freedom, which prohibits the Member States and the EU in principle from taking active steps to prevent people from taking up employment and thus from choosing and exercising a profession.[111] In the case law of the CJEU, however, there is no precise definition of the term "business". From a generous assumption on numerous gainful activities under the freedoms of the internal market, which is to be determined in the case law of the CJEU and the courts of the Member States, it can be concluded, however, that the freedom to conduct a business under Art. 15 para. 1 CFR is to be understood in a comprehensive sense.[112] Consequently, any economic activity, i.e. remunerated activity serving the purpose of acquisition, is also to be considered as a profession within the meaning of Art. 15 CFR if it is neither purely temporary nor absolutely minor in nature, whereby economic success is irrelevant in this respect.[113]

According to the case law of the CJEU, however, freedom to conduct a business does not apply in all its forms "without limits"; rather, it must be viewed in terms of its social function.[114] An encroachment on the freedom to conduct a business that requires justification is present in every sovereign act which has a perceptible negative effect on the choice or exercise of an occupation. With regard to the dissemination of online content and the corresponding enforcement of rights, online platforms and other service providers, in particular, may be severely restricted in their rights.

---

110 *Blanke*, in: *Stern/Sachs*, Art. 15, para. 14.
111 *Blanke*, in: *Stern/Sachs*, Art. 15, para. 24 et seq.
112 *Blanke*, in: *Stern/Sachs*, Art. 15, para. 28.
113 *Penski/Elsner*, in: DÖV 7/2001, p. 265, 271.
114 *Blanke*, in: Stern/Sachs, Art. 15, para. 43.

The business model of many providers is aimed precisely at being able to offer a large number of contents to a large audience without prior verification. Regulations that impose obligations on the platforms in this respect and, if necessary, provide for liability in the event of non-compliance thus constitute interference with their freedom of occupation.

The justification for such an intervention is based on Art. 52 para. 1 CFR. According to this, each interference must be based on a legal basis issued by the competent legislator. In addition, each infringement must comply with the principle of proportionality, therefore pursue a legitimate objective, be necessary and appropriate and must not affect the essence of the fundamental right.[115] Furthermore, it can be stated that Art. 15 CFR, with regard to the unity of the CFR, finds a direct barrier in other legal values guaranteed by the CFR.[116] Thus, a service provider can only exercise its freedom from Art. 15 CFR to such an extent that the fundamental rights of other rights holders whose contents are disseminated, for example, via platforms in the online area are also sufficiently taken into account. For example, the right to intellectual property contained in Art. 17 para. 2 CFR, which includes copyright, publishing, patent and trademark rights, or the right of a company to dispose of the information concerning its systems and products, should be mentioned here.[117]

2.1.2.6. Right to Property

The right to property is guaranteed in Art. 17 CFR and in Art. 1 of Protocol No. 1 to the ECHR (P1ECHR).

According to Art. 17 para. 1 CFR, everyone has the right to own, use, dispose of and bequeath his or her lawfully acquired possessions. The term "possessions", i.e. the material scope of protection of the right to property, thus encompasses all monetary asset positions, i.e. in addition to the ownership of movable and immovable property, all acquired property rights which are exclusively assigned to a person by the legal system, provided that these have arisen by virtue of his own performance or at any rate from the assets of a natural or legal person.[118] Moreover, Art. 17 para. 2 CFR states that also intellectual property shall be protected. Corresponding to

---

115 *Blanke*, in: Stern/Sachs, Art. 15, para. 44.
116 *Blanke*, in: Stern/Sachs, Art. 15, para. 44.
117 *Vosgerau*, in: Stern/Sachs, Art. 17, para. 44.
118 *Vosgerau*, in: Stern/Sachs, Art. 17, para. 43.

Art. 17 para. 1 CFR, Art. 1 para. 1 P1ECHR states that every natural or legal person is entitled to the peaceful enjoyment of his possessions. However, the ECHR not only protects within the framework of this wording the ownership of property but in principle also includes certain rights and interests which constitute an asset and can, therefore, be equated with (tangible) property.[119] This also includes, although not explicitly mentioned here as in the CFR, intellectual property rights (copyright, trademark and patent rights), because these are rights which are assigned to the individual as exclusive rights and which she or he can generally freely dispose of.[120]

In the context of the cross-border dissemination of online content, different actors have to be considered in light of the right to property. On the one hand, the rights of those whose content is distributed via online platforms are significantly affected. The intellectual property just mentioned will often be affected here, whether in the sense of an original copyright or a license, which also has an asset value in the sense of the definition mentioned above. On the other hand, however, platforms are also affected which first make the content available to an audience. Regulations that impose obligations or restrictions on platforms or other distributors can interfere with the basic right to property of the platform provider. Although the CJEU has already frequently dealt with the protection of the property of companies and in principle also subjects companies to the right to property, it has not explicitly recognised, so far, a right to the established and exercised business which goes beyond the individual operating resources already covered by the property right and would aim at the company as a whole.[121] However, according to the case law of the ECHR, economic interests affecting the running of a business are also considered to be within the scope of protection of the right to property. According to the CFR, these "soft factors" should in any case also participate in the protection of property when the existence of the (ownership protected) company itself is at stake. Due to extensive obligations imposed on platform operators with regard to the distribution of online content, the business model of various providers can be severely endangered and is thus a position capable of protection in the sense of this fundamental right.

---

119 *Meyer-Ladewig/von Raumer*, in: Meyer-Ladewig/Nettesheim/von Raumer, Art. 1 Protocol No. 1 to the ECHR, para. 11.
120 On the character of intellectual property rights as property in the sense of Art. 1 P1ECHR cf. already *Peukert*, EuGRZ 1981, p. 97; *Vosgerau*, in: Stern/Sachs, Art. 17 para. 44.
121 *Vosgerau*, in: Stern/Sachs, Art. 17, para. 35.

In this context, the enforcement of rights by means of instruments provided for this purpose by the legal system can mean an interference in the legal position of another legal subject. An interference of the right to property is given if either an ownership position is withdrawn or its use, disposal, inheritance or exploitation is subject to restrictions. In this respect, the CJEU, in its previous case-law, has essentially adopted the concept of ownership interference from the ECHR. An intervention may, however, be justified under the requirements provided for this purpose. When examining the justification, a distinction must be made between the withdrawal of ownership and restrictions on its use based on the wording of Art. 17 CFR (and also Art. 1 P1ECHR). For the distribution of online content, the restriction of the use of proprietary protective positions is decisive. A mere restriction on the use of property is justified if it serves objectives which are in the public interest of the Union, if it does not present itself as unacceptable, i.e. excessive, with regard to the purpose pursued and if it therefore does not affect the substance of the property right.

2.1.3. Fundamental Rights Protection Obligations

With regard to the ECHR, the fundamental existence of obligations to protect ("positive obligations" or *"obligations positives"*) – derived from duties to act – can be established by interpreting a series of judgments of the ECtHR.[122] At the same time, however, on the basis of the ECHR there is a scope for implementation by the states in the exercise of their protection obligations, so that the protection obligation does not necessarily have to be followed by a statutory regulation; instead, investigation obligations and information obligations can also be considered.[123]

The ECtHR has, for example, recognised such "positive obligations" for Art. 8 ECHR[124] and Art. 10 ECHR. With regard to the former, obligations of the contracting states may result from human rights, particularly in the

---

122 Cf. ECtHR, judgement of 16.3.2000, no. 23144/93, para. 42; *Dröge*, Positive Verpflichtungen der Staaten in der Europäischen Menschenrechtskonvention, pp. 1 et seq., 71 et seq., 179 et seq.; *Jaeckel*, Schutzpflichten im deutschen und europäischen Recht, pp. 128 et seq.; *Klatt*, in: ZaöRV 71, 2011, p. 691, 692 et seq.; *Koenen*, Wirtschaft und Menschenrechte, p. 58; *Ress*, in: ZaöRV 64, 2004, p. 621, 628.
123 Cf. *Koenen*, Wirtschaft und Menschenrechte, p. 59 et seq.
124 ECtHR, judgement of 27.10.1994, no. 18535/91, para. 31; judgement of 12.11.2013, no. 5786/08, para. 78.

area of the right to sexual self-determination, respect for good reputation, the right to one's own image and the protection of personal data. With regard to the freedom of the media, the contracting parties must effectively guarantee pluralism, particularly in the audiovisual media, through an appropriate framework.[125] Freedom of expression can also trigger such obligations.[126] Furthermore, the ECtHR assumes positive obligations under Art. 2, 3, 6 and 11 ECHR[127], whereby such positive obligations to act can also be considered for other rights. In a decision concerning Art. 10 ECHR, the ECtHR explained the criteria for the assumption of a positive duty to protect:

> "In determining whether or not a positive obligation exists, regard must be had to the fair balance that has to be struck between the general interest of the community and the interests of the individual, the search for which is inherent throughout the Convention. The scope of this obligation will inevitably vary, having regard to the diversity of situations obtaining in Contracting States, the difficulties involved in policing modern societies and the choices which must be made in terms of priorities and resources. Nor must such an obligation be interpreted in such a way as to impose an impossible or disproportionate burden on the authorities"[128].

This shows that a weighing up of fundamental rights at the level of justification, which is regularly required in the framework of fundamental rights, can already play a role in the assessment of the warranty content of fundamental rights. The more an existing grievance interferes with fundamental rights, the more government action will be necessary.

With regard to human dignity – as an inviolable good and as the highest principle which also affects other human rights – and its relevance in the area of online content (cf. Chapter 2.1.2.1), one will be able to ascertain serious grievances concerning human dignity in the digital environment, especially if one includes the *dark web*. With regard to Art. 3 ECHR, the ECtHR already ruled on the emergence and scope of state protection obligations which, however, directly only concern the actual (physic or psy-

---

125 ECtHR, judgement of 22.4.2013, no. 48876/08 para. 134; judgement of 17.9.2009, no. 13936/02 para. 100 et seq.
126 ECtHR, judgement of 29.02.2000, no. 39293/98; judgement of 16.03.2000, no. 23144/93.
127 For an overview see ECtHR, judgement of 16.3.2000, no. 23144/93, para. 42.
128 ECtHR, judgement of 16.3.2000, no. 23144/93, para. 43.

chic) threat or existence of inhuman or degrading acts and not their depiction or making available on the Internet. Accordingly, protective measures are necessary if state authorities know or must know of such a danger, which applies in particular and to a special extent to the danger of child abuse.[129] In this case, they must intervene effectively and with due regard to the interests of the victims, which also implies legislative measures.[130] Although the (psychological) burden of depicting acts violating human dignity in the context of online content and the resulting (renewed) impairment of human dignity may not be comparable with the actual (psychological and physical) burden of the depicted act, there is at least a connection and a similarity. Against this background, it seems contradictory to impose protective duties on the state, for example, if torture is committed against a person, but not if a video of this act of torture is published on the Internet. As shown above, both can affect human dignity, albeit in different ways.

With regard to the question of positive protection obligations of the Member States under the CFR, two things should first be mentioned: On the one hand, such obligations can only be imposed on Union law bodies if they have original Union law competence in this area and if their action in accordance with the principle of subsidiarity is precisely required, and the Member States can only be imposed if they implement Union law. Another approach would conflict with Art. 51 para. 2 CFR, according to which the CFR does not extend the scope of Union law beyond the competences of the Union and has no influence on existing competences.[131] On the other hand, Art. 51 para. 1 sentence 2 CFR states an obligation for the Member States to promote, but it should not in principle be interpreted in such a way that positive legal protection obligations of the Member States result from the fundamental rights in general. Rather, in principle, each individual fundamental right of the Union must be examined with regard to its content under the law of compulsory protection.[132] If such state protection obligations exist at Union level, there is much to suggest that these can also include warranty obligations in the organisation and design of procedures as well as information obligations.[133]

---

129 ECtHR, judgement of 28.10.1998, no. 23452/94, para. 116 et seq.
130 ECtHR, judgement of 22.3.2016, no. 646/10, para. 72 et seq.
131 Cf. Explanations relating to the Charter of Fundamental Rights, OJ C 303, 14.12.2007, pp. 17–35.
132 *Ladenburger/Vondung*, in: Stern/Sachs, Art. 51 para. 21 et seq.
133 *Weber*, in: Stern/Sachs, Art. 7 para. 5 with further references.

The CJEU has so far been rather cautious in its explicit acceptance of state protection obligations under the fundamental rights of the Charter. It has indicated such obligation, for example, for the right to property[134]; the CJEU has, however, in particular with regard to intellectual property, tended to focus on secondary legislation dealing with the right to property and has not dealt with the question of positive protection obligations (despite its possibility to deal with).[135] The same applies to the protection of private life under Art. 7 CFR against the background of secondary data protection law.[136] With regard to the rights of the child, for example, which are guaranteed in Art. 24 CFR, Art. 14 and Art. 24 para. 2 CFR provide for the participation of the state in the upbringing of children and thus also in the concretisation of the best interests of the child, whereby Art. 24 para. 3 indicates that this guardian function is the responsibility of the Member States and not of the Union itself.[137] Thus, the fundamental duties of protection in favour of the best interests of the child are stipulated here, the concrete contents of which, however, have to be determined by the national legislature.[138]

Due to the relationship between ECHR and CFR described at the beginning of this section, but also due to the CJEU's reference to the principles developed by ECtHR in the framework of its case law on fundamental rights of the Union, it will, however, also be possible to transfer the ECtHR's doctrine of the duty to protect to Union level, provided that this does not contradict the special characteristics described in Art. 51 and, in particular, that there remains a margin for manoeuvre for the Member States.

---

134 CJEU, judgement of 24.3.1994, C-2/92, *The Queen v Ministry of Agriculture, Fisheries and Food, ex parte Dennis Clifford Bostock*, para. 18 et seq.
135 Cf., e.g., CJEU, judgement of 29.1.2008, C-275/06, *Productores de Música de España (Promusicae) v Telefónica de España SAU*.
136 Cf. on this CJEU, judgement of 8.4.2014, joint cases C-293/12 and C-594/12, *Digital Rights Ireland Ltd v Minister for Communications, Marine and Natural Resources and Others and Kärntner Landesregierung and Others*.
137 *Ennuschat*, in: Stern/Sachs, Art. 24 para. 12.
138 Cf. *Grabenwarter*, in: DVBl. 2001, p. 1, 6.

2.2. Fundamental Freedoms

2.2.1. Freedom of Establishment and Freedom to Provide Services

Freedom of establishment (Art. 49 et seq. of the Treaty of the Functioning of the European Union, TFEU[139]) includes the right to take up and pursue self-employment in another Member State in accordance with the provisions laid down by the latter for its own nationals, as well as the right to set up and manage businesses. The applicability of the material scope of protection requires the existence of an economic activity with cross-border implications. Both characteristics must be interpreted broadly.[140] With regard to the cross-border dissemination of online content, a profit-making purpose will usually be necessary. It can be assumed that this is normally the case, at least on the part of the disseminator of content. The notion of "establishment" implies a certain stability and durability and thus distinguishes the freedom of establishment from the freedom to provide services (Art. 56 et seq. TFEU). In the case of the former, it is important that the entrepreneur participates permanently in the economic market of another Member State by establishing a presence. By contrast, in the latter case, the provision of a cross-border service is of primary importance. The TFEU does not define durability any further. The CJEU has laid down various criteria, such as period and frequency, residential situation of the service provider or place of payment.[141] However, the notion of establishment has been refined in the area of media law, which is of particular relevance here. Art. 2 of the AVMSD contains a list of indicative facts according to which the place of establishment of a media service provider can be determined (and therefore which Member State is responsible for its regulation). The following facts are of particular relevance: the location of the head office and the place where editorial decisions are made or where a significant proportion of the staff responsible for the programming is based. Although these requirements only apply directly within the framework of the AVMSD, they can also be used for assessment purposes within the framework of freedom of establishment for media service providers.

---

139 Treaty on the Functioning of the European Union, OJ C 326, 26.10.2012, pp. 47390. Provisions of the TFEU relevant in the context of this study are listed in the Online Annex, available at www.nomos-shop.de/44382, I.
140 *Korte*, in: Calliess/Ruffert, Art. 49 TFEU para. 12, 19 et seq.
141 *Korte*, in: Calliess/Ruffert, Art. 49 TFEU para. 26.

The players potentially involved in the dissemination of online content – broadcasters, on-demand providers, VSPs, intermediaries, search engines, apps, access providers, etc. – are heterogeneous. Thus they cannot be categorised as falling under the protective scope of the freedom of establishment per se. Rather, the protections offered by the freedom to provide services (Art. 56 et seq. TFEU) will more regularly apply for these actors, especially if they are information society services within the meaning of the ECD[142]. The freedom to provide services does not require a permanent change of seat nor integration into a legal system and thus corresponds more readily to the spontaneous cross-border (factor) mobility of online activity.[143] According to Art. 57 TFEU, services shall be considered to be "services" within the meaning of the Treaties where they are normally provided for remuneration, insofar as they are not governed by the provisions relating to freedom of movement for goods, capital and persons. However, in addition to this negative definition, which relies on a distinction from other fundamental freedoms, participation in commercial transactions by self-employed persons is regularly taken into account.[144] In its case-law, the CJEU has characterised the crossing of borders and remuneration as indispensable characteristics of a service. The notion of service must be interpreted broadly and can already be assumed to exist if the activities constitute part of economic life.[145] This includes "cultural activities" such as radio and television[146] as well as gambling[147]. It (usually) does not matter who pays the fee, whether it is the customer/user or a third party such as an advertising partner. This is particularly relevant for advertising-financed offers such as private broadcasting, for the countless offers on the Internet that are financed via advertising business models such as VSPs or for social networks like Facebook or adult content platforms.

---

142 Cf. on this recently the Opinion of Advocate General Szpunar delivered on 30.4.2019, C-390/18, *AirBnB*, para. 19 et seq.

143 *Kluth*, in: Calliess/Ruffert, Art. 56 TFEU, para. 1.

144 *Randelzhofer/Forsthoff*, in: Grabitz/Hilf/Nettesheim, Art. 49, 50 TFEU, para. 80.

145 CJEU, judgement of 12.12.1974, C-36/74, *B.N.O. Walrave and L.J.N. Koch v Association Union cycliste internationale, Koninklijke Nederlandsche Wielren Unie and Federación Española Ciclismo*, para. 4; of 5.10.1988, C-196/87, *Udo Steymann v Staatssecretaris van Justitie*, para. 9.

146 Fundamentally: CJEU, judgement of 30.4.1974, C-155/73, *Giuseppe Sacchi*.

147 CJEU, judgement of 22.3.1994, C-275/92, *Her Majesty's Customs and Excise v Gerhart Schindler and Jörg Schindler*; judgement of 6.11.2003, C-243/01, *Criminal proceedings against Piergiorgio Gambelli and Others*.

It has not yet been expressly clarified by the CJEU whether payment with user data, for example in return for the use of a free digital service, is to be regarded as payment in this sense. As a result of new efforts at EU level, in particular by the Directive (EU) 2019/770 on certain aspects concerning contracts for the supply of digital content and digital services[148], which recognises data as quasi-contractual consideration in the case of digital services[149], an interpretation in this sense is very likely.[150] However, such offers will regularly rely, at least partially, on advertising finance, which is enhanced by the collection, analysis and use of user data in the context of, for example, personalised advertising.[151]

However, either the freedom of establishment or the freedom to provide services will regularly be affected. It follows from the case law of the CJEU that an economic activity – which regularly exists in the online activities considered here – falls under either the freedom of establishment or the freedom to provide services.[152] The provisions on services are complementary to those on the right of establishment: the wording of Art. 56 para. 1 TFEU already requires that the provider and recipient of the service in question are "established" in two different Member States. Art. 57 TFEU stipulates that the provisions on services apply only if the provisions on the

---

148 Directive (EU) 2019/770 of the European Parliament and of the Council of 20 May 2019 on certain aspects concerning contracts for the supply of digital content and digital services, OJ L 136, 22.5.2019, pp. 1–27. According to Recital 36 of this directive, however, this directive should (expressively) be without prejudice to other Union law governing a specific sector or subject matter, such as telecommunications, e-commerce and consumer protection. It should also be without prejudice to Union and national law on copyright and related rights, including the portability of online content services.

149 Art. 3 para. 1 of Directive (EU) 2019/770 states: "This Directive shall also apply where the trader supplies or undertakes to supply digital content or a digital service to the consumer, and the consumer provides or undertakes to provide personal data to the trader [...]."

150 Cf. on this Directive also *Schmidt-Kessel/Erler/Grimm/Kramme*, in: ZPEU 13(1), 2016, p. 2; and *Bokor*, Die Richtlinienvorschläge der Kommission zu Verträgen über digitalen Inhalt und Online-Warenhandel, available at https://www.bunde stag.de/resource/blob/422554/6f0bd347b413226ad2ffe992dc5cfa9f/bokor-data.p df.

151 Cf. on data driven business models *Seufert* (ed.), Media Economics revisited: (Wie) Verändert das Internet die Ökonomie der Medien?, pp. 38 et seq.

152 CJEU, judgement of 30.11.1995, C-55/94, *Reinhard Gebhard v Consiglio dell'Ordine degli Avvocati e Procuratori di Milano*, para. 2.

right of establishment are not applicable.[153] When examining whether exemptions to the freedom of establishment or the freedom to provide services are justified, it is not necessary to make a separate assessment for each freedom when looking at the context of the online dissemination of the relevant content. The requirements for justifying exemptions to the two fundamental freedoms do not differ significantly from each other. In the following, solely the effects of the freedom to provide services in the area of online content dissemination will be discussed.

The freedom to provide services contains a prohibition of discrimination and a prohibition of restrictions.[154] In addition to the active freedom to provide services, i.e. the freedom of the service provider to provide his service in another Member State under the same conditions as a service provider established there, it also protects the passive freedom to provide services[155], i.e. the recipient's right to receive a service in another Member State from a service provider established there.

In this context it has often been discussed whether – and if so, to what extent – the freedom to provide services requires the implementation of the country-of-origin principle.[156] According to the CJEU, a provision is already restrictive and thus a limitation of the freedom to provide services if it requires an additional administrative or economic effort on the part of the service provider. This is meant to protect the service provider from a double burden (obligations under the laws of the country of origin and the country of destination).[157] The country-of-origin principle, on which, inter alia, the AVMSD and the ECD are based, avoids such double burdens (in principle), since it binds the service provider (in principle) only to the obligations provided in his country of origin. Art. 56 et seq. TFEU are primari-

---

153 Ibid., para. 22; Cf. also judgements of 12.12.1996, C-3/95, *Reisebüro Broede v Gerd Sandker*, para. 19; judgement of 11.3.2010, C-384/08, *Attanasio Group Srl gegen Comune di Carbognano*, para. 39.

154 Established jurisprudence since CJEU, judgement of 3.12.1974, C-33/74, *Johannes Henricus Maria van Binsbergen v Bestuur van de Bedrijfsvereniging voor de Metaalnijverheid*; for the freedom of establishment in parallel, cf. *Korte*, in: Calliess/Ruffert, Art. 49 TFEU para. 49.

155 Cf. on this *Randelzhofer/Forthoff*, in: Grabitz/Hilf/Nettesheim, Art. 49/50 TFEU para. 51.

156 Cf. on this in detail *Waldheim*, Dienstleistungsfreiheit und Herkunftslandprinzip; *Albath/Giesel*, in: EuZW 2, 2006, p. 38, 39 et seq.; *Hörnle*, in: International and Comparative Law Quarterly 54(1), 2005, p. 89.

157 CJEU, judgement of 15.3.2001, C-165/98, *Criminal proceedings against André Mazzoleni and Inter Surveillance Assistance SARL, as the party civilly liable, third parties: Eric Guillaume and Others*, para. 24.

ly intended to dismantle barriers to market access; however, they do not specify how equivalence is to be established for service providers. The CJEU derives from the freedom to provide services at least an obligation of the Member States to examine whether equivalence and recognition exists, i.e. whether control measures already carried out (equivalent and recognisable) in the country of origin may not be carried out again[158]. However, this does not mean that the legal situation of the country of origin takes precedence in principle. It merely obliges the Member State to take account of it. The freedom to provide services therefore does not necessarily require the application of the country-of-origin principle. This seems logical insofar as, on the one hand, the country-of-origin principle can also have a restrictive effect on the service provider, where for example the legal situation in the country of destination is more favourable. On the other hand, this is supported in particular in the interest of consumer protection, which prohibits that service providers be bound per se only by the law of their country of origin. This is meant to prevent situations whereby consumers would be subject to a legal uncertainty due to a lack of knowledge of the legal situation in the origin Member State and the service provider itself.[159]

Finally, it should also be noted that a restriction on the freedom to provide services needs to be justified. In addition to the justifications expressly provided for by the TFEU – public security, public order and public health – other restrictive measures may also be justified if they are necessary in order to pursue an objective in the public interest and if they are applied appropriately and do not go beyond what is necessary in order to achieve that objective (i.e. meet the proportionality test).[160] Exceptions to the country-of-origin principle and the scope of application of the country-of-destination principle must always be measured against these criteria, in particular when drafting national or European legislation.

For example, the objective of ensuring the quality of services or protecting customers from harm may be such an objective of general interest. The resulting obligations for undertakings, such as registration obligations, must not extend to the provision of occasional services and must not give

---

158 Cf. on this, e.g., CJEU, *Gebhard v Consiglio dell'Ordine degli Avvocati e Procuratori di Milano*, supra (fn 152).

159 *Kluth*, in: Calliess/Ruffert, Art. 56 TFEU para. 3 et seq.

160 CJEU, judgement of 13.1.1993, C-19/92, *Dieter Kraus v Land Baden-Württemberg*, para. 32; judgement of 26.10.1995, C-272/94, *Criminal proceedings against Michel Guiot and Climatec SA, as employer liable at civil law*, para. 11.

rise to additional administrative or contribution costs.[161] Other objectives of general interest recognised by the CJEU which are relevant in the context of this study are cultural policy[162], the protection of intellectual property[163], consumer protection[164] and the protection of minors[165]. Whether these objectives are pursued by appropriate and proportionate means is a matter for the individual case but depends in particular on the intensity of the restriction imposed.

2.2.2. Free Movement of Goods

The free movement of goods (Art. 28 et seq. TFEU) will only be briefly discussed in the present context, as it has only minor relevance for the cross-border dissemination of online content. It covers the free exchange of goods (movable physical items with a basic monetary value) within the Union and therefore protects against restrictions on the movement of goods. Online content is typically distributed in a digital format. The CJEU analyses the nature of a service by referring to the main activity of the service. For example, in the case of television broadcasts, the main activity is not the transmission but the production of content and thus subject to the rules on the freedom to provide services.[166] Although content can be fixed on physical media such as hard disks or the smartphone memories, in the context of online distribution this is normally only carried out by the user on an occasional basis. The online distribution of content is usually about consumption and not ownership. The freedom to provide services applies to non-physical products such as digital media content which is not distributed on a storage medium.

---

161 CJEU, judgement of 30.11.1999, C-58/98, *Josef Corsten*, para. 38 et seq.

162 CJEU, judgement of 25.7.1991, C-353/89, *Commission of the European Communities v Kingdom of the Netherlands*.

163 CJEU, judgement of 18.3.1980, C-62/79, *SA Compagnie générale pour la diffusion de la télévision, Coditel, and others v Ciné Vog Films and others*.

164 CJEU, judgement of 4.12.1986, C-220/83, *Commission of the European Communities v French Republic*.

165 CJEU, judgement of 8.9.2009, C-42/07, *Liga Portuguesa de Futebol Profissional and Bwin International Ltd v Departamento de Jogos da Santa Casa da Misericórdia de Lisboa*.

166 CJEU, *Sacchi*, supra (fn. 146).

2.3. Other Elements of EU Primary Law

2.3.1. Fundamental Principles and Goals of the EU

The Treaty on European Union (TEU)[167] is, alongside the TFEU, the basis for the European Union. It lays down its constituent structural principles and thus defines its essential legitimating foundations. All regulatory measures of the EU and its Member States must therefore always be viewed in the light of the TEU: they must meet its requirements and take its fundamental values into account. Art. 2 and 3 of the TEU elaborate the basic values and objectives of the EU. They are of particular importance.

Art. 2 TEU establishes the foundational values of the Union: respect of human dignity, freedom, democracy, equality, the rule of law and respect of human rights, including the rights of minorities. The respect of human rights not only substantiates human dignity and the principle of freedom but also the rule of law within the EU.[168] It thus builds a bridge to the fundamental rights addressed in the first section of this chapter.

These values are common to all Member States, i.e. in a society in which pluralism, non-discrimination, tolerance, justice, solidarity and equality between women and men prevail. Even though Art. 2 TEU is therefore primarily aimed at the EU itself, as can be seen from sentence 2, these fundamental values also have significance under Union law with regard to the legal systems of the Member States. Thus, on the one hand, the aforementioned fundamental values acquire significance as a substantive prerequisite in the accession procedure under Art. 49 TEU. On the other hand, their non-compliance in the procedure under Art. 7 TEU can lead to a restriction or suspension of Member State rights, including voting rights.[169] In addition to the fundamental requirement of Member States to remain loyal to the Union, derived from Art. 4 para. 3 subpara. 2, this is a further,

---

167 Treaty on European Union (TEU), OJ C 326, 26.10.2012, pp. 13–390. Provisions of the TEU relevant in the context of this study are listed in the Online Annex, available at www.nomos-shop.de/44382, I.

168 *Calliess*, in: Calliess/Ruffert, Art. 2 TEU para. 27.

169 This procedure is currently of importance for the first time with regard to the Member States Poland and Hungary, whereby the (political) discussion also refers to restrictions on freedom of the media and diversity of opinion in these Member States. Cf. *Ukrow*, in: vorgänge No. 224, 4/2018, p. 57, 62. Cf. also the Opinion of Advocate General Sharpston, delivered on 31.10.2019, C-715/17, C-718/17 and C-719/17 in the proceedings against Poland, Hungary and the Czech Republic.

more concrete mechanism for coordinating measures within the EU along the lines of adherence to fundamental values.

Art. 3 TEU sets out the objectives to be achieved through integration of the Union. These objectives are meant to provide a goal-oriented framework for action and ensure that integration is not just pursued for its own sake.[170] The provision therefore lays down a final EU programme, which must be achieved by EU institutions with respect to the latter's limited competencies and in the relevant thematic and legal areas through coordinated policy action by Member States. This can also result in standstill obligations for the Member States, which may prohibit them from counteracting the integration targets set by the EU.[171] According to Art. 4 para. 3 subpara. 3 TEU, the Member States shall instead assist the Union in carrying out its task and shall refrain from any measure which could jeopardise the attainment of the objectives of the Union.

Art. 3 TEU lists several objectives which are also relevant in the context of this study. According to Art. 3 para. 2 TEU, the Union shall, among other things, establish an internal market, work towards the sustainable development of Europe on the basis of balanced economic growth and a highly competitive social market economy, and promote scientific and technical progress. With regard to the distribution of online content and the digital economy as a whole, the strategy for a digital single market for Europe as a manifestation of these objectives is particularly important.[172] The Commission considers that the Digital Single Market should provide better access to digital goods and services, create an optimal environment for digital networks and services, and ensure that Europe's economy benefits from the digital revolution as a growth engine. Distributors/providers of online content are therefore meant to benefit as a priority from a (better) economic and regulatory environment that is to be created as part of this strategy. The EU has already tackled some reform projects under the umbrella of the Digital Single Market strategy. These include in particular the promotion of electronic commerce by abolishing geo-blocking, the modernisation of EU copyright law to adapt to the digital age and the updating of

---

170 *Ruffert*, in: Calliess/Ruffert, Art. 3 TEU para. 3; in principle regarding the objectives cf. *Müller-Graf*, in: Pechstein/Nowak/Häde, Art. 3 TEU para. 1; *Heintschel von Heinegg*, in: Vedder/Heintschel von Heinegg, Art. 3 TEU para. 3.

171 *Ruffert*, in: Calliess/Ruffert, Art. 3 EUV para. 4, 7.

172 Communication from the Commission to the European Parliament, the Council, the European Economic and Social Committee and the Committee of Regions, A Digital Single Market Strategy for Europe, COM(2015) 192 final, https://eur-lex.europa.eu/legal-content/EN/TXT/?uri=celex%3A52015DC0192.

EU rules on audiovisual content, implemented through the adoption of the Geo-blocking Regulation[173], the new DSM Directive and the reformed AVMSD. Meanwhile, other reform projects, such as the adaptation of the rules on privacy in electronic communications to the new digital environment, are still pending.[174] A closer look at the reforms that have already taken place shows, however, that not only the interests of the digital economy have been taken into account but that the interests of other stakeholders, in particular consumers, have played a central role, too. For example, combating illegal online content and protecting the most vulnerable users has been a key concern of the AVMSD reform, reflected for example in new rules for video-sharing platforms.

This in turn corresponds to a further objective of Art. 3 para. 3 subpara. 2 TEU, according to which the Union fights social exclusion and discrimination and promotes social justice and the protection of the rights of children.

Finally, Art. 3 para. 3 subpara. 4 TEU plays a role in the context of media policy as a whole and therefore in the context of this study. According to this, the EU shall respect its rich cultural and linguistic diversity and shall ensure that Europe's cultural heritage is safeguarded and enhanced. This provision therefore addresses the role of media as economic and cultural heritage in safeguarding diversity. Thereby the EU's objective is not to create a uniform European culture but rather to preserve existing cultural diversity, which draws its strengths precisely from its historically grown diversity. Against this background, measures at national level which are necessary for the protection of national and regional languages and cultures

---

173 Regulation (EU) 2018/302 of the European Parliament and of the Council of 28 February 2018 on addressing unjustified geo-blocking and other forms of discrimination based on customers' nationality, place of residence or place of establishment within the internal market and amending Regulations (EC) No 2006/2004 and (EU) 2017/2394 and Directive 2009/22/EC, OJ L 60I, 2.3.2018, pp. 1–15.

174 Cf. on this the Proposal for a Regulation of the European Parliament and of the Council concerning the respect for private life and the protection of personal data in electronic communications and repealing Directive 2002/58/EC (Regulation on Privacy and Electronic Communications), COM/2017/010 final – 2017/03 (COD), which, according to the Commission's original objective, was to enter into force at the same time as the GDPR but is still in the trilogue procedure.

are advocated at European level, as they ultimately make a contribution to cultural diversity – one of Europe's fundamental values.[175]

In the context of this study, Art. 2 and 3 TEU therefore mean two things: Firstly, the Member States must comply with the basic values established by the EU and meet the targets set. Different basic values and targets must be reconciled. Secondly, this gives rise to a responsibility on the part of the EU: On the one hand, where standstill obligations for the Member States exist, resulting from Art. 3 in conjunction with Art. 4 para. 3 TEU, the Union must – where it is assigned a competence – at least react to existing grievances which endanger the objectives. On the other hand, it should also be mentioned that no direct concrete duties to act can be derived from Art. 2 and 3 TEU.

2.3.2. Relevant EU Competencies

2.3.2.1. Legal Bases for an EU Competence in the Media Sector

However, the establishment of goals in accordance with Art. 3 TEU does not result in an allocation of powers. The EU can therefore only act within the framework of its competence to implement these goals.[176] All competences not conferred on the Union by the Treaties remain with the Member States in accordance with Art. 5 TEU, which addresses the principle of limited power, whereby the Union acts only within the limits of the powers conferred on it by the Member States in the Treaties to attain the objectives set out therein. These are exclusive competences (Art. 3 TFEU), shared competences (Art. 4 TFEU) or competences to support, coordinate or supplement the actions of the Member States (Art. 6 TFEU). The nature of each competence also determines the respective powers to act of both the Union and the Member States.

Exclusive competences, under which, in principle[177], only the EU can take legislative actions, exist in particular for "the establishing of the competition rules necessary for the functioning of the internal market". Art. 101 et seq. TFEU are expressions of the exercise of this competency. They also form the core of EU competition policy, which contains provi-

---

175 Cf. further *Ukrow/Cole*, Aktive Sicherung lokaler und regionaler Medienvielfalt, pp. 56 et seq.
176 *Ruffert*, in: Calliess/Ruffert, Art. 3 TEU para. 37.
177 However, the EU can continue to empower Member States to act.

sions on prohibitions of cartels, abuse of market power and on combating state restrictions on competition in the form of monopolisation and state aid.

Although the functioning of the internal market is a prerequisite for a matter to be allocated exclusive EU competence, the internal market (Art. 114 TFEU) itself does not fall under the exclusive competence of the EU.[178] On the contrary, Art. 4 para. 2 TFEU – like consumer protection – defines it as a shared competence[179], under which both the Union and the Member States have the possibility of adopting legally binding acts, whereby the Member States can only take action to the extent that the Union has not taken action.[180]

Finally, under Art. 6 lit. c only support, coordination and complementary measures can be taken by the EU in the field of culture, which is therefore fundamentally and intrinsically the responsibility of the Member States. In principle, the EU is free to choose which instruments it uses for support and coordination, which may also include the enactment of binding legislation in the form of regulations or directives. However, it is limited to the extent that the basic power to regulate must remain with the Member States. Harmonisation of national legislation is therefore excluded.[181]

For the cultural sector this means that Art. 167 para. 1–3 TFEU enable, and at the same time limit, the active cultural policy of the EU. Thus, the EU should contribute to the development of the cultures of the Member States and promote cooperation between them, supporting and supplementing their activities where necessary, amongst others in the field of artistic and literary creation, "including in the audiovisual sector". This is relevant insofar as the regulation and law enforcement concerning the dissemination of online content normally concerns the media – in the sense of a broad understanding of the term – or at least involves media indirectly. Within the framework of Art. 167 para. 1–3 TFEU, however, EU cultural policy is not intended to counteract, unify or replace the policy of the Member States. It is (merely) to play a role as a guardian of European cul-

---

178 *Frenz*, Handbuch Europarecht, para. 2217 with further references.
179 *Calliess*, in: EuzW 1995, p. 693, 694 et seq.; *Ludwigs*, in: EuZW 19(2004), p. 577.
180 *Calliess*, in: Calliess/Ruffert, Art. 2 AEUV para. 12 with reference to other views which assume that competence under Art. 4 is originally in the hands of the Member States and is only superseded by Union action.
181 *Calliess* in: Calliess/Ruffert, Art. 2 AEUV para. 28.

tural creation and otherwise act in an entirely subsidiary manner.[182] Art. 167 para. 4 TFEU, a "cross-cutting cultural clause", establishes a rule for EU action outside the areas of cultural policy referred to in para. 1–3. According to this, the Union shall take cultural aspects into account when acting under other provisions of the Treaties. This, however, does not affect the EU's basic competence order, for example in the sense of an "*exception culturelle*". Art. 167 para. 5 TFEU determines the instruments and procedures available to the EU. Only recommendations adopted by the Council on a proposal from the Commission, as well as support measures adopted by the European Parliament and the Council in accordance with the ordinary legislative procedure and after consulting the Committee of the Regions, but excluding any harmonisation of the laws and regulations of the Member States[183], can be considered. The latter negative clause prevents the EU from recourse to the general titles of competence under the approximation of laws, particularly in the area of the internal market (Art. 114 TFEU), and regards special provisions on the harmonisation of laws.[184] Thus, this provision does not present itself as a general prohibition of harmonisation for measures *with an impact* on the cultural sphere but rather as a prohibition of harmonising cultural measures.

It follows from this system in Art. 167 TFEU that the EU, based on a legal basis from its catalogue of competences, can also act (regulating) beyond the obligations under Art. 167 TFEU.[185] However, the prerequisite resulting from the cultural cross-cutting clause is that it must take cultural aspects into account, which regularly amounts to a balancing of cultural and other regulatory interests (e.g. economic aspects). Moreover, it follows from the TFEU system that cultural aspects must not be at the centre of a regulation under Union law.[186]

In the case of questions and problems relating to the cross-border dissemination of online content, it is not possible to define a specific, relevant

---

182 Cf. on this in detail and with further references *Ukrow/Cole*, Aktive Sicherung lokaler und regionaler Medienvielfalt, pp. 60 et seq.
183 The importance of this exclusion was also emphasised by the Court of the European Union in its judgment of 10 May 2016; cf. EC, judgement of 10.5.2016, T-529/13, para. 101 et seq., *Izsák and Dabis*.
184 *Blanke*, in: Calliess/Ruffert, Art. 167 para. 19; similar: *Niedobitek*, in: Streinz, Art. 167 TFEU, para. 55.
185 *Lenski*, Öffentliches Kulturrecht, p. 142.
186 Established jurisprudence of the CJEU, cf., e.g., CJEU, judgement of 17.3.1993, C-155/91, *Commission of the European Communities v Council of the European Communities*.

area of law. Rather, various matters are involved here, different objectives can be pursued with legislation, and even addressees and contents may not be uniform. Thus, substantive legal rules on lawfulness or liability play just as much a role as more formalistic legal questions of law enforcement and jurisdiction. Accordingly, the rules that are relevant in this context are spread out among a number of different sets of laws such as the AVMSD, the DSM Directive and the ECD, which interact with each other and cannot be considered separately. It is therefore not surprising that in the area of "media policy" and in view of the complex nature of media goods and services, which can be defined neither solely as cultural goods nor simply as economic goods, competences are based on various legal bases in the TFEU: namely Art. 28, 30, 34, 35 (free movement of goods), 45–62 (free movement of persons, services and capital), 101–109 (competition policy), 114 (technological harmonisation or the use of similar technological standards, for instance, in Internet productions), 165 (education), 166 (vocational training), 167 (culture), 173 (industry) and 207 (common commercial policy).[187]

2.3.2.2. The Specific Legal Bases for the ECD

At the time of its adoption the ECD was based mainly on Art. 47 para. 2 in conjunction with Art. 55 and 95 of the Treaty establishing the European Community[188], i.e. competences arising out of the completion of the internal market.

The legislative competence established by Art. 47 para. 2 and Art. 55 of the EC Treaty (now Art. 53 para. 1 and 62 TFEU) in the field of recognition of qualifications, taking up and pursuing self-employed activities and providing services falls under the area of shared competence under Art. 4 para. 2 lit. a TFEU. It allows the Union to recognise and coordinate national law in this area, in particular in the form of Directives[189] as the strongest

---

187 Cf., e.g., European Parliament, Fact Sheets on the European Union, 2019, http://www.europarl.europa.eu/ftu/pdf/en/FTU_3.6.2.pdf.

188 Treaty establishing the European Community, as amended by the Treaty of Amsterdam amending the Treaty on European Union, the Treaties establishing the European Communities and certain related acts, OJ C 340, 10.11.1997, pp. 1–144.

189 The adoption of a regulation based solely on Art. 53, 62 TFEU would not be possible. Cf. on this *Korte*, in: GewArch 6(2013), p. 230, 232.

legislative instrument possible in this framework.[190] The aim of this competence is to help those wishing to set up or provide services with the expansion of their services from the origin Member State to other destinations within the EU. Legal harmonisation was meant to improve the exercise of cross-border activities, an objective which is also protected and advocated by the fundamental freedoms. The starting point for any coordinative action is therefore a legal provision in the Member States which contains substantive provisions on an economic activity covered by the freedom of establishment or the freedom to provide services. This may also concern the coordination of administrative procedures[191], but it must also comply with the other requirements of Art. 53 TFEU.

This area has been substantiated to an extensive degree by CJEU case law, which prohibits the use of these provisions as general competence under the objective to regulate the internal market.[192] The CJEU has required, for one, the identification of a (sufficiently probable) obstacle to free movement caused by diverging national legal provisions, and, secondly, the cessation of a positive internal market effect by the coordinative measure in the sense that it facilitates the exercise of the freedom of establishment or the freedom to provide services. The creation and functioning of the internal market must always be the focus and objective of the coordinative action, although the pursuit of other objectives, such as those based on special authorisation (even decisive ones[193]), remains possible, provided that this does not circumvent rules of competence which have not been allocated.

---

190 *Korte*, in: Calliess/Ruffert, Art. 53 para. 1.
191 *Korte*, in: Calliess/Ruffert, Art. 53 TFEU para. 11, with further references.
192 Cf. this and the following fundamentally: CJEU, judgement of 5.10.2000, C-376/98, *Federal Republic of Germany v European Parliament and Council of the European Union*.
193 Ibid., para. 3.

2.4. EU Secondary Law

This section looks at secondary legislation (already adopted and proposed) that plays a role in the field of regulation of online content. The diversity of content, dissemination channels and problems on the Internet is matched by the diversity of issues covered by the legislative acts.

The ECD is the main secondary legislation to be dealt with in the context of this study because of the horizontal approach it follows. It will therefore be dealt with in detail in the following (Chapter 3). In this chapter, only a first quick overview of the genesis of the Directive will be given.

The AVMSD will be presented extensively because it is the most recent revision of a content-related regulatory instrument of the EU, which from the outset of the ECD was regarded as being closely related (see, e.g., Recital 44 of the AVMSD). Especially due to the extension of the scope to VSPs it is relevant to study the Directive in more detail as it can be seen as an important step towards a more inclusive regulation of online service providers by the EU. While the ECD historical background relates to an Internet context which was completely different in terms of the important market players, the AVMSD reform was decided in light of the acknowledgment of the role of content dissemination by platforms.

The consideration of the General Data Protection Regulation and related legal acts in the field of data protection law is relevant, as it pursues both a cross-sectorial approach, which all data processors must follow in principle, and a cross-border approach, which links to the consumers of services made available online and thus also addresses providers who are not established in the EU. In addition, the particularly differentiated and far-reaching harmonised provisions on supervisory structures serve as an example for the presentation of a new, very far-reaching harmonisation approach at EU level, which is otherwise unfamiliar to regulation in the media sector.

2.4.1. e-Commerce Directive

Adopted in 2000, the ECD was intended to create for the first time a coherent framework for Internet commerce. The core of the Directive is to eliminate legal uncertainties for cross-border online services and to ensure the free movement of information society services between the Member States.[194]

2.4.1.1. Historical Background

Already in April 1997, in the context of its Communication "A European Initiative in Electronic Commerce", the Commission identified an urgent need to engage in an early political debate with the aim to provide a stimulus to electronic commerce.[195] Driven by the "Internet Revolution", electronic commerce, as a rapidly developing sector, would have a major impact on Europe's competitiveness on the global market. Regulatory measures should therefore ensure that fragmentation of this promising market is avoided and that the benefits of the further development of information and communication technology, the liberalisation of telecommunications markets, the introduction of the euro and the internal market are exploited.

The main focus of the Communication was on economic aspects. The Commission referred to estimates that the value of Internet transactions could reach up to ECU[196] 200 billion in 2000. The proposed actions therefore aim to "provide a stimulus to electronic commerce and to avoid a fragmentation of this promising market". However, the Commission does not address concrete regulatory proposals. In particular, no statement is made on a possible design of the liability system in the e-commerce sector. A legal framework based on the initiative should, in particular, offer coherent regulation that encourages companies to invest in appropriate products, services and infrastructure and which gives consumers the opportunity to gain confidence. This should ensure that the global and European legal frameworks fit together. A number of other issues should also be addressed in this context. The Communication identifies areas such as data protection, protection of intellectual property rights, data security and a clear and neutral tax environment.

---

194 The provisions of the ECD relevant in the context of this study are reprinted in the Online Annex, available at www.nomos-shop.de/44382, II. A.

195 Communication from the Commission to the Council, the European Parliament, the Economic and Social Committee and the Committee of the Regions, A European Initiative in Electronic Commerce, COM(97)157 final, p. 4.

196 The European Currency Unit (ECU) was a basket of the currencies of the European Community Member States, used as the unit of account of the European Community before being replaced by the euro on 1 January 1999.

However, the Communication was already assuming a broad regulatory framework at this stage. "Electronic Commerce", for example, defines all electronic business activities of companies among themselves, with their customers or with the administration. This includes both so-called indirect electronic commerce, i.e. the electronic ordering of tangible goods even when physically delivered, as well as direct electronic commerce, i.e. the online ordering, payment and delivery of intangible goods and services such as computer software, entertainment content or information services.

On 18 November 1998, a first proposal for the ECD was submitted, shortly after the Digital Millennium Copyright Act[197], which incorporated a similar liability regime as the later ECD, was signed in the U.S.[198]

As key areas of regulation, the proposal identifies the responsibility of intermediaries, electronic contracts, commercial communications, transparency and enforcement, and the country-of-origin principle. In particular, the chosen framework should be simple, minimalist and predictable.[199] The primary objective of the liability rules is to prevent distortion of competition between cross-border services through different civil and criminal responsibilities. Similar to the Directive adopted later, providers are therefore not responsible as long as they merely act as intermediaries for information provided by third parties.

> *(16) Whereas, both existing and emerging disparities in Member States' legislation and case-law concerning civil and criminal liability of service providers acting as intermediaries prevent the smooth functioning of the internal market, in particular by impairing the development of cross-border services and producing distortions of competition; whereas service providers have a duty to act, under certain circumstances, with a view to preventing or ceasing illegal activities; whereas the provisions of this Directive should constitute the appropriate basis for the development of rapid and reliable procedures for removing and disabling access to illegal information; whereas such mechanisms could be developed on the basis of voluntary agreements be-*

---

197 The Digital Millennium Copyright Act of 1998, Pub. L. No. 105-304, 112 Stat. 2860 (Oct. 28, 1998).

198 *Weidert/Molle*, in: Ensthaler/Weidert, p. 396 para. 39; regarding DCMA and ECRL see also *Freytag*, MMR 4/1999, p. 207, 207 et seq.

199 As described in the Report on the proposal for a European Parliament and Council Directive on certain legal aspects of electronic commerce in the internal market (COM(98)0586 – C4-0020/99 – 98/0325(COD)), Committee on Legal Affairs and Citizens' Rights, under point B. Explanatory Statement, 1. Introduction.

tween all parties concerned; whereas it is in the interest of all parties in-volved in the provision of Information Society services to adopt and imple-ment such procedures; whereas the provisions of this Directive relating to lia-bility should not preclude the development and effective operation, by the different interested parties, of technical systems of protection and identifica-tion;[200]

The European Parliament occasionally expressed concern about a too broad limitation of liability and the impact of harmful content on the Internet.[201] In principle, however, the rules proposed in Art. 12–14 were seen as achieving an appropriate balance between the interests of potential rights holders and intermediaries during the discussion at the time.

Following a further draft[202], the Council's General Approach of 28 February 2000 was approved by the European Parliament and the Directive was published on 17 June 2000.

The Directive establishes the freedom to provide information society services (ISS) throughout the EU on the one hand and harmonises national rules on transparency and information obligations for online service providers, liability limitations and obligations for intermediaries on the other. The specific scope of the Directive covers "information society services". For that matter, it refers to the definition as laid down in the so-called Technical Standards Transparency Directive[203]. According to this it is any service normally provided for remuneration, at a distance, by elec-

---

200 Proposal for a European Parliament and Council Directive on certain legal aspects of electronic commerce in the internal market, COM/98/0586 final, Recital 16.

201 Opinion for the Committee on Legal Affairs and Citizens' Rights on the proposal for a European Parliament and Council Directive on certain legal aspects of electronic commerce in the internal market (COM(98)0568 – C4-0020/99 – 98/0325(COD)) (report by Ms Oddy), Committee on Culture, Youth, Education and the Media, available at http://www.europarl.europa.eu/sides/getDoc.do?pub Ref=-//EP//TEXT+REPORT+A4-1999-0248+0+DOC+XML+V0//EN.

202 Amended proposal for a European Parliament and Council Directive on certain legal aspects of electronic commerce in the Internal Market, COM/99/0427 final, OJ C 248 E, 29.08.2000, pp. 69–96.

203 Directive 98/48/EC of the European Parliament and of the Council of 20 July 1998 amending Directive 98/34/EC laying down a procedure for the provision of information in the field of technical standards and regulations, OJ L 217, 5.8.1998, pp. 18–26, as repealed by codified Directive (EU) 2015/1535 of the European Parliament and of the Council of 9 September 2015 laying down a procedure for the provision of information in the field of technical regulations and of rules on Information Society services OJ L 241, 17.9.2015, pp. 1–15.

tronic means and at the individual request of a recipient of services. Thereby, the term covers a wide range of economic online activities, including those that are financed, for example, by advertising.[204] Art. 1 para. 5 ECD explicitly excludes the areas of taxation, data protection, cartel law and gambling. With reference to the example of the Television without Frontiers Directive[205], the ECD is intended – in its words – to achieve a high level of Community integration in order to make full use of the opportunities offered by the internal market.[206]

At the same time, the free movement of ISS is understood as a manifestation of the right to freedom of expression within the meaning of Art. 10 para. 1 ECHR.[207] The Directive follows the main features already mentioned in the 1997 Communication of a light and flexible regulatory framework ("light touch approach"), a technology-neutral and horizontal design and a comprehensive scope applicable to both B2B and B2C relations.[208]

2.4.1.2. Further Developments

Since the adoption of the ECD almost 20 years ago, no reform of the Directive has been proposed, although the implementation of the ECD has been reviewed/evaluated several times. In addition, the provisions of the ECD have been supplemented over time by a number of sectorial Directives and Regulations relating to individual sub-areas and by a number of Recommendations and Communications from the Commission, which refer to the ECD but leave the Directive untouched in its scope.

Art. 21 ECD provides for a regular review of the implementation of the rules and their technical and economic circumstances. In 2003, the Commission presented its first report on the application of the Directive to the

---

204 ECD, Recital 18.
205 Council Directive 89/552/EEC of 3 October 1989 on the coordination of certain provisions laid down by law, regulation or administrative action in Member States concerning the pursuit of television broadcasting activities.
206 ECD, Recital 4.
207 ECD, Recital 46.
208 *Valcke/Dommering*, in: Castendyk/Dommering/Scheuer, European Media Law, p. 1084.

European Parliament, the Council and the Economic and Social Committee.[209]

According to the report, the Directive already achieved "substantial and positive effects" by applying the internal market principle and the freedom to provide services to electronic commerce. However, the report also stressed that, in view of the continuing technological innovation and the rapid growth of electronic commerce, the Commission should keep a close eye on the application of the Directive. With regard to the liability of intermediaries, the Commission emphasises the regime applicable under the Directive. The liability rules would be limited to what is strictly necessary and essential both to ensure the provision of basic services and to create a framework that would provide possibilities for the Internet and e-commerce to develop. However, the use of a general policy to combat illicit content on a larger scale, and not merely in the case of specific infringements, would give rise for concern.

In 2007, the Commission commissioned two studies on the legal and economic impact of the ECD.[210] In particular, the "Study on the liability of Internet intermediaries" examined the legal framework and the jurisprudence on liability limitations under the ECD until 2007. As specifically problematic areas the authors identified the enforcement of orders to filter and block illegal content along the different interpretation of the requirement of "knowledge" by intermediaries and the measures to disclose customer data in order to prosecute infringements.

In addition, in 2011 and 2012, two public consultation procedures, taking into account economic matters and the procedure regarding illegal content, were carried out by the Commission.[211] Further studies were inter alia commissioned by the European Parliament. One example is a study

---

209 Report from the Commission to the European Parliament, the Council and the European Economic and Social Committee – First Report on the application of Directive 2000/31/EC of the European Parliament and of the Council of 8 June 2000 on certain legal aspects of information society services, in particular electronic commerce, in the Internal Market (Directive on electronic commerce), COM/2003/0702 final.

210 *Verbiest/Spindler/Riccio*, Study on the Liability of Internet Intermediaries; and *Nielsen and others*, Study on the Economic Impact of the Electronic Commerce Directive.

211 Summary of the results of the Public Consultation on the future of electronic commerce in the Internal Market and the implementation of the Directive on electronic commerce (2000/31/EC); Public Consultation on the Procedures for notifying and acting on illegal content hosted by online intermediaries, available at: https://ec.europa.eu/newsroom/dae/document.cfm?doc_id=42071.

carried out at the request of the European Parliament's Committee on the Internal Market and Consumer Protection (IMCO), inquiring the extent to which Internet intermediaries should be held liable in future for the illegal activities of their users.[212]

As mentioned above, the broad regulatory approach of the ECD was supplemented by various sector-specific rules, for instance in the area of consumer protection law.[213] Most recently, as part of the Strategy for a Digital Single Market for Europe, several e-commerce-related rules were adopted or announced, such as a revised Payment Services Directive[214], new rules to prevent unjustified geo-blocking[215], revised consumer protection rules[216] and new VAT rules for the online sale of goods and services[217].

---

212 Cf., e.g., *van Eecke/Truyens*, Legal analysis of a Single Market for the Information Society; *Sartor*, Providers Liability: From the eCommerce Directive to the future.

213 Directive 2011/83/EU of the European Parliament and of the Council of 25 October 2011 on consumer rights, amending Council Directive 93/13/EEC and Directive 1999/44/EC of the European Parliament and of the Council and repealing Council Directive 85/577/EEC and Directive 97/7/EC of the European Parliament and of the Council Text with EEA relevance, OJ L 304, 22.11.2011, pp. 64–88.

214 Directive (EU) 2015/2366 of the European Parliament and of the Council of 25 November 2015 on payment services in the internal market, amending Directives 2002/65/EC, 2009/110/EC and 2013/36/EU and Regulation (EU) No 1093/2010, and repealing Directive 2007/64/EC, OJ L 337, 23.12.2015, pp. 35–127.

215 Regulation (EU) 2018/302 of the European Parliament and of the Council of 28 February 2018 on addressing unjustified geo-blocking and other forms of discrimination based on customers' nationality, place of residence or place of establishment within the internal market and amending Regulations (EC) No 2006/2004 and (EU) 2017/2394 and Directive 2009/22/EC, OJ L 60I, 2.3.2018, pp. 1–15.

216 Proposal for a Directive of the European Parliament and of the Council on representative actions for the protection of the collective interests of consumers, and repealing Directive 2009/22/EC, COM/2018/0184 final; Proposal for a Directive of the European Parliament and of the Council amending Council Directive 93/13/EEC of 5 April 1993, Directive 98/6/EC of the European Parliament and of the Council, Directive 2005/29/EC of the European Parliament and of the Council and Directive 2011/83/EU of the European Parliament and of the Council as regards better enforcement and modernisation of EU consumer protection rules, COM/2018/0185 final.

217 Council Directive (EU) 2017/2455 of 5 December 2017 amending Directive 2006/112/EC and Directive 2009/132/EC as regards certain value added tax obligations for supplies of services and distance sales of goods, OJ L 348, 29.12.2017,

In addition, the Commission adopted recommendations and communications on complementing the rules on electronic commerce. These include, for example, the Commission's 2012 Communication regarding "A coherent framework for building trust in the Digital Single Market for e-commerce and online services"[218] on the potential of online services for growth and jobs and the more recent Recommendations on measures to effectively tackle illegal content online.[219]

Without fundamentally abandoning the principle enshrined in the ECD that Internet service providers acting as intermediaries are not liable for the content they transmit, store or make available, the Commission, already in its Communication on the Strategy for a Digital Single Market for Europe and in light of combatting illegal online content, noted that, given the growing amount of digital content available on the Internet, "today's rules are likely to come under increasing pressure". Against this backdrop, a trend towards greater responsibility, especially for platform operators, can be observed beyond soft law instruments, particularly in the context of the recently adopted reform of copyright law in the Digital Single Market and the proposal for a Regulation on preventing the dissemination of terrorist content online[220].

In her political guidelines for the period 2019 to 2024, Commission President designate Ursula von der Leyen announced that she will enact a new Digital Service Act to update the Union's liability and safety rules for digital platforms, services and products.[221]

---

pp. 7–22; Council Regulation (EU) 2017/2454 of 5 December 2017 amending Regulation (EU) No 904/2010 on administrative cooperation and combating fraud in the field of value added tax, OJ L 348, 29.12.2017, pp. 1–6.

218 Commission Communication to the European Parliament, the Council, The Economic and Social Committee and the Committee of Regions, A coherent framework for building trust in the Digital Single Market for e-commerce and online services, COM/2011/0942 final.

219 Commission Recommendation 2018/334 of 1 March 2018 on measures to effectively tackle illegal content online, OJ 2018 L 63/50; cf. on this in detail Chapter 2.5.2.

220 Proposal for a Regulation of the European Parliament and of the Council on preventing the dissemination of terrorist content online, A contribution from the European Commission to the Leaders' meeting in Salzburg on 19–20 September 2018, COM/2018/640 final.

221 Political guidelines for the next Commission (2019–2024), "A Union that strives for more: My agenda for Europe", 16 July 2019.

2.4.1.3. Main Goals and Principles of the Original ECD

The adoption of the ECD was justified on grounds of legal obstacles that hindered the free exercise of internal market principles, in particular, the right of establishment (Art. 49 TFEU)[222] and the freedom to provide services (Art. 56 TFEU)[223]. Recital 5 ECD mentions a number of obstacles, such as the divergent national rules concerning information society service providers and the extent to which Member States may control services originating from another Member State.

The ECD functions in accordance with the principle of proportionality. The details of this approach are laid down in Recital 10. The ECD limits itself to regulating only those legal aspects and matters that pose problems for the functioning of the internal market. In that respect, the Directive pursues a minimum harmonisation approach. This means that the ECD approximates the rules applicable to information society services only to the extent that obstacles to the free operation of the internal market are to be removed and the general interest principles are to be safeguarded, in particular the protection of minors, consumers and public health. Generally speaking, for ISS as defined in the Technical Standards Transparency Directive – mentioned above – the basic idea was that Member States are barred from introducing a prior authorisation request. But in order to make the single market function the basic idea is that there is one jurisdiction and the responsible Member States ensure an effective supervision. Besides some rules informing the users better about the identity of the providers, the most important element was the introduction of a liability (exemption) regime, which has had significant impact on the topics covered by this study. Further, there are only limited rules on supervision or enforcement, but Art. 18 ECD does foresee that, e.g., States need to ensure that there are efficient court procedures that allow for termination of infringements and prevention of further impairments of the interests of the concerned parties.

Art. 1 para. 2 ECD defines the areas affecting information society services which, according to the EU at the time, necessitated regulatory intervention. Necessary areas for action were Member State provisions concerning the establishment of service providers, commercial communications, electronic contracts, the liability of intermediaries, codes of conduct,

---

222 Ex-Art. 43 of the Treaty of the EC (TEC).
223 Ex-Art. 49 TEC.

out-of-court dispute settlements, court actions and cooperation between Member States.

At the same time, the ECD complements the legislative body of the EU Consumer acquis. Where its provisions affect other rules laid down in this body of EU law, the Directive may enhance them but shall not diminish the level of protection, in particular where it concerns public health and consumer interests. Against that background, Recital 11 of the ECD refers to EU legislation (at the time) that needs to be taken into account. Some of the more substantial provisions referred to were the Council Directive 93/13/EEC on unfair terms in consumer contracts, Directive 97/7/EC on the protection of consumers in respect of distance contracts[224], Directive 84/450/EEC concerning misleading advertising[225] and Directive 92/59/EEC on general product safety.[226]

The Directive does not affect national or Community measures that promote cultural and linguistic diversity and measures to defend pluralism. Finally, Recitals 63 and 64 underline that the Directive should not stand in the way of Member States' efforts to utilise the means provided by electronic communications for the attainment of social, democratic and cultural goals.

The minimum harmonisation approach also plays out in the choice of regulatory tools favoured by the EU legislator in this field. In order to minimise regulatory intervention, the ECD emphasises the use of self-regulatory measures, such as codes of conduct. This is important in the more recent context when discussing the role of the Commission in establishing processes and agreements with industry to fight unlawful content online, which will be discussed further below. Recital 32 and Art. 16 encourage Member States to promote and create voluntary codes of conduct through the involvement of industry and professionals. In addition, Art. 17 promotes the use of out-of-court dispute settlements.

---

224 Replaced by Directive 2011/83/EU of the European Parliament and of the Council of 25 October 2011 on consumer rights, amending Council Directive 93/13/EEC and Directive 1999/44/EC of the European Parliament and of the Council and repealing Council Directive 85/577/EEC and Directive 97/7/EC of the European Parliament and of the Council, OJ L 304, 22.11.2011, pp. 64–88.

225 Replaced by Directive 2006/114/EC of the European Parliament and of the Council of 12 December 2006 concerning misleading and comparative advertising, OJ L 376, 27.12.2006, pp. 21–27.

226 Replaced by Directive 2001/95/EC of the European Parliament and of the Council of 3 December 2001 on general product safety, OJ L 11, 15.1.2002, pp. 4–17.

2.4.2. Audiovisual Media Services Directive

2.4.2.1. Historical Development up to the Latest Revision in 2018

The AVMSD in its current version is based on a three decades long evolution during which it has been repeatedly adapted to current market conditions as well as technical and social developments.[227] The foundation for a common market for cross-border television was established at European level 30 years ago with the Television without Frontiers Directive (TwFD)[228]. On the one hand, the agreement of minimum conditions which applied to every television broadcaster under the jurisdiction of a Member State of the European Economic Community (now the European Union) and, on the other hand, the country-of-origin principle, according to which only one Member State shall be responsible for regulating a broadcaster, formed the core of the TwFD. Broadcasters were permitted to broadcast throughout Europe without any further control if the national legal requirements were complied with. The Directive is still based on these basic principles, which are as relevant today as they were when it was adopted.[229] Nevertheless, the Directive has been revised once every decade.

In an effort to adapt the provisions of the TwFD to a new advertising environment and to the technological developments in the field of television broadcasting, Directive 1997/36/EC[230] introduced, inter alia, provisions on the regulation of teleshopping, clarified the rules on jurisdiction (the Member State responsible for television channels is determined by the location of the head office and the place where programming decisions are made) and deepened rules on the protection of human dignity. Moreover, a Contact Committee to monitor the implementation of the Directive and the developments in that sector, and a forum for the exchange of views

---

227 Cf. on this and this Chapter overall: *Weinand*, Implementing the EU Audiovisual Media Services Directive.

228 Council Directive 89/552/EEC of 3 October 1989 on the coordination of certain provisions laid down by Law, Regulation or Administrative Action in Member States concerning the pursuit of television broadcasting activities, OJ L 298, 17.10.1989, pp. 23–30.

229 Cf. in particular on the country-of-origin principle: *Cole*, The Country of Origin Principle.

230 Directive 97/36/EC of the European Parliament and of the Council of 30 June 1997 amending Council Directive 89/552/EEC on the coordination of certain provisions laid down by law, regulation or administrative action in Member States concerning the pursuit of television broadcasting activities, OJ L 202, 30.7.1997, pp. 60–70.

were established under the Directive. Furthermore, the revised Directive placed greater emphasis on the protection of minors by specifying, for example, that Member States must ensure that programs which are likely to impair the development of minors and are broadcast in unencrypted form are to be preceded by an acoustic warning or identified by a visual symbol.

However, the most significant changes (also in the context of this study) until the AVMSD's most recent revision were those introduced in 2007. Directive 2007/65/EC[231] adapted the provisions to the new technical environment, generated by the growing importance of the Internet, and thus took account of the increasing convergence of the media. Accordingly, the Directive was given its current name, which no longer focused solely on "television without frontiers" but also on audiovisual media services. In addition to redefining the provisions on responsibility against the background of the country-of-origin principle and the consideration of self- and co-regulation mechanisms, the rules on cooperation between regulators and the implementation of provisions for on-demand services were the most significant innovations.

While the Contact Committee had already been set up with the 1997 reform, the revised Directive from 2007 took a further step with the adoption of Art. 23a, according to which Member States shall take appropriate measures to provide each other and the Commission with the information necessary for the application of the provisions of the AVSMD. The entry into force of that provision was crucial, in particular, due to the fact that cross-border content became more and more relevant.[232] In 2014, Art. 23a built the basis for the establishment of the European Regulators Group for Audiovisual Media Services (ERGA), which should serve as an advisory body to the Commission in its implementation of activities concerning areas coordinated by the AVMSD and which should facilitate coordination and cooperation between the national regulatory bodies in the Member States. In its decision establishing the ERGA, the Commission outlined, inter alia, that, "[i]n order to achieve a successful development of an internal market for audiovisual media services notably in view of increased cross-border dissemination and the regulatory challenges linked to on-demand

---

231 Directive 2007/65/EC of the European Parliament and of the Council of 11 December 2007 amending Council Directive 89/552/EEC on the coordination of certain provisions laid down by law, regulation or administrative action in Member States concerning the pursuit of television broadcasting activities, OJ L 332, 18.12.2007, pp. 27–45.
232 Cf. Recitals 32 and 66 of Directive 2007/65/EC.

services", a coherent application of the AVMSD in all Member States is essential and that "[t]o achieve this goal it is crucial to facilitate a closer and more regular cooperation between the competent independent regulatory bodies of the Member States and the Commission"[233].

Considering that legal uncertainty and a non-level playing-field exist for European companies delivering audiovisual media services as regards the legal regime governing emerging on-demand audiovisual media services, the competent EU institutions also found it necessary that, in order to avoid distortions of competition, to improve legal certainty, to help complete the internal market and to facilitate the emergence of a single information area, at least a basic tier of coordinated rules applies to all audiovisual media services, both television broadcasting and on-demand audiovisual media services (cf. Recital 7). However, the basic principles of Directive 89/552/EEC, namely the country-of-origin principle and common minimum standards, had proved their worth and therefore were retained. While the ECD, which had already been in force for five years at the time of the Commission's AVMSD reform proposal at the end of 2005, dealt with the much broader spectrum of electronic commerce and addressed information society services, the scope of AVMSD, which has always been primarily related to the function of (cross-border) television to protect the general interest[234], had to be adjusted. Therefore, the definition established for audiovisual media services covered mass media only in their function to inform, entertain and educate the general public. Any form of private correspondence, services whose principal purpose is not the provision of programs (e.g. websites that contain audiovisual elements only in an ancillary manner, such as animated graphical elements, short advertising spots or information related to a product or non-audiovisual service), games of chance involving a stake representing a sum of money, including lotteries, betting and other forms of gambling services, online games and search en-

---

233 Commission Decision of 3.2.2014 on establishing the European Regulators Group for Audiovisual Media Services, C(2014) 462 final, available at https://ec. europa.eu/digital-single-market/en/news/commission-decision-establishing-euro pean-regulators-group-audiovisual-media-services, p. 2, Whereas (3).

234 Cf. already the considerations in the TwFD: "Whereas broadcasts transmitted across frontiers by means of various technologies are one of the ways of pursuing the objectives of the Community; whereas measures should be adopted to permit and ensure the transition from national markets to a common programme production and distribution market and to establish conditions of fair competition without prejudice to the public interest role to be discharged by the television broadcasting services; [...]."

gines were excluded from the scope of the AVMSD as were electronic versions of newspapers and magazines, private websites and services consisting of the provision or dissemination of audiovisual content generated by private users for the purposes of sharing and exchange within communities of interest.[235] Thus, only audiovisual content produced and provided with a certain level of editorial responsibility (to be further defined by the Member States) was covered, whereas the ECD, for example, covered *any* service normally provided for remuneration, at a distance, by electronic means and at the individual request of a recipient. With the extension of the scope to include on-demand services in the online environment on the one hand and the restrictive definition on the other, both the convergence of the media was taken into account and the fact that audiovisual services in particular are the focus of harmonisation because of their increased suggestive power.[236]

For reasons of clarity and rationality, the Directive was subsequently codified in order to incorporate the three amending Directives into a new single text, Directive 2010/13/EU.[237]

In 2013, the Commission published a Green Paper on "Preparing for a Fully Converged Audiovisual World: Growth, Creation and Values"[238], which gave a major boost to the process of reforming the audiovisual sector again. The Green Paper should launch a broad public debate on the impact of the change in the audiovisual media landscape, which is characterised by an ever-increasing convergence of media services and the way these services are used and delivered, and on the impact of the borderless Internet in particular on market conditions, interoperability and infrastructure. The Commission received a number of submissions in the con-

---

235 Cf. Directive 2007/65/EC, Recital 16 et seq.

236 Cf. on the suggestive power of audiovisual media the report by Andreas Grünwald on possible options for the review of the European Convention on Transfrontier Television: Standing Committee on Transfrontier Television of the Council of Europe, Doc. TTT(2003)002, 24 April 2003.

237 Directive 2010/13/EU of the European Parliament and of the Council of 10 March 2010 on the coordination of certain provisions laid down by law, regulation or administrative action in Member States concerning the provision of audiovisual media services (Audiovisual Media Services Directive), OJ L 95, 15.4.2010, pp. 1–24, and the Corrigendum to Directive 2010/13/EU, OJ L 263, 6.10.2010, pp. 15–15.

238 Opinion of the European Economic and Social Committee on the 'Preparing for a Fully Converged Audiovisual World: Growth, Creation and Values (Green Paper)' COM(2013) 231 final, OJ C 341, 21 11.2013, pp. 87–91.

sultation procedure it launched[239] as well as expressions from other EU institutions, notably from the European Parliament[240] and the Council[241]. In particular, the need for a renewed adaptation of the AVMSD rules to the ongoing convergence of the media was stressed in the several opinions, emphasising that the horizontal (sector convergence), vertical (value chain convergence) and functional convergence (convergence of applications/services) all impact the audiovisual industry and that technical convergence means that media law and network policy issues are increasingly overlapping.[242] Some even argued that any de-regulation of the current services within the scope of the AVMSD would need to look at the growing asymmetry between media companies, media platforms and media aggregators in both the regulatory and fiscal playing fields.[243] Consequently, in 2015 the European Commission explicitly announced in its Strategy for a Digital Single Market that it would review the AVMSD with regard to its scope and the nature of the rules applicable to all market players, in particular the measures to promote European works, the rules on the protection of minors and the advertising rules.[244]

All this led to a reform proposal by the European Commission in 2016 amending Directive 2010/13/EU on the coordination of certain provisions

---

239 The results of the consultation on the Green Paper are available at https://ec.eur opa.eu/digital-single-market/en/news/consultation-green-paper-preparing-fully-c onverged-audiovisual-world-growth-creation-and-values.

240 European Parliament resolution of 12 March 2014 on Preparing for a Fully Converged Audiovisual World (2013/2180(INI)), available at http://www.europa rl.europa.eu/sides/getDoc.do?pubRef=-//EP//TEXT+TA+P7-TA-2014-0232+0+DO C+XML+V0//EN.

241 Council conclusions on European Audiovisual Policy in the Digital Era Education, Youth, CULTURE and SPORT Council meeting Brussels, 25 November 2014, available at https://www.consilium.europa.eu/uedocs/cms_data/docs/press data/en/educ/145950.pdf.

242 Cf. European Parliament resolution of 12 March 2014, loc. Cit. (fn. 240), para. C. and D.

243 Cf. Commission, summaries of the replies to the public consultation launched by the Green Paper "Preparing for a Fully Converged Audiovisual World: Growth, Creation and Values", available at https://ec.europa.eu/digital-single-m arket/en/news/publication-summaries-green-paper-replies, p. 40; in this context it was even outlined that "[i]t is at this juncture that an evaluation of the crossover between AVMSD and the eCommerce Directive would be necessary".

244 Communication from the Commission to the European Parliament, the Council, the European Economic and Social Committee and the Committee of the Regions, A Digital Single Market Strategy for Europe, COM(2015) 192 final, available at https://eur-lex.europa.eu/legal-content/EN/TXT/?uri=celex%3A52015 DC0192, para. 3.2.

laid down by law, regulation or administrative action in Member States concerning the provision of audiovisual media services in view of changing market realities, which finally resulted in the amending Directive (EU) 2018/1808 after an intensive two-year trilogue procedure.[245] Member States must transpose the reformed rules into national law by 19 September 2020.

The importance of this last reform lies, among other things, in the further extension of its scope: while audiovisual media services and their providers remain the focus and starting point of the Directive, certain types of distributors are now also addressed. This applies directly to video-sharing platforms, which have been included in the scope of the Directive and will be given greater responsibility under the new provisions (in particular Art. 28b). The extension has taken place mainly in the light of the fact that more or less new players on the market are competing with traditional service providers, such as television, for the attention of the same recipients and the same advertisers (Recital 4). This shows similarities to the inclusion of VoD offers within the framework of the 2007 reform but goes beyond the adaptation of the former rules, to the extent that the feature of television-likeness, which still played a role at that time regarding VoD services, is now dispensed. Whereas previously the (partly) harmonisation of the legal framework was based on a similarity of formats, the current approach is more based on similarities with regard to the audience concerned.[246] In the future, VSP providers will have to follow the same rules as other audiovisual media service providers with regard to sponsorship, product placement, surreptitious advertising, subliminal influence, and tobacco and alcohol advertising. Only the consequence of the applicability of the rules is different from that of linear and non-linear providers, which here also depends on the question of the economic advantage of the VSP provider. In their dealings with users, VSP providers merely have to push for compliance with the legal requirements by means of suitable measures, whereas they have to ensure compliance with their own commercial communication in a binding manner. Art. 28b also establishes a catalogue of obligations to be observed by VSP providers in order to protect both minors and the general public from certain harmful content, including, for example, the establishment of age verification mechanisms, reporting and

---

245 For a detailed overview on the trilogue procedure cf. the different synopses of the EMR, available at https://emr-sb.de/gb/synopsis-avms/.
246 On this and the following see *Cole/Etteldorf*, in: Medienhandbuch Österreich 2019, p. 56, 57 et seq.

complaint systems. In order to implement those objectives, Member States should support the use of co-regulation and the promotion of self-regulation through codes of conduct – an instrument that has taken on much greater overall weight with the reform of the Directive.

Indirectly, however, some rules of Directive (EU) 2018/1808 also affect other platforms that make audiovisual content accessible. This applies in particular to the new rules on searchability and signal integrity of audiovisual content (Art. 7a and 7b), which oblige Member States to take measures to ensure the appropriate prominence of audiovisual media services of general interest and require that audiovisual media services provided by media service providers are not, without the explicit consent of those providers, overlaid for commercial purposes or modified.

Finally, the legal framework for non-linear service providers has been (partially) aligned with the previous legal framework for linear services. This is the case in the areas of the promotion of European works and the protection of minors in the media, where Art. 6a introduced a provision that applies to all media service providers.

The historical development of the former TwFD shows that, over time, the Directive has been constantly adapted to new technical and social developments. Media convergence has been identified and addressed. Particularly noteworthy are the aforementioned rules on searchability and overlay protection, as they document the AVMSD's efforts to ensure a comprehensive protection of audiovisual content, the consequences of which go beyond the actual core area of application and also include access to other providers like distributors. At its core, however, the AVMSD still deals with the regulation of cross-border audiovisual content, which is an important part of the European structure against the background of the creation of a Digital Single Market. The AVMSD's regime is thus subject to equal limits, both in terms of its scope of application outside audiovisual media service providers and in terms of enforcement. The possibilities and limits arising from this (also for the national regulatory authorities) will be examined in the following section.

2.4.2.2. Overview of Relevant Rules for the Online Context

2.4.2.2.1. Personal Scope of Application

The AVMSD[247] initially covered two types of services in particular: audio-visual media services within the meaning of Art. 1 para. 1 lit. a and video-sharing platforms within the meaning of Art. 1 para. 1 lit. aa AVMSD.

The first term covers both audiovisual commercial communications and services (linear and non-linear) as defined by Art. 56 and 57 TFEU, where the principal purpose of the service or a dissociable section thereof is devoted to providing programs, under the editorial responsibility of a media service provider, to the general public in order to inform, entertain or educate by means of electronic communications networks within the meaning of lit. a of Art. 2 of Directive 2002/21/EC. In the online sector, the definition covers, for example and above all, streaming offers or media libraries of traditional broadcasters as well as on-demand offers of other providers. However, individual channels or profiles on platforms such as Twitch or YouTube can also fall under this term if they are designed in the way that Art. 1 para. 1 lit. a describes.

Meanwhile, with the 2018 reform, a separate definition was created for abovementioned platforms that base their business models on the fact that their users themselves create the content to make it available via the platform. According to Art. 1 para. 1 lit. aa, video-sharing platform service means a service as defined by Art. 56 and 57 TFEU, where the principal purpose of the service or of a dissociable section thereof or an essential functionality of the service is devoted to providing programmes, user-generated videos, or both, to the general public, for which the video-sharing platform provider does not have editorial responsibility, in order to inform, entertain or educate by means of electronic communications networks within the meaning of lit. a of Art. 2 of Directive 2002/21/EC, whereby the organisation of such providing is determined by the video-sharing platform provider, including by automatic means or algorithms in particular by displaying, tagging and sequencing.

Although there are many criteria in this definition that should characterise a VSP covered by the AVMSD, the definition is very broad. For example, there is no exception for small platform providers as in the new

---

247 The provisions of the AVMSD relevant in the context of this study are reprinted in the Online Annex to this study, available at www.nomos-shop.de/44382, II. B.

DSM Directive.[248] Rather, the size or economic power of a platform is only taken into account within the framework of the measures that the provider has to take to implement the requirements of the AVMSD. This means that not only large platforms such as YouTube or Twitch, which was presumably the actual goal of the new rules, will be covered, but also smaller, national platforms such as the ones currently being set up in many Member States in the form of start-ups. In addition, there is no restriction to specific content, which means that niche-specific offers such as pornography platforms with user-generated videos or (audiovisual) forums of a themed community (e.g. websites with do-it-yourself instructions or videos on pet education) have to comply with the new rules, too. Finally, the scope is not limited to "audiovisual platforms" alone. This is emphasised in the Recitals to the AVMSD mentioning in particular "social media services" (Recital 4) and "electronic versions of newspapers and magazines" (Recital 6). It is precisely in the area of such offers that the criterion of "essential functionality" will be of importance in future, for the assessment of which the Commission[249] has already announced that it will issue corresponding guidelines.[250]

As mentioned above, however, the 2018 AVMSD reform also introduced provisions that do not directly address other platform providers in the sense of (also definitory) including them within the scope of the Directive but indirectly affect the structure of their offerings. This applies in particular to the provisions of Art. 7a and b AVMSD. According to those provisions, Member States may take measures to ensure the appropriate prominence of audiovisual media services of general interest and shall take appropriate and proportionate measures to ensure that audiovisual media services provided by media service providers are not, without the explicit consent of those providers, overlaid for commercial purposes or modified. At the core of these provisions are the content providers whose content is to be protected and made retrievable, as well as the users to whom the content is to be made easily accessible and who are nevertheless to remain in control of certain functions.[251] However, the implementation of these re-

---

248 Art. 17 para. 6 of DSM Directive.
249 Cf. the report of the Commission of 21.3.2019 on the preparatory work for AVMSD guidelines, available at https://ec.europa.eu/digital-single-market/en/ne ws/preparatory-work-avmsd-guidelines-report-stakeholder-workshop.
250 Cf. on this also *Kogler*, in: K&R 9/2018, p. 537, 540; *Cole*, AVMSD Jurisdiction Criteria after the 2018 Reform.
251 Cf. on this *Cole*, Die Neuregelung des Artikel 7b Richtlinie 2010/13/EU (AVMD-RL).

quirements into national law must nevertheless address the providers of these platforms, as only they can ensure that these offerings are easy to find and that they are protected against overlays by designing them accordingly. How the Member States transpose the rules on taking "appropriate and proportionate" measures (in compliance with fundamental rights and primary law requirements) is in principle up to them. Not least because of the indeterminate legal terms "media services of general interest" or "legitimate interests of users", which exist in these regulations and which can be concretised by the Member States through laws of the legislator or guidelines of the regulatory authorities, it is to be expected that a uniform implementation throughout the EU will not take place in this area either. This is all the more true in view of the fact that the Member States also have at their disposal the instruments of self- and co-regulation.

2.4.2.2.2. Country-of-Origin Principle

2.4.2.2.2.1. Importance of the Principle and Changes Related to It in the Recent Reform

The core principle of the AVMSD and its predecessor, the TwFD, has always been the country-of-origin principle, which determines the regulatory approach towards providers of linear and non-linear audiovisual media services. This principle laid down in Art. 2 para. 1 AVMSD states that a provider that falls under the jurisdiction of one EU Member State can rely on complying with the legal framework of (only) that specific state in order to be authorised to disseminate content across all EU Member States. Art. 2 para. 3 and 4 thereby lays down under which circumstances jurisdiction can be assumed. The flipside of this approach was to ensure that a certain number of key issues relevant for all Member States would be harmonised by the Directive, in which way they would become the minimum standard that is respected across the EU.[252] In the online context, therefore, the country-of-origin principle is linked in particular to the minimum harmonisation of audiovisual content (Chapter 2.4.2.2.3).

Although this was problematised[253] within the framework of the reform, the country-of-origin principle was retained in its entirety in the AVMSD when it was reformed in 2018. Only minor changes were made to

---

252 *Cole*, AVMSD Jurisdiction Criteria after the 2018 Reform, p. 5.
253 Cf. *Kogler*, in: K&R 9/2018, p. 537.

the jurisdiction criteria.[254] Furthermore, and what is particularly relevant in the context of this study, Art. 3 AVMSD, which contains rules and exceptions regarding the country-of-origin principle, has been amended. This concerns in particular the harmonisation of the rule on linear and non-linear services and the streamlining of the procedure before the European Commission (Art. 3 para. 6).

As can be seen in detail from the synoptic illustration of the provisions of Art. 3 before and after the 2018 reform in the annex[255], there have been some significant changes here. This applies in particular to the harmonisation of the provisions for linear and non-linear providers in this area. While Art. 3 para. 4 of Directive 2010/13/EU still contained a special provision for taking (not only in the case of linear services temporary) measures against non-linear offers, which almost identically adopted the wording of the corresponding possibility of deviation from the country-of-origin principle from the ECD (Art. 3 para. 4), Art. 3 para. 4 has now given way to uniform regulation under Art. 3 para. 2 and 3, which no longer continues the synchronisation between AVMSD and ECD in this area. Art. 3 para. 2 and para. 3 apply to all audiovisual media services and distinguish, other than before, according to the type of infringement, although in both cases only temporary measures may be imposed by the Member States. The strict distinction between violations of Art. 6 para. 1 lit. a and Art. 6a para. 1 (in Art. 3 para. 2 AVMSD), on the one hand, and Art. 6 para. 1 lit. b and other state interests (in Art. 3 para. 3 AVMSD), on the other, appears only in its current form in the final compromise proposal, while the Commission's proposal still contained an overall uniform rule.[256] The decisive difference between the two provisions is essentially that Art. 3 para. 2 requires a twofold violation of the provisions mentioned therein for action to be taken, while under Art. 3 para. 3 AVMSD a one-time violation is sufficient for Member States to impose measures.

---

254 For a detailed overview and a genesis of the provisions cf. *Cole*, AVMSD Jurisdiction Criteria after the 2018 Reform.

255 Online Annex, available at www.nomos-shop.de/44382, II.B.

256 Cf. on this the synopsis provided by the EMR giving an overview on the trilogue, available at https://emr-sb.de/wp-content/uploads/2019/03/EMR-Synopsis -AVMSD_final_EN.pdf.

2.4.2.2.2.2. Home State Jurisdiction Rule

Art. 3 para. 1 states that a media service provider always has the right to re-transmit its content to other EU Member States without any restriction being imposed by the state receiving such a retransmission. However, there are possible exceptions to this obligation as well as a safeguard mechanism to avoid a "race to the bottom" through what is known as "forum shopping": if specific violations of the Directive do not lead to measures imposed by the supervisory authority in the country of origin, authorities in the receiving state can derogate from the retransmission requirement, subject to a procedure laid down in the Directive. Furthermore, in the case of linear services, it may under certain circumstances be assumed that a provider that transmits from abroad but only targets an audience in the home country is circumventing the latter's laws, and the relevant supervisory authority may then take action.[257]

The country-of-origin principle and thus the fundamental guarantee of freedom of reception under Art. 3 para. 1 AVMSD only apply in the area coordinated by the Directive. However, in the area of cross-border distribution of (audiovisual) content online, which is relevant in the context of this study, there are hardly any conceivable areas where coordination can be completely neglected by the Directive (in particular with regard to the protection of minors from harmful media, protection against violence and hatred, and terrorist content). The CJEU, too, has so far been rather cautious on this point. In the *Commission v Belgium*[258] case, for example, the Court rejected a reference to cultural policy objectives, in particular the safeguarding of pluralism and the protection of morality, public order and public security, and a reference to a lack of coordination by the Directive, since at least part of the area was coordinated. In the *De Agostini* case, the CJEU left an appeal to consumer protection principally open, as this area was not fully coordinated at EU level (at that time), but denied that possibility with regard to the protection of minors.[259]

In this context, a recent decision of the CJEU on the scope of Art. 3 para. 1 AVMSD requires particular attention. In its judgment of 4 July

---

257 Cf. on this and the following also *Cappello (ed.)*, Media law enforcement without frontiers, IRIS Special 2018-2.

258 CJEU, judgement of 10.9.1996, C-11/95, *Commission of the European Communities v Kingdom of Belgium*.

259 CJEU, judgements of 09.7.1997, joint cases C-34/95, C-35/95 and C-36/95, *Konsumentombudsmannen (KO) v De Agostini (Svenska) Förlag AB and TV-Shop i Sverige AB)*, para. 57 et seq.

2019, the Court ruled in the *Baltic Media Alliance* case[260] that the AVMSD does not preclude a provision in Member State legislation which allows for a temporary obligation to transmit or retransmit a television channel from another Member State only in form of pay-TV packages. This could be lawful for reasons of public order such as combating incitement to hatred. The CJEU thus ruled in favour of the Lithuanian Radio and Television Commission (*Lietuvos radijo ir televizijos komisija*, LRTK), which had issued a corresponding ruling to the Baltic Media Alliance. It had taken action against the United Kingdom-based television channel Baltic Media, which inter alia broadcasts the television channel NTV Mir Lithuania that is aimed at the Lithuanian public and contains predominantly Russian-language content. On the grounds that various broadcasts on the channel had incited hostility and hatred towards the Baltic States based on nationality, LRTK obliged the broadcaster to broadcast the channel NTV Mir Lithuania only in pay-TV packages for a period of twelve months. LRTK held that, in particular, the broadcasts targeted the Russian-speaking minority in Lithuania with false information about the collaboration of Lithuanians and Latvians in the Holocaust and alleged nationalist and neo-Nazi domestic policies of the Baltic States that ostensibly posed a threat to the Russian minority in the territories of these countries. The Court ruled that this does not constitute an obstacle within the meaning of Art. 3 para. 1 AVMSD if certain modalities – such as in this case the obligation to broadcast the channel only on pay-TV – do not prevent retransmission in the actual sense of the channel. Such a measure would not introduce a second check of the channel concerned in addition to the check to be carried out by the sending Member State, which is precisely what the country-of-origin principle seeks to prevent. Art. 3 para. 1 would only refer to the area coordinated by the AVMSD, which in turn is limited to the "provision of audiovisual media services". According to the CJEU, such interpretation may be derived from the wording and the history of that provision. Since the Court considered Art. 3 para. 1 to be irrelevant, it no longer found it necessary to examine Art. 3 para. 2 of the AVMSD in detail.

---

260 CJEU, judgement of 4.7.2019, C-622/17, *Baltic Media Alliance Ltd v Lietuvos radijo ir televizijos komisija.*

2.4.2.2.2.3. Exceptional Derogation of Free Flow of Information

Powers of the Member States to derogate temporarily from the principle of freedom of reception are found in Art. 3 para. 2 and 3 AVMSD. These rights apply when an audiovisual media service manifestly, seriously and gravely infringes Art. 6 para. 1 lit. a or Art. 6a para. 1 or prejudices or presents a serious and grave risk of prejudice to public health (Art. 3 para. 2 AVMSD) and when an audiovisual media service manifestly, seriously and gravely infringes Art. 6 para. 1 lit. b or prejudices or presents a serious and grave risk of prejudice to public security, including the safeguarding of national security and defence (Art. 3 para. 3 AVMSD). The relevant rules also set out further conditions and a specific procedure to be followed by the Member State concerned, involving the competent Member State, the Commission and the ERGA. The cooperation procedure provided for here makes it difficult in practice to take action against foreign providers, despite a possibility to derogate in urgent cases under Art. 3 para. 5 AVMSD.[261] This applies in particular against the background of the mentioned national peculiarities with regard to the interpretation of undefined legal concepts, the implementation of the provisions at national level and the distribution of responsibilities and competences regarding enforcement. If the Commission confirms conformity with Union law after the receiving state has notified the steps it has taken, "reception" of the content may be prevented. However, this does not include supervisory measures in form of direct enforcement measures addressed to the foreign provider but include rather possibilities to prevent the dissemination of offers, for instance by linking domestic infrastructure operators instead of imposing a fine.[262]

2.4.2.2.2.4. Exception in Case of Circumvention

Finally, the circumvention of Art. 4 para. 2 AVMSD, which applies to all audiovisual media services since the 2018 reform, should be mentioned.

---

261 Cf. the describing part and the country reports in: *Cappello (ed.)*, Media law enforcement without frontiers, IRIS Special 2018-2.
262 Cf. on this already *Ukrow*, Zur Zuständigkeit der Landesmedienanstalten/KJM für ausländische Anbieter, p. 193.

The provision codifies the relevant CJEU case-law on circumvention.[263] Where a Member State has exercised its freedom to adopt more detailed or stricter rules of general public interest (Art. 4 para. 1 AVMSD) and assesses that a media service provider under the jurisdiction of another Member State provides an audiovisual media service that is wholly or mostly directed towards its territory, it may request the Member State having jurisdiction to address any problems identified in relation to this paragraph. According to the requirements mentioned in Art. 4 para. 2, both Member States shall cooperate sincerely and swiftly with a view to achieving a mutually satisfactory solution. If a satisfactory solution is not found, the receiving Member State may adopt appropriate measures against the media service provider if, inter alia, it has adduced evidence showing that the media service provider in question has established itself in the Member State having jurisdiction in order to circumvent the stricter rules. But even this is only possible if a certain procedure has been followed (Art. 4 para. 4: the Commission and the competent Member State have been notified, opportunity to submit comments for the media service provider, Commission issued a decision on the compatibility with Union law, etc.).

Art. 4 serves as a backstop in cases when a provider has relocated to another Member State in order to avoid having to comply with stricter rules that a Member State has enacted while the provider was targeting mainly the territory of that Member State.[264] However, as Art. 4 constitutes an exception to a (fundamental) freedom, it needs to be interpreted narrowly.[265] The Commission sets a high threshold for evidence about a circumvention as it needs to be clearly distinguished from a "simple" use of the right to decide on establishment and profit from the country-of-origin principle which the Directive grants providers.[266]

---

263 For an overview cf. *Cole*, in: Fink/Cole/Keber, Europäisches und Internationales Medienrecht, para. 37 and 62.

264 Cf. on this *Cole*, AVMSD Jurisdiction criteria after the 2018 reform; *Cole*, The Country of Origin Principle, p. 120; *Herold*, in: Journal of Consumer Policy, 31(1), 2008, p. 5, 6.

265 Cf. Recital 43 of Directive 2010/13/EU and CJEU, judgement of 28.10.1999, C-6/98 *Arbeitsgemeinschaft Deutscher Rundfunkanstalten (ARD) v PRO Sieben Media AG, supported by SAT 1 Satellitenfernsehen GmbH, Kabel 1, K 1 Fernsehen GmbH*; on this *Cole/Haus*, in: JuS 5/2001, p. 435, 435 et seq.

266 Cf. Commission decision C(2018) 532 final, 31.1.2018, on the Swedish intention to impose a ban on alcohol advertising on two UK broadcasters which was considered as not compatible with EU rules.

2.4.2.2.3. Minimum Harmonisation Concerning Specific Types of Content

The minimum standards relevant in the context of this study, which audiovisual content must comply with also in the online sector, concern primarily the protection of minors, the protection against violence, hatred and terrorist content as well as the design of audiovisual commercial communication. Therefore, Art. 6, 6a and 9 of the AVMSD will be presented in the following, in particular the specifications which audiovisual media services must comply with, whereby VSP providers pursuant to Art. 28b para. 1 and 2 of the AVMSD (will) also meet corresponding requirements. This minimum harmonisation is the basis for cooperation between the regulatory authorities, since it contains a standard that all parties are obliged to maintain.

Directive 2010/13/EU	Directive (EU) 2018/1808
Art. 6	**Art. 6**
Member States shall ensure by appropriate means that audiovisual media services provided by media service providers under their jurisdiction do not contain any incitement to hatred based on race, sex, religion or nationality.	**1. Without prejudice to the obligation of Member States to respect and protect human dignity,** Member States shall ensure by appropriate means that audiovisual media services provided by media service providers under their jurisdiction do not contain any: **(a)** incitement to **violence or** hatred **directed against a group of persons or a member of a group based on any of the grounds referred to in Art. 21 of the Charter; (b) public provocation to commit a terrorist offence as set out in Art. 5 of Directive (EU) 2017/541. 2. The measures taken for the purposes of this Art. shall be necessary and proportionate and shall respect the rights and observe principles set out in the Charter.**

Art. 6 AVMSD was significantly expanded with the 2018 reform. Member States shall ensure by appropriate, proportionate and necessary means that audiovisual media services do not contain incitement to violence or hatred against certain persons or groups of persons or public provocation to commit terrorist offences. While the provision on terrorist content is new, the incitement provision has been amended only in respect of the offences covered so as to extend to all grounds of discrimination referred to in Art. 21 of the CFR, thus achieving a more uniform approach in EU law

also in the formulation of prohibited grounds of discrimination. In addition to race, sex, religion or nationality (as in the past), the grounds of discrimination now include skin colour, ethnic or social origin, genetic characteristics, language, belief, political or other opinion, membership of a national minority, property, birth, disability, age and sexual orientation. Reference to Art. 21 CFR can also be found in a corresponding obligation for VSPs and may be seen as response to developments with regard to the exchange of discriminatory statements in online offers.[267]

Particularly noteworthy is the introductory sentence on human dignity, which not only emphasises that Member States have obligations derived from this fundamental right beyond the scope of Art. 6 AVMSD but also underlines the connection between Art. 6 AVMSD and considerations regarding human dignity. The additional ground of discrimination in connection with incitement to violence or hatred in Art. 6 para. 1 lit. a AVMSD limits the considerations made above on human dignity on the one hand, but on the other hand it also imposes an explicit obligation on the Member States in the sense of minimum harmonisation. When considering the emergence and growth of videos of populist associations within social networks or on VSPs, online content violating these requirements is probable.[268] Some Member States[269] have already addressed[270] the issue of hate speech at legislative level, independently of the provisions under Art. 6 AVMSD (and partly also independently of the limitation to audiovisual content), not without receiving strong criticism in view of the privatisation of enforcement and the latter's compatibility with higher-level law, notably fundamental rights and the ECD.[271] Art. 6 AVMSD thus creates a basis which, at least partially, counteracts the divergences in the na-

---

267 *Cole/Etteldorf*, in: Medienhandbuch Österreich 2019, p. 56, 60.
268 Cf. on this for example *Dittrich*, Social Networks and Populism in the EU – Four Things You Should Know.
269 For example the German Network Enforcement Act (cf. Chapter 2.4.4) or the French Loi visant à lutter contre les contenus haineux sur internet, http://www. assemblee-nationale.fr/15/ta/ta0310.asp.
270 For an overview on developments in Austria, Germany, Hungary, Italy, Poland and the United Kingdom cf. Art. 19 Free World Centre, Responding to 'hate speech': Comparative overview of six EU countries, available at https://www.Art. 19.org/wp-content/uploads/2018/03/ECA-hate-speech-compilation-report_March-2018.pdf.
271 For the discussion on the German Network Enforcement Act cf. for example the documentation of the hearing of the Legal Committee of the German Bundestag on 15 May 2019, available at https://www.bundestag.de/dokumente/textarchiv/2019/kw20-pa-recht-netzwerkdurchsetzungsgesetz-636616.

tional legal systems of those Member States that decided to adopt separate legislation in that field.

Directive (EU) 2018/1808
Art. 6a
1. Member States shall take appropriate measures to ensure that audiovisual media services provided by media service providers under their jurisdiction which may impair the physical, mental or moral development of minors are only made available in such a way as to ensure that minors will not normally hear or see them. Such measures may include selecting the time of the broadcast, age verification tools or other technical measures. They shall be proportionate to the potential harm of the programme. The most harmful content, such as gratuitous violence and pornography, shall be subject to the strictest measures.
2. Personal data of minors collected or otherwise generated by media service providers pursuant to paragraph 1 shall not be processed for commercial purposes, such as direct marketing, profiling and behaviourally targeted advertising.
3. Member States shall ensure that media service providers provide sufficient information to viewers about content which may impair the physical, mental or moral development of minors. For this purpose, media service providers shall use a system describing the potentially harmful nature of the content of an audiovisual media service. For the implementation of this paragraph, Member States shall encourage the use of co-regulation as provided for in Art. 4a(1).
4. The Commission shall encourage media service providers to exchange best practices on co-regulatory codes of conduct. Member States and the Commission may foster self-regulation, for the purposes of this Art., through Union codes of conduct as referred to in Art. 4a(2).

With regard to the protection of minors in the media, former Art. 12 (previously for non-linear media services) and Art. 27 (previously for linear media services) were deleted and instead Art. 6a, as a provision relating to the protection of minors, which applies to all audiovisual media service providers, was standardised and simplified. It requires Member States to take appropriate measures to ensure that content of audiovisual media services which is detrimental to the development is made available only in such a way as to ensure that it cannot normally be heard or seen by minors. The choice of transmission time or means of age verification are cited as examples of implementation, and co-regulatory systems are advocated. With this formulation, television broadcasters are moving away from the complete prohibition of certain content that may seriously impair the development of minors, hitherto contained in Art. 27, towards a more openly formulated provision that covers both linear and non-linear offerings dealing with pornography or gratuitous acts of violence in an equal manner.[272] However, as regards the possible measures, Art. 6a requires that the most harmful content (such as gratuitous violence and pornography) shall be subject to the strictest measures, including bans on broadcasting. On the other hand, there is no precise specification or balancing criteria to be applied. In addition, providers should make available sufficient information on content that may impair the physical, mental or moral development of minors, which will enable parents (but also regulators) to exercise better control. Personal data of minors must not be used for commercial purposes such as direct marketing or profiling – a provision which also takes into account the relevant considerations of the General Data Protection Regulation, which lays down that data of children enjoy special protection (e.g. Recital 38 of the GDPR).

For the cross-border distribution of online content, the provision regarding content which may impair the physical, mental or moral development of minors is particularly relevant. Each Member State must ensure (and in principle had to ensure under old law) that both linear and non-linear offers from VSPs (Art. 28b para. 1 lit. a) have no negative influence on the development of the personality of children and adolescents. However, the Directive does not define how this is to be ensured or what is to be understood as content that may impair minors' physical, mental or moral development. Numerous Member States have therefore developed different systems, in particular based on self-regulation and co-regulation, within which content and, in particular, age labels are reviewed.[273] In practice, when a specific content or offer is considered to impair the development of minors and should possibly be labelled or sanctioned (in the hardest case a ban), it is assessed on the basis of nationally established criteria (while there is a general statutory requirement such as under Art. 6a AVMSD). For example the Spanish Self-regulation Code for TV Content and Children, signed by several free-to-air linear providers, relies on several

---

272 In detail on the move away from the ban on pornography: *Ukrow*, Por-No Go im audiovisuellen Binnenmarkt?

273 Cf. in particular on self- and co-regulation systems: *Cappello (ed.)*, Self- and Co-regulation in the new AVMSD, IRIS Special 2019-2; on the legal situation under Directive 2010/13/EU see *Nikoltchev (ed.)*, Protection of Minors and Audiovisual Content On-Demand, IRIS plus 2012; *Capello (ed.)*, The protection of minors in a converged media environment, IRIS plus 2015-1; and ERGA report on Protection of Minors in the Audiovisual Media Services: Trends & Practices, 2016, available at https://ec.europa.eu/digital-single-market/en/news/erga-report-protec tion-minors-converged-environment.

categories of impairing content (violence, sex, fear or anguish, drugs and toxic substances, discrimination, imitable behaviour and language)[274], and the German approved self-regulatory body for the telemedia sector defines impairing content as offers that are suitable for exerting a negative influence on the development of the personality of children and adolescents that contradicts the human image of the Basic Law whereby concretising this in its decisions[275]. While some content available on the Internet will certainly be considered as impairing the development of minors in all Member States (particularly in the area of pornography and violence) and is already stipulated by European fundamental rights, there will still be nuances of national differences.

Art. 9 of the AVMSD regulates advertising restrictions. The 2018 reform partially harmonised the legal framework for linear and non-linear services. The criteria under Art. 22, which until now only had to be complied with by television broadcasters in commercial communications for alcoholic beverages and which relate in particular to the prohibition of alcohol advertising aimed at minors and the positive presentation of alcohol consumption, now also apply to on-demand audiovisual media services. With regard to aspects relating to the protection of minors, the use of co-regulation and the promotion of self-regulation, in particular through codes of conduct, should be supported by the Member States in the advertising of alcoholic beverages. The same shall apply to inappropriate audiovisual commercial communication contained in or accompanying children's programs concerning food and beverages that contain nutrients or substances with a nutritional or physiological effect, in particular fat, trans-fatty acids, salt or sodium and sugar. This rule aims at effectively reducing the (positive) impact of such advertising on children and thus indirectly also the consumption of such foods and was therefore probably also connected with alarming reports of the World Health Organization on the worldwide increasing overweight among children in the run-up to the reform.[276]

The rules on the recognisability of advertising and the use of subliminal techniques have remained unchanged. Art. 1 para. 1 lit. c and g AVMSD, in particular, retains the rules which transpose the abovementioned con-

---

274 Cf. ERGA report on Protection of Minors in the Audiovisual Media Services, supra (fn. 273), p. 20.
275 For an overview of the decisions dealing with impairing content cf. https://www.fsm.de/de/downloads.
276 Report of the Commission on Ending Childhood Obesity (ECHO), 25.1.2016, available at https://www.who.int/end-childhood-obesity/en/.

siderations of human dignity, discrimination and protection of minors into the field of audiovisual commercial communication. Therefore, what
has been mentioned applies – with some exceptions – accordingly: here,
too, the national transpositions diverge[277]. With regard to alcoholic beverages, tobacco products and electronic cigarettes as well as prescription
medicines, strong harmonisation across Europe exists as there is little or no
room for manoeuvre in the Member States.

2.4.2.2.4. Supervision and Sanctions

Until the 2018 revision, the AVMSD contained no specific provisions on
supervision[278] but merely required (or at least assumed) the existence of
national regulatory authorities at certain provisions in the Directive.[279] Although the AVMSD, even after the 2018 reform, neither contains particular structural supervisory requirements nor explicitly requires Member
States to set up an independent regulatory body or to define the terms of
that independence, it is nevertheless noteworthy that Recital 94 and
Art. 30 presume that the regulatory entities responsible for implementing
the Directive's provisions are "independent regulatory bodies". This is an
important step in the context of media regulation. The reluctance that nevertheless exists is certainly not least due to the fact that the EU only has
limited competences in the field of cultural and media law (cf. already
Chapter 2.3.2), that the (constitutional) traditions of the Member States
have grown very differently, particularly in the media sector, and that, finally, in many Member States there are different supervisory structures (especially in federal systems) that would hardly be open to "standardisation"
or harmonisation at European level. It is therefore the Member States that

---

277 For a detailed analysis cf. the study Defining a framework for the monitoring of
     advertising rules under the Audiovisual Media Services Directive, prepared for
     the European Commission by Ramboll Management Consulting and the Insti-
     tute of European Media Law, available at https://ec.europa.eu/digital-single-mar
     ket/en/news/audiovisual-and-media-services-directive-avmsd-study-advertising-ru
     les.
278 Cf. on this ERGA's statement on the independence of NRAs in the audiovisual
     sector, ERGA(2014)03, October 2014, available at https://ec.europa.eu/digital-si
     ngle-market/en/avmsd-audiovisual-regulators, and ERGA, Report on the inde-
     pendence of NRAs.
279 Cf. for example Art. 5 para. 1 lit. d, Art. 7 para. 2 and 3, Art. 28b para. 5
     AVMSD.

must take the appropriate measures to ensure effective implementation of the Directive (in accordance with the duties imposed by the TFEU). They are free to choose the appropriate instruments according to their legal traditions and established structures, and, in particular, the form of their competent independent regulatory bodies in order to be able to carry out their work in implementing the AVMSD impartially and transparently.[280]

At national level, this can lead to very different forms of supervision, which can affect both structural issues (e.g. term of office of members of the supervision, allocation of funds, affiliation to state authorities or ministries, etc.) and competence issues (responsibility of different authorities for different areas of the AVMSD, allocation of enforcement powers, etc.).[281] This in turn can lead to legal uncertainties, especially in the regulation of cross-border online content (in conjunction with the country-of-origin principle on which the AVMSD is based), especially if the national regulatory authorities reach organisational or competence limits within the framework of the cooperation to which they are entitled under Art. 30 AVMSD.[282] For example, in a study carried out by the ERGA and published in 2015, five European regulatory authorities indicated that they did not have the necessary power to enforce their decisions autonomously and four national European regulatory authorities stated that in some cases the intervention of the Ministry/Government is needed for their decisions to take effect.[283] A further comparative study, in addition to the comprehensive study for the Commission in 2015[284], carried out by the EMR for the European Audiovisual Observatory, showed, for example, large differences in the selection, design and framework of sanctions: While the German media authority may take action against illegal telemedia offers, this is not possible for the Swedish media authority in this form; while the Latvian regulator has a sanction framework of 14,000 euros for the violation of content-related provisions, the German regulator can impose penalties of up to 500,000 euros; and while the Italian regulator can also take blocking

---

280 Cf. Recital 94 of Directive 2010/13/EU.
281 Cf. on this in detail: AVMS-RADAR, study prepared for the European Commission by the EMR and the University of Luxembourg, p. 40 et seq.
282 Cf. on this in general and for a comparative analysis of selected Member States: *Cappello (ed.)*, Media law enforcement without frontiers, IRIS Special 2018-2; and *Cappello (ed.)*, The independence of media regulatory authorities in Europe, IRIS Special, IRIS Special 2019-1.
283 ERGA, Report on the independence of NRAs, pp. 51, 52.
284 AVMS-RADAR, study prepared for the European Commission by the EMR and the University of Luxembourg.

measures against platforms and websites, this is not possible in Sweden.[285] Moreover, self-regulation and co-regulation systems also have a different importance in the Member States, which is particularly evident in the area of advertising. While some regulators can take immediate action against providers themselves if they consider advertising to be inadmissible, regulators in other Member States have to maintain co-regulatory mechanisms in which it is foreseen that regulators have to first include opinions by self-regulatory institutions before being able to take action or in some cases are blocked from acting themselves.[286]

2.4.3. Data Protection and ePrivacy

With regard to data protection and the protection of privacy, the relevant secondary legislation determining the legal framework in the online environment is primarily the General Data Protection Regulation (GDPR)[287], which entered into force in May 2018, and the ePrivacy Directive[288]. Directive (EU) 2016/680[289] on the protection of natural persons with regard to the processing of personal data by competent authorities for the purposes of the prevention, investigation, detection or prosecution of criminal offences or the execution of criminal penalties, which repealed a Framework Decision[290] and was issued at the same time as the GDPR, applies to the exchange of personal data by national police and criminal justice authori-

---

285 *Cappello (ed.)*, Media law enforcement without frontiers, IRIS Special 2018-2, pp. 97 et seq.

286 Cf. *Capello (ed.)*, Self- and Co-regulation in the new AVMSD, IRIS Special 2019-2.

287 The provisions of the GDPR relevant in the context of this study are reprinted in the Online Annex, available at www.nomos-shop.de/44382,II. C.

288 Directive 2002/58/EC of the European Parliament and of the Council of 12 July 2002 concerning the processing of personal data and the protection of privacy in the electronic communications sector (Directive on privacy and electronic communications), OJ L 201, 31.7.2002 pp. 37–47.

289 Directive (EU) 2016/680 of the European Parliament and of the Council of 27 April 2016 on the protection of natural persons with regard to the processing of personal data by competent authorities for the purposes of the prevention, investigation, detection or prosecution of criminal offences or the execution of criminal penalties, and on the free movement of such data, and repealing Council Framework Decision 2008/977/JHA, OJ L 119, 4.5.2016, pp. 89–131.

290 Council Framework Decision 2008/977/JHA of 27 November 2008 on the protection of personal data processed in the framework of police and judicial cooperation in criminal matters, OJ L 350, 30.12.2008, pp. 60–71.

ties. The Directive is intended to improve the exchange of personal data within the framework of law enforcement and to better protect the data of offenders, victims and witnesses by, inter alia, no longer requiring law enforcement authorities to apply different data protection rules depending on the origin of the personal data. Outside of the purposes mentioned in the Directive, however, the GDPR also applies to law enforcement authorities. Since the Directive essentially incorporates the principles laid down in the GDPR and plays a role in the context of this study only insofar as it concerns the criminal investigation and prosecution in the area of online-crimes, it is not supposed to be dealt with in the following in more detail.

2.4.3.1. Data Processing and the Media Privilege

Data processing activities are omnipresent on the Internet and the use of data is manifold. Electronic commerce requires personal data to process contracts concluded online, websites need personal data to ensure their operation and security[291], just as the way in which the business model of so-called intermediaries and other platforms depend on and are geared by the processing of personal data.[292] To cite one of the most famous examples, representing a number of business models in the digital economy, the social network Facebook stores and uses user data to offer personalised advertising. The frequently quoted sentence "Senator, we sell ads" by Facebook CEO Mark Zuckerberg at his hearing before the US Congress,[293] however, became famous against the rather sad background of the Cambridge Analytica scandal and the associated possibilities of influencing political elections.[294] This case shows not least the connection between data processing or power over data and the freedom of opinion and the freedom of the media directly connected with the formation of political opinion. Therefore,

---

291 Thus, when a website is called up, the service host regularly requests device data which, among other things, contains the IP address as a personal date in order to protect against unauthorised or damage-intended (e.g. DOS attacks) calls to the website, for example.

292 *Hans/Ukrow/Knapp/Cole*, (Neue) Geschäftsmodelle der Mediaagenturen.

293 Facebook chief executive Mark Zuckerberg appeared before the Senate's Commerce and Judiciary committees on 10 April 2019. For a transcription cf. https://www.washingtonpost.com/news/the-switch/wp/2018/04/10/transcript-of-mark-zuckerbergs-senate-hearing/.

294 For an analysis cf., e.g., *Dutt/Deb/Ferrara*, "Senator, We Sell Ads": Analysis of the 2016 Russian Facebook Ads Campaign.

when, as in the context of this study, online content is mentioned, a distinction must first be made at this point between journalistic data processing and other (economic, technical, organisational and administrative) data processing activities against the background of the so-called media privilege.[295]

Pursuant to Art. 85 para. 1 GDPR, Member States are obliged to balance the right to the protection of personal data with the right to freedom of expression and information, including processing for journalistic purposes, by means of legal provisions. If necessary, they should provide for derogations or exceptions from Chapters II to VII and Chapter IX in accordance with Art. 85 para. 2 GDPR. Against the background of media freedom, the GDPR thus recognises that the provisions on the protection of personal data cannot automatically apply to the processing of personal data for journalistic purposes, which is inevitably linked to the exercise of media freedom. These positions of the media protected by fundamental rights (in the form of freedom of reporting and research) and of the public (in the form of freedom to receive and disseminate information and ideas without official intervention and regardless of national borders) may, for example, require that the processing of personal data for journalistic purposes also is permitted outside the grounds set out in Art. 6 para. 1 GDPR or that rights of persons affected under Chapter III of the Regulation are restricted. This balancing act[296], i.e. the assessment of the extent to which the balancing of data subjects' interests and media/information interests requires modifications with regard to data protection provisions, is the responsibility of the Member States, which, however, have a wide margin of manoeuvre in this respect. In the field of journalistic data processing, European secondary law therefore does not provide a framework but leaves this largely to[297] the Member States. In order to do justice to the

---

295 Cf. *Cappello (ed.)*, Journalism and media privilege, IRIS Special 2017-2.

296 *Schiedermair*, in: Ehmann/Selmayr, Art. 85 GDPR para. 9.

297 By being bound by the fundamental rights of the Union, it also applies to the adoption of such legal provisions by the Member States that they must observe the rulings of the CJEU on the balancing of the right to informational self-determination with freedom of the media and freedom of information and that they must comply with the provisions of Art. 85 in the light of fundamental rights and the case-law of the ECJ; see, in particular, CJEU, judgements of 6.11.2003, C-101/01, *Criminal proceedings against Bodil Lindqvist*, para. 85 et seq.; of 16.12.2008, C-73/07, *Tietosuojavaltuutettu gegen Satakunnan Markkinapörssi Oy und Satamedia Oy*, para. 54 et seq.; of 13.5.2014, *Google Spain*, supra (fn. 79), para. 73 et seq.

tasks and functions of the media protected by fundamental rights, the concept of journalistic purposes must be interpreted broadly (Recital 153). With regard to the interpretation of the predecessor rule in Art. 9 of the DPD, the core of which was not touched within the GDPR either, the CJEU also confirmed this and clarified that exemptions should not only apply to media companies but to everyone who is active in journalism.[298] Therefore, Art. 85 GDPR can only be understood as meaning that the regulatory mandate to the national legislator does not only refer to the areas of "traditional press" and "traditional press activity". The GDPR therefore does not seek to seize activities whose goal exists in the passing on of information, opinions and conceptions to the public – as this was already planned by the definition in Recital 121 of an earlier draft of the Regulation[299].[300] This addresses the role of the media as an economic asset on the one hand and a cultural asset on the other.[301] The media privilege thus applies, for example, to private broadcasting when data collection is carried out for research purposes, e.g. for the production of articles as an intrinsic journalistic activity, but can also apply in individual cases to billing activities if these data are inseparably linked to a journalistic service (e.g. fee data of freelancers in particular in investigative journalism).[302] In the online context, the media privilege will therefore primarily affect the content itself, insofar as it also deals with personal data (e.g. within reports, news or documentaries and overall with regard to the perception of rights of depicted persons and actors), but not the mere accessibility of this content (e.g. via intermediaries such as search engines). In its landmark decision of 2014 in the *Google Spain* case, the CJEU stated that Directive 95/46/EC granted media privilege to Google Spain at the time: "Furthermore, the processing by the publisher of a web page consisting in the publication of information relating to an individual may, in some circum-

---

298 CJEU, C-73/07, ibid., para. 56 and 58; cf. ECtHR, judgement of 27.6.2017, no. 931/13.

299 Proposal for a Regulation of the European Parliament and of the Council on the protection of individuals with regard to the processing of personal data and on the free movement of such data (Data Protection Basic Regulation), COM(2012), 11 final, available at https://eur-lex.europa.eu/LexUriServ/LexUriSe rv.do?uri=COM:2012:0011:FIN:DE:PDF.

300 Cf. also *Cappello (ed.)*, Journalism and media privilege, IRIS Special 2017-2, pp. 13 et seq., on the scope of the media privilege as a whole.

301 Cf., e.g., *Von Rimscha/Siegert*, Medienökonomie pp. 227 et seq.

302 Cf. also in detail *Soppe*, in: ZUM 63(6), 2019, p. 467, 472, with further references.

stances, be carried out 'solely for journalistic purposes' and thus benefit, by virtue of Art. 9 of Directive 95/46, from derogations from the requirements laid down by the directive, whereas that does not appear to be so in the case of the processing carried out by the operator of a search engine. It cannot therefore be ruled out that in certain circumstances the data subject is capable of exercising the rights [...] of Directive 95/46 against that operator but not against the publisher of the web page."[303] The purely economic operation of websites, media libraries, apps etc. is therefore generally subject to the provisions of European data protection law.

2.4.3.2. ePrivacy Directive and GDPR

In a further step the question about the relationship between the GDPR and the ePrivacy Directive is to be raised – in the ordered brevity. Art. 95 GDPR answers this question expressly in such a way that the GDPR "shall not impose additional obligations on natural or legal persons in relation to processing in connection with the provision of publicly available electronic communications services in public communication networks in the Union in relation to matters for which they are subject to specific obligations with the same objective set out in Directive 2002/58/EC". This means that there is a lex generalis-lex specialis relationship where the special provisions of ePrivacy Directive prevail over the general rules of the GDPR in areas which they specifically seek to regulate.[304] The European Data Protection Board (EDPB)[305] recently opted in this direction, holding in particular that the sanctions framework of the GDPR cannot be applied to cases that fall under the ePrivacy Directive.[306] The Directive applies to the processing of personal data in connection with the provision of publicly available electronic communications services in public communications net-

---

303 CJEU, *Google Spain v AEPD*, supra (fn. 79), para. 85.

304 However, that would not mean that generally further rules of the GDPR would be inapplicable. Thus, for example, Art. 6 does not contain any special defaults to the right of access, so that for this matter the provisions of the GDPR are still applicable.

305 EDPB, Opinion 5/2019 on the interplay between the ePrivacy Directive and the GDPR, in particular regarding the competence, tasks and powers of data protection authorities, adopted on 12 March 2019, available at https://edpb.europa.eu/sites/edpb/files/files/file1/201905_edpb_opinion_eprivacydir_gdpr_interplay_en_0.pdf.

306 Cf. on this in detail *Etteldorf*, in: EDPL 5(2), 2019, p. 224, 226 et seq.

works and thus partly relies on the definitions in the Framework Directive for electronic communications networks and services.[307] Therefore, to fall under the scope of the ePrivacy Directive, services have to meet four criteria: (1) there is an electronic communications service[308]; (2) that service is offered over an electronic communications network[309], (3) both service and network are publicly available[310] and (4) service and network are offered in the EU.[311] Consequently only services consisting wholly or mainly in the conveyance of signals – as opposed to, e.g., the provision of content – fall within the scope of the ePrivacy Directive. However, convergence

---

307 Directive 2002/21/EC of the European Parliament and of the Council of 7 March 2002 on a common regulatory framework for electronic communications networks and services (Framework Directive), OJ L 108, 24.4.2002, pp. 33–50.

308 Art. 2 lit. d ePrivacy Directive specifies that "communication" means "any information exchanged or conveyed between a finite number of parties by means of a publicly available electronic communications service" and excludes broadcasting services which may – in theory – reach an unlimited audience. The term "electronic communications service" is currently defined by Art. 2 lit. d Framework Directive as "a service normally provided for remuneration which consists wholly or mainly in the conveyance of signals on electronic communications networks, including telecommunications services and transmission services in networks used for broadcasting, but exclude services providing, or exercising editorial control over, content transmitted using electronic communications networks and services; it does not include information society services [...] which do not consist wholly or mainly in the conveyance of signals on electronic communications networks".

309 An electronic communications network is defined in the Framework Directive as "transmission systems and, where applicable, switching or routing equipment and other resources, including network elements which are not active, which permit the conveyance of signals by wire, radio, optical or other electromagnetic means, including satellite networks, fixed (circuit- and packet-switched, including Internet) and mobile terrestrial networks, electricity cable systems, to the extent that they are used for the purpose of transmitting signals, networks used for radio and television broadcasting, and cable television networks, irrespective of the type of information conveyed."

310 A service for the public is a service available to all members of the public on the same basis, and not only publicly owned services. Cf. EDPS, Opinion 5/2016, Preliminary EDPS Opinion on the review of the ePrivacy Directive (2002/58/EC), available at https://edps.europa.eu/sites/edp/files/publication/16-07-22_opinion_eprivacy_en.pdf, p. 12; and Communication by the Commission to the European Parliament and the Council on the status and implementation of Directive 90/388/EEC on competition in the markets for telecommunications services, COM(95) 113 final, 04.04.1995, p. 14.

311 Cf. on the several conditions in detail *van Hoboken/Zuiderveen Borgesius*, in: JIPITEC 6(3), 2015, p. 198.

sometimes results in services that are very similar from a functional perspective but remain subject to different legal regimes depending on whether they are provided in form of an electronic communications service, an information society service or an audiovisual service.[312] Without going into detail on the scope of the ePrivacy Directive[313], it should be noted that – in the light of the objective of this Directive to ensure the protection of fundamental rights and freedoms of the public when they make use of electronic communication networks – at least some of its provisions also apply on providers of information technology networks (in particular Art. 5(3), 9 and 13).[314] Regarding the dissemination of content in the online environment this means that Art. 5 para. 3 and 13 of the ePrivacy Directive apply to website operators (e.g. for cookies) or other businesses (e.g. for direct marketing). For example, website operators have to obtain the (active)[315] consent of the user if they want to store (and subsequently use for e.g. personalised advertising) certain cookies on the end devices of website users, which in particular enables web tracking and is therefore essential for many advertising-based business models on the Internet. Consent is also required if advertisers want to address potential customers via electronic means of communication (e.g. e-mail) with direct marketing purposes.

This means that the distributors of online content as responsible parties (platform providers, website operators, etc.) must observe secondary legal requirements resulting from the implementation of the ePrivacy Directive in the Member States if they process personal data. However, like the AVMSD, the ePrivacy Directive contains no provisions on law enforcement, sanctions and the establishment of supervisory authorities. Rather, it is up to the Member States, who must ensure that the requirements are implemented, to decide how they are to be implemented. Similar to the AVMSD, this has led to a different implementation of the requirements[316],

---

312 *Dumortier/Kosta*, ePrivacy Directive: assessment of trans-position, effectiveness and compatibility with proposed Data Protection Regulation, p. 8.

313 For a detailed analysis cf. ibid.

314 Art. 29 Data Protection Working Party, Opinion 2/2010 on online behavioural advertising, 22 June 2010, WP 171, p. 9; Opinion 1/2008 on data protection issues related to search engines, WP148, p. 12.

315 Cf. in particular CJEU, judgement of 1.10.2019, C-673/17, *Bundesverband der Verbraucherzentralen und Verbraucherverbände - Verbraucherzentrale Bundesverband e.V. v Planet49 GmbH*.

316 Cf. National transposition measures communicated by the Member States, OJ L 201, 31.7.2002, pp. 37–47.

in particular with regard to the implementation of certain rules in general[317] or the responsibility of authorities to monitor the requirements. In Germany, Sweden and the UK, for example, there is a division of competences between the DPAs and the telecoms regulator in the area of electronic communications.[318] In addition, there is no forum under the ePrivacy Directive, such as the ERGA or EDPB, where an exchange could take place on the implementation and enforcement of the requirements of the Directive. Occasionally – and not established or prescribed by the Directive – coordination here can only take place via related instruments such as the EDPB or the Body of European Regulators for Electronic Communications (BEREC), although this is not expressly intended by the European legislator in the context of data processing within electronic communications networks. Especially in the online sector, which is the linchpin of the ePrivacy Directive, this is problematic due to the cross-border nature of online offerings. The same considerations as set out in point 2.4.2.2.4 apply.

The ePrivacy Directive is also currently undergoing a reform process. A proposed ePrivacy Regulation[319], introduced by the Commission in January 2017, should enter into force at the same time as the GDPR but is still – not least because of the controversial cookie regulation it contains – in the trilogue process. Therein particular rules are contained to the supervision, law enforcement and sanctioning of offences, referring to the corresponding regulations of the GDPR, so that in the future there will probably be a very broad synchronisation of these sets of rules.

Outside the regulatory framework of the ePrivacy Directive, the GDPR applies. Due to its character as a regulation, it is directly applicable in all Member States and has thus strongly harmonised the data protection laws throughout Europe. The Member States only have a few areas in which they have room for manoeuvre and which are expressly mentioned. The

---

317 In Germany, for example, there is no implementation of Art. 5 para. 3 of ePrivacy Directive according to the Positioning of the Conference of the Independent Data Protection Authorities of the Federal Government and the Länder on "Zur Anwendbarkeit des TMG für nicht-öffentliche Stellen ab dem 25. Mai 2018", available at https://www.ldi.nrw.de/mainmenu_Datenschutz/submenu_Technik/Inhalt/TechnikundOrganisation/Inhalt/Zur-Anwendbarkeit-des-TMG-fuer-nicht-oeffentliche-Stellen-ab-dem-25_-Mai-2018/Positionsbestimmung-TMG.pdf.

318 *Dumortier/Kosta*, ePrivacy Directive: assessment of transposition, effectiveness and compatibility with proposed Data Protection Regulation, pp. 33 et seq.

319 Proposal for a Regulation of the European Parliament and of the Council concerning the respect for private life and the protection of personal data in electronic communications and repealing Directive 2002/58/EC (Regulation on Privacy and Electronic Communications), COM/2017/010 final - 2017/03 (COD).

GDPR contains comprehensive provisions on principles, legality requirements and information obligations in connection with the processing of
personal data. In addition, data subjects are granted comprehensive rights
of control and access to processing operations. Although this certainly also
plays an increased role in the online sector, that area will not be discussed
in detail here, since questions of legality are ultimately questions of detail
for the specific individual case.[320] However, the market place principle anchored in the GDPR, the comprehensive rules on supervision and sanctioning, and the system of cooperation within the EDPB are to be addressed in the following sections.

2.4.3.3. Market Location Principle

Under the conditions established by Art. 3 para. 2 lit. a and b GDPR, the
scope of the GDPR extends to processing of personal data of data subjects
located in the EU, without consideration of physical or operational structures of companies. With the introduction of this market location principle, the EU legislator thus extends the scope of application of European data protection law to data protection-relevant business activities of companies that do not have branches in the EU and would normally fall outside the territorial scope of application of EU law.[321] The aim was to
ensure (Recital 23) that a natural person would not be deprived of his or
her right to the protection of personal data simply because the processing
is carried out by foreign providers. Thus, the GDPR takes its protection
goal into account, which lies decisively in the protection of "fundamental
rights and freedoms of natural persons and in particular their right to the
protection of personal data" (Art. 1 para. 2 GDPR). The object of protection therefore determines the scope of application. However, it is not related to citizenship, residence or other types of legal status of the individual
whose personal data are being processed, but only to the location of the

---

320 Although compliance with data protection law is rightly doubtful, especially on
large online platforms such as Facebook, in view of recent rulings by the CJEU;
cf. for example CJEU, judgement of 5.6.2018, C-210/16, *Unabhängiges Landeszentrum für Datenschutz Schleswig-Holstein v Wirtschaftsakademie Schleswig-Holstein
GmbH*, regarding facebook fanpage; judgement of 29.7.2019, C-40/17, *Fashion
ID GmbH & Co.KG v Verbraucherzentrale NRW eV*, concerning the facebook like
button.
321 Cf. on the market location principle *Schantz*, in: NJW 26(69), 2016, p. 1841,
1842.

data subject in the Union.[322] The GDPR understands the Union thus as protected area, in which certain rights are guaranteed independently of Union citizenship.

The connecting factors for the market place principle and thus the applicability of GDPR are "the offering of goods or services, irrespective of whether a payment of the data subject is required, to such data subjects in the Union" (Art. 3 para. 2 lit. a GDPR) or "the monitoring of their behaviour as far as their behaviour takes place within the Union" (Art. 3 para. 2 lit. b GDPR). Only in these cases, which are triggered by an independent and targeted action of the processing body, it is, according to the intention of the Union legislator, also in the interest of the enterprises to be subject to EU law.

In order to clarify in which situations goods or services within the meaning of Art. 3 para. 2 lit. a GDPR are directed towards a person, Recital 23 lists several criteria. According to that list, the mere accessibility of the controller's, processor's or an intermediary's website in the Union, of an email address or of other contact details, or the use of a language generally used in the third country where the controller is established, is insufficient to ascertain such intention. But factors such as whether it is apparent that the controller or processor envisages offering services to data subjects in one or more Member States in the Union, which language or currency is used or if customers or users who are in the Union are mentioned can play a decisive role. In its Guidelines on the territorial scope[323], the EDPB mentions further criteria which could be taken into account like the use of a specific top-level-domain (".eu", ".de", etc.), the mention of dedicated addresses or phone numbers to be reached from an EU country, the international nature of an offer, the direction of advertisement or travel instructions for EU citizens. Furthermore, the EDPB considers that there needs to be a connection between the processing activity and the offering of good or service, but both direct and indirect connections are relevant and to be taken into account. It is notable that the aforementioned criteria show similarities to the criteria for assessing whether a broadcast by a media service provider established in another Member State is wholly or mostly directed towards the territory of another Member State in Recital 42 of the AVMSD (in the version of Directive 2010/13/EU).

---

322 Cf. Recital 14.
323 EDPB, Guidelines 3/2018 on the territorial scope of the GDPR (Art. 3), adopted on 16 November 2018, available at https://edpb.europa.eu/sites/edpb/files/consu ltation/edpb_guidelines_3_2018_territorial_scope_en.pdf, p. 18.

Regarding the second alternative under Art. 3 para. 2 GDPR, Recital 24 clarifies that "[t]he processing of personal data of data subjects who are in the Union by a controller or processor not established in the Union should also be subject to this Regulation when it is related to the monitoring of the behaviour of such data subjects insofar as their behaviour takes place within the Union", and it names in particular "profiling" as activity the provision relies on. However, there are also other (mainly online) activities which could trigger the scope of Art. 3 para. 2 lit. b GDPR, such as behavioural advertisement, geo-localisation activities, fingerprinting, personalised diet and health analytics services, market surveys and other behavioural studies based on individual profiles.[324]

In order to fulfil the requirements under Art. 3 para. 2 GDPR, foreign providers must not only comply with the rules under the GDPR but also take into account the national regulations, which are the result of the discretion given to the Member States.[325] This extends the reach of the market location principle even further.

Beyond the applicability of Art. 3 para. 2 GDPR, however, action against EU foreign providers will continue to be based on requests for administrative assistance[326] or the exertion of influence on affiliated companies over which an original jurisdiction exists.[327]

---

324 See also EDPB, Guidelines 3/2018 on the territorial scope of the GDPR (Art. 3), supra (fn. 323), p. 18.

325 See also EDPB, Guidelines 3/2018 on the territorial scope of the GDPR (Art. 3), supra (fn. 323), p. 12.

326 Cf. on this for example the case of the data protection authority Schleswig-Holstein (Unabhängiges Landeszentrum für Datenschutz Schleswig-Holstein), described in 31th Activity report, 2009, chapter 7.4, printed papers 16/2439, available at https://www.datenschutzzentrum.de/tb/tb31/kap07.html#74. This case was about the website "rottenneighbor.com" where users could post (regularly negative) things about their neighbours by adding their location data. The German authorities approached the competent US Federal Trade Commission (FTC) and asked for remedy.

327 Cf. on this in detail already *Ukrow*, Zur Zuständigkeit der Landesmedienanstalten/KJM für ausländische Anbieter, p. 177.

2.4.3.4. Supervision and Sanctioning

Other than many other laws in the field of media and information-technical systems[328], the GDPR contains very extensive rules on supervision. Although the concrete establishment and structural design of the supervisory authorities is left to the Member States, it is determined to a greater or lesser extent by EU requirements. This was done considering that the "effective protection of personal data throughout the Union requires [...] equivalent powers for monitoring and ensuring compliance with the rules for the protection of personal data and equivalent sanctions for infringements in the Member States" (Recital 11).

Points of contact which contain rules on the independent supervisory authorities are in principle[329] Art. 51 et seq. GDPR. Art. 51 of the GDPR requires each Member State to ensure that one or more independent authorities are responsible for monitoring the application of the Regulation in order to protect the fundamental rights and freedoms of natural persons with regard to processing and to facilitate the free movement of personal data within the Union. That complies with the goals mentioned in the GDPR (cf. Art. 1 GDPR). However, the focus is on the protection of fundamental rights and freedoms as a direct and actual purpose of the establishment of supervisory authorities. The supervisory authority must be in a position (factually and technically) to include fundamental-rights concerns in the monitoring of data processing operations of the responsible bodies subject to its supervision. Accordingly, Art. 53 para. 2 GDPR provides that *each member* of the supervisory authority must have the qualification, experience and expertise required for the fulfilment of its tasks and the exercise of its powers, in particular in the area of the protection of personal data, whereby the closer arrangement is left to the Member States (Art. 54 para. 1 lit. b GDPR). The term "members" here refers to the management level of the respective supervisory authority, which may vary depending on the implementation in the Member States.[330] They are the holders of the guaranteed independence and democratic legitimacy which must be en-

---

328 E.g. the AVMSD, the DSM Directive or the ECD.

329 According to Art. 85 para. 2 GDPR, Member States shall provide for exemptions or derogations from Chapter VI (independent supervisory authorities) in the field of the media privilege.

330 For this *Ziebarth*, in: Sydow, Art. 52 para. 21; in Germany, for example, the supervisory authorities of the Länder have only one member in this sense (Landesbeauftragte für den Datenschutz), while in Belgium a collegial body is appointed.

sured by the Member States when appointing them (under Art. 53 para. 1 of the GDPR, it must be ensured that each member of the supervisory authorities is appointed by means of a transparent procedure, whether by Parliament, the Government, the head of state or an independent body entrusted with the appointment under the law of the Member State).

Altogether, the independence of the supervisory authorities takes a special role in the context of the GDPR. Art. 52 GDPR lays down a number of requirements in order to guarantee the independence of the supervisory authorities, regulating in particular the freedom of the supervisory authorities from instructions from outside or inside, the personnel sovereignty and the necessity of the equipment with staff, technical and financial resources, premises and infrastructures. This also takes into account the fundamental rights requirements of Art. 8 para. 3 CFR. It should be emphasised at this point that adequate funding is intended to ensure independence, the establishment of a harmonised level of data protection and an effective protection of fundamental rights and is therefore of crucial importance.[331] Art. 53 GDPR supplements the provisions of Art. 52 GDPR, in particular to ensure the independence of members of supervisory authorities. For example, they must be appointed by an independent body through a transparent procedure, certain terms of office must be respected and there is some protection against unjustified dismissal.

The tasks and powers of the supervisory authorities are laid down in Art. 57 et seq. of the GDPR. Art. 57 GDPR, which lists various individual tasks, specifies the general monitoring activity already assigned to the supervisory authorities pursuant to Art. 51 GDPR, e.g. monitoring and enforcement of the ordinance (para. 1 lit. a) or the decision on complaints by persons concerned (para. 1 lit. f), on the one hand, but on the other hand also sets further requirements going beyond mere monitoring, e.g. raising public awareness (para. 1 lit. d) or the obligation to contribute to the activities of the EDPB (para. 1 lit. t). The supervisory authorities are therefore, on the one hand, "external supervisory bodies" in the sense of monitoring both without and (in the event of complaints) with regard to specific occasions; on the other hand, they perform[332] educational tasks comparable to media regulation authorities in the audiovisual sector. Art. 58 GDPR ensures that each supervisory authority has the necessary investigative, corrective and advisory powers at its disposal.

---

331 *Ziebarth*, in: Sydow, Art. 52 para. 40 et seq.
332 Cf. *Brink*, in: Wolff/Brink, § 38 BDSG para. 2.

In principle, the imposing of administrative fines for infringements of the GDPR is left to the Member States, whereby those fines shall be effective, proportionate and dissuasive (Art. 83 para. 1 GDPR). However, with regard to administrative fines that are imposed for infringements of the GDPR[333] by private entities[334], Art. 83 GDPR contains a comprehensive framework. On the one hand this is supposed to ensure that each supervisory authority (for the special cases of Denmark and Estonia cf. Recital 151) has the power to impose administrative fines and, on the other hand, to strengthen and harmonise administrative fines.[335]

2.4.3.5. Jurisdiction and Cooperation of Authorities

As regards the competence of the supervisory authorities, Art. 55 para. 1 GDPR provides that each supervisory authority shall be competent for the performance of the tasks assigned to and the exercise of the powers conferred on it in accordance with the GDPR on the territory of its own Member State. This basically establishes the one-stop shop principle, which enables companies to address their concerns to the supervisory authority of the Member State in which they are established. The connection between Art. 3 para. 2 GDPR and the rules to the competence regarding the responsible supervisory authority also means that foreign service providers do not automatically benefit from the one-stop shop mechanism.[336] This principle applies only to processing entities established in the Union.[337]

In the case of cross-border situations that are the rule in the online environment, however, Art. 56 GDPR provides for rules deviating from the competence of the Member State of establishment. Nevertheless, Art. 56 does not apply to processing operations necessary to fulfil a legal obliga-

---

333 Regarding penalties for infringements of national rules, the Member States are enabled to lay down rules for (criminal and administrative) penalties, whereby the principle of *ne bis in idem*, as interpreted by the Court of Justice, should be taken into account; cf. Recital 149.

334 Regarding public authorities and bodies, each Member State may lay down the rules on whether and to what extent administrative fines may be imposed; cf. Art. 83 para. 7 GDPR.

335 Cf. Recital 150.

336 See also EDPB, Guidelines 3/2018 on the territorial scope of the GDPR (Art. 3), adopted on 16 November 2018, available at https://edpb.europa.eu/sites/edpb/fil es/consultation/edpb_guidelines_3_2018_territorial_scope_en.pdf, p. 12.

337 Cf. Art. 29 Working Party, WP244, 13 December 2016, Guidelines for identifying a controller or processor's lead supervisory authority.

tion to which the controller is subject (Art. 55 para. 2 in conjunction with Art. 6 para. 1 lit. c GDPR). This reflects the idea that Member States are empowered in this area to allow (relatively extensive) derogations from the GDPR, in particular to allow for the integration of national specificities in other sectors related to data protection law.

Art. 56 para. 1 GDPR regulates the competence of the lead supervisory authority in a way that the supervisory authority of the main establishment or of the single establishment of the controller or processor shall be competent to act as lead supervisory authority for the cross-border processing carried out by that controller or processor.

An exception to Art. 56 para. 1 is to be found under Art. 56 para. 2: By derogation from the one-stop shop principle, each supervisory authority shall be competent to handle a complaint lodged with it or a possible infringement of the GDPR if the subject matter relates only to an establishment in its Member State or substantially affects data subjects only in its Member State. As examples for processing activities concerning only processing carried out in a single Member State, Recital 127 names the processing of employees' personal data in the specific employment context of a Member State. In the cases referred to in Art. 56 para. 2 and 3, the supervisory authority shall observe a special procedure: In order to ensure the effective enforcement of a decision vis-à-vis the controller or processor, it shall inform the lead supervisory authority without delay about the matter, and the lead supervisory authority shall decide whether or not it will handle the case, by taking into account whether there is an establishment of the controller or processor in the Member State of the supervisory authority which informed it (Recital 127). If the lead supervisory authority decides to handle the case, the procedure of cooperation between the supervisory authorities provided in Art. 60 GDPR shall apply, and the notifying supervisory authority should have the possibility to submit a draft decision, of which the lead supervisory authority should take utmost account when preparing its decision under the one-stop shop mechanism.

Art. 60 comprehensively regulates the cooperation procedure between the lead supervisory authority and the other supervisory authorities concerned in cases of cross-border data processing. The lead supervisory authority shall, inter alia, endeavour to reach consensus and provide other supervisory authorities involved with comprehensive information. The provision also includes procedural steps that give other supervisory authorities the possibility to make an objection against resolutions of the lead supervisory authority.

If a consensus ultimately cannot be reached, Art. 63 GDPR et seq. also provides for a consistency mechanism involving the EDPB. The EDPB was established under Art. 68 GDPR as a body of the Union with its own legal personality, composed of the head of the supervisory authority of each Member State[338]. Its main role is to ensure the consistent application of the GDPR throughout the European Economic Area – a task which is substantiated under Art. 70 para. 1 GDPR in more detail and in no less than 25 specific provisions. The EDPB will also be involved in advising the Commission, drawing up codes of conduct and certification mechanisms. In this role, the EDPB adopts, after extensive consultations, inter alia guidance in the form of guidelines, recommendations, best practices and opinions, thus clarifying the terms of the Regulation in order to provide a consistent interpretation of the rights and obligations of stakeholders. However, in cross-border cases where the cooperation procedure has led to no consensus, the EDPB has the power to rule on the matter by means of a binding decision, inter alia:

> "– where, in a case referred to in Art. 60 para. 4, a supervisory authority concerned has raised a relevant and reasoned objection to a draft decision of the lead authority or the lead authority has rejected such an objection as being not relevant or reasoned. The binding decision shall concern all the matters which are the subject of the relevant and reasoned objection, in particular whether there is an infringement of this Regulation" (Art. 65 para. 1 lit. a);
> "– where there are conflicting views on which of the supervisory authorities concerned is competent for the main establishment" (Art. 65 para. 1 lit. b).

According to Art. 65 para. 2 GDPR, this decision shall be adopted within one month from the referral of the subject matter by a two-thirds majority of the members of the Board. That period may be extended by a further month on account of the complexity of the subject matter. The decision shall further be reasoned and addressed to the lead supervisory authority and all the supervisory authorities concerned and binding on them.

---

338 Where more than one supervisory authority is established in a Member State, that Member State shall designate the supervisory authority which is to represent those authorities in the Board and shall set out the mechanism to ensure compliance by the other authorities with the rules relating to the consistency mechanism referred to in Art. 63, Art. 51 para. 3 GDPR.

This gives the EDPB strong powers, compared to other authorities established at European level in the field of cross-border cooperation between supervisory authorities such as the ERGA, which, although linked to a complex and burdensome procedure, can lead to a final agreement in conflict cases.

2.4.4. Intellectual Property Rules

In the context of online content and related legal requirements, copyright plays an important role. Relevant legislative texts on EU level are the InfoSoc Directive of 2001[339], the Directive 2004/48/EC of the European Parliament and of the Council of 29 April 2004 on the enforcement of intellectual property rights (Enforcement Directive)[340] and the DSM Directive[341], which is the legislative act that was recently adopted and amended the InfoSoc Directive and Directive 96/9/EC and has to be transposed by the Member States until 7 June 2021.

2.4.4.1. The InfoSoc and Enforcement Directives

The InfoSoc Directive, adopted on 22 May 2001, aims to harmonise key copyright and related rights issues in the EU and implements[342], inter alia, the 1996 WIPO Copyright Treaty. It contains a general regulatory framework, in particular with regard to reproduction and dissemination rights and most importantly concerning the communication to the public and making available to the public rights. These are property rights of the respective rights holders, who may permit or prohibit such acts in whole or in part and who are granted the right to bring an action for damages and/or a court order, among other things, with respect to infringements of their rights. In addition, the Directive contains a comprehensive list of copyright exceptions and limitations, which are exhaustively listed.

---

339 Directive 2001/29/EC, supra (fn. 15).
340 Directive 2004/48/EC of the European Parliament and of the Council of 29 April 2004 on the enforcement of intellectual property rights, OJ L 157, 30.4.2004, pp. 45–86.
341 Directive (EU) 2019/790, supra (fn. 16).
342 WIPO Copyright Treaty (WCT) – Joint Declarations, OJ L 89, 11.4.2000, pp. 8–14.

The Enforcement Directive of 2004 serves in particular to strengthen the rights of rights holders in order to ensure a high level of protection for intellectual property. It includes a wide range of enforcement instruments under private law, for example with regard to the preservation of evidence, information rights, interim measures or court orders.

2.4.4.2. The DSM Directive

The DSM Directive, which entered into force on 6 June 2019 after lengthy discussions, is based on, and supplements, the other relevant Directives with the aim of adapting copyright law in the EU to the requirements of the digital society. It includes rules on copyright contract law, text and data mining, ancillary copyright for press publishers, but also rules on the use of protected content by online services. In this latter area, the DSM Directive clearly departs from the principles of limited responsibility laid down in the ECD. It is especially interesting to consider in the legislative history of that Directive that there were numerous changes made to the text of this part of the Directive between the Commission's original proposal of 2016 and the finally adopted Directive of 2019. The core has remained, however, and that is bringing the possibility of direct platform liability more into focus when the DSM Directive will have been transposed. For this reason, the provisions of the relevant Art. 17 of the DSM Directive shall be examined in more detail in the context of this opinion.[343]

The rules contained in the DSM Directive on the use of protected content by online content-sharing service providers provide detailed guidelines on the liability of this type of platforms in the area of copyright.

The newly designed area of liability regulation within the framework of Art. 17 of the DSM Directive refers less to its own regime than to an explicit renunciation of liability privileges under the ECD in certain cases with regard to copyright infringing content on such online platforms. The DSM Directive currently in the process of being transposed in national law thus takes a step towards greater accountability of online platforms, albeit not on a cross-sectorial basis, as is the case for the ECD, but only in relation to certain areas of copyright law. The standard of liability and its enforcement in the cases covered by the DSM Directive shall subsequently be governed in particular by the standards laid down in the InfoSoc Directive

---

343 The provisions of the DSM Directive relevant in the context of this study are reprinted in the Online Annex, available at www.nomos-shop.de/44382, II. D.

and the Enforcement Directive. Because of the significant departure of the previously untouched liability regime of the ECD for platforms, it is worthwhile taking a brief look into the genesis of Art. 17.

The Commission's proposal on Art. 17 DSM Directive, at that time still Art. 13 of the proposal, which was not included in the final version of the DSM Directive, provided for a different wording, which could also be associated much more strongly with proactive obligations of the platform providers. Among other aspects, this wording referred to measures "such as the use of effective content recognition technologies"[344]. Recital 39 of the proposal claimed such technologies to be appropriate and proportionate measures to ensure protection of works. This wording fuelled the discussion about the future obligation of platform providers to establish so-called upload filters to ensure that copyright infringing material cannot be uploaded.[345] The argument was made that, to effectively recognise infringing content on a platform, a technology applied will have to examine the entirety of the content on the platform. This could, therefore, be seen in a way that Art. 13 of the proposal envisaged a general monitoring obligation.[346] This understanding of the proposal's wording was supported by the Commissions Impact Assessment on the modernisation of EU copyright rules[347], in which the Commission referred to "fingerprinting"[348] and

---

344 Proposal for a Directive of the European Parliament and of the Council on copyright in the Digital Single Market, COM/2016/0593 final, available at https://eur-lex.europa.eu/legal-content/EN/TXT/?uri=COM:2016:0593:FIN.

345 Cf. on this in detail *Henrich*, Nach der Abstimmung ist (fast) vor der Umsetzung; *Kuczerawy*, EU Proposal for a Directive on Copyright in the Digital Single Market: Compatibility of Art. 13 with the EU Intermediary Liability Regime.

346 *Kuczerawy*, EU Proposal for a Directive on Copyright in the Digital Single Market: Compatibility of Art. 13 with the EU Intermediary Liability Regime, p. 10.

347 Commission staff working document, impact assessment, on the modernisation of EU copyright rules Accompanying the document Proposal for a Directive of the European Parliament and of the Council on copyright in the Digital Single Market and Proposal for a Regulation of the European Parliament and of the Council laying down rules on the exercise of copyright and related rights applicable to certain online transmissions of broadcasting organisations and retransmissions of television and radio programmes, as of 14.9.2016, SWD(2016) 301 final, available at https://ec.europa.eu/digital-single-market/en/news/impact-assessment-modernisation-eu-copyright-rules, PART 3/3, p. 164.

348 Fingerprinting allows easily recognisable features of the content to be extracted and thus identified as unique features of that content. These features are then compared against a reference database.

"watermarking"[349] as two main types of content recognition technologies, in particular mentioning YouTube's Content ID system[350] as a prominent example for fingerprinting technologies.[351] However, the Commission's proposal was criticised for a number of factors. Concerns were raised in particular in light of the freedom of platforms to conduct a business, the freedom of expression of content creators and the right to protection of personal data (see Chapter 2.1.2). Above all, fears were voiced because of a possible collision with Art. 15 ECD, which prohibits Member States from imposing general obligations to monitor the information which service providers covered by the ECD transmit or store, and with the related case law of the CJEU (cf. on this in detail Chapter 3.3.7.3).[352] This led to an intensive search for a compromise in the course of the trilogue regarding former Art. 13:[353]

---

349 Watermarking is an invisible tattooing operation that only allows identifying tattooed copies. Digital watermarks are embedded into the content and make each copy of the content a unique copy.

350 The technological tool Content ID developed by Google allows the screening of visual and phonographic data of videos on YouTube and their automatic matching with other videos uploaded. In case a new video is uploaded on YouTube and a match is found against a "hash", the owner of the original content can decide whether content has to be blocked, content can be viewed freely and viewing statistics are gathered or content is being monetised (add advertisements); cf. https://support.google.com/youtube/answer/2797370?hl=en.

351 *Senftleben et al.*, in: European Intellectual Property Review 40(3), 2018, p. 149, 150 et seq.

352 See for example *Senftleben et al.*, in: European Intellectual Property Review 40(3), 2018, p. 149, 149 et seq.

353 Cf. the synopsis prepared by the Council, available at https://eur-lex.europa.eu/l egal-content/EN/HIS/?uri=CELEX:32019L0790.

COMMISSION'S PROPOSAL	Amendments of the Parliament[354]	General Approach of the Council[355]
1. Information society service providers that store and provide to the public access to large amounts of works or other subject-matter uploaded by their users shall, in cooperation with rightholders, take measures to ensure the functioning of agreements concluded with rightholders for the use of their works or other subject-matter or to prevent the availability on their services of works or other subject-matter identified by rightholders through the cooperation with the service providers. Those measures, such as the use of effective content recognition technologies, shall be appropriate and proportionate. The service providers shall provide rightholders with adequate information on the functioning and the deployment of the measures, as well as, when relevant, adequate reporting on the recognition and use of the works and other subject-matter.	1. **Without prejudice to Art. 3(1) and (2) of Directive 2001/29/EC, online content sharing** [...] service providers **perform an act of communication** to the public [...]. **They** shall **therefore conclude fair and appropriate licensing agreements with right holders.** 2. [...] **Licensing agreements which are concluded by online content sharing** service providers **with right holders for the acts of communication** referred to in paragraph 1, **shall cover the liability for works uploaded by the users of such online content sharing services in line with the terms and conditions set out in the licensing agreement, provided that such users do not act for commercial purposes. 2a. Member States shall provide that where right holders do not wish to conclude licensing agreements, online content sharing service providers and right holders shall cooperate in good faith in order to ensure that unauthorised protected works or other subject matter are not available on their services. Cooperation between online content service providers and right holders shall not lead to preventing the availability of non-infringing works or other protected subject matter, including those covered by an exception or limitation to copyright.**	1. *Member States shall provide that an* online content sharing service provider performs an act *of communication to the public or an act of making available to the public when it gives the public access to copyright protected works or other protected subject matter uploaded by its users. An* online content sharing service provider *shall obtain an authorisation from* the rightholders referred to in Art. 3(1) *and (2) of* Directive 2001/29/EC *in order to communicate or make available to the public works or other subject matter. Where no such authorisation has been obtained, the service provider shall prevent the availability on its service of those works and other subject-matter, including through the application of measures referred to in paragraph 4. This subparagraph shall apply without prejudice to exceptions and limitations provided for in Union law. Member States shall provide that when an authorisation has been obtained, including via a licensing agreement, by an online content sharing service provider, this authorisation shall also cover acts of uploading by the users of the service falling within Art. 3 of Directive 2001/29/EC when they are not acting on a commercial basis.* [...]

---

354 Amendments adopted by the European Parliament on 12 September 2018 on the proposal for a directive of the European Parliament and of the Council on copyright in the Digital Single Market COM(2016)0593, available at http://www.europarl.europa.eu/doceo/document/TA-8-2018-0337_EN.html.

355 Document 9134/18 as of 25.5.2018, available at https://www.consilium.europa.eu/media/35373/st09134-en18.pdf.

3. When an online content sharing service provider performs an
act of communication to the
public *or an act of making available to the public, it shall not be
eligible for the exemption of liability provided for in Art. 14 of Directive 2000/31/EC for unauthorised
acts of communication to the public and making available to the
public, without prejudice to the
possible application of Art. 14 of
Directive 2000/31/EC to those services for purposes other than copyright relevant acts.*

4. *In the absence* of the authorisation referred to in the second
subparagraph of paragraph 1,
Member States shall provide
that an online content sharing
service provider *shall not be liable for acts of communication to
the public or making available to
the public within the meaning of
this Art. when:*

*(a) it demonstrates that it has
made best efforts to prevent the
availability of specific works or
other subject matter by implementing effective and proportionate
measures, in accordance with paragraph 5, to prevent the availability
on its services of the specific works
or other subject matter identified
by rightholders and for which the
rightholders have provided the service with relevant and necessary
information for the application of
these measures; and*

*(b) upon notification by righthold-
ers of works or other subject matter, it has acted expeditiously to remove or disable access to these
works or other subject matter and
it demonstrates that it has made its
best efforts to prevent future availability through the measures referred to in point (a).*

The Parliament avoided an explicit mentioning of content recognition technologies but suggested nonetheless to oblige the service providers to ensure that unauthorised protected works are not available on their services. The Parliament addressed concerns regarding the collision with fundamental rights by a cooperation clause. The Council took a different approach. On the one hand, it implied a kind of notice and staydown mechanism in Art. 13 para. 4 lit. b) (Council Approach) requiring the service provider not only to remove the content in case of a notification but also to take additional measures to ensure that it is not subsequently reposted, either by the same user or by other users. On the other hand, it also required "best efforts" to prevent the availability of specific works or other subject matter by implementing effective and proportionate measures (Art. 13 para. 4 lit. a) of the Council Approach). However, such efforts would only be prescribed, according to the Council's approach, where the rights holders have provided the service with the relevant and necessary information for the application of these measures.

The differing positions led to a final compromise in Art. 17 of the DSM Directive which was no longer as strict as the Commission's original proposal but also included the approaches of Parliament and Council. Although Recital 66 DSM Directive now (only) states that "the obligations established in this Directive should not lead to Member States imposing a general monitoring obligation", the debate on content recognition technologies or other proactive measures is still relevant due to the relative general wording of Art. 17 DSM Directive, which continues to rely on appropriate and proportionate measures by demanding "best efforts" to ensure the unavailability of specific works. In this regard Art. 17 in its final version, which will be described in the following in more detail, still reflects a gradual shift in the perception of such platforms from being "mere conduits" to "active gate-keepers" of content uploaded and shared by users.[356]

Art. 17 DSM Directive, which regulates the liability of platforms, is applicable to "online content sharing service providers". These are platforms on which users can post large amounts of content and which make this available to the public, the main purpose of which must be to store and publish content uploaded by users.[357] The definition in Art. 2 para. 6 DSM Directive refers to the commercial nature of such a platform. Non-profit online encyclopaedias, science or education directories and open-source developer platforms are excluded. Moreover, providers of telecommunications or cloud services and online sales platforms are excluded, too. The storage and publication of content uploaded by users must be the "primary purpose" or "one of the primary purposes" of the platform concerned. The

---

356 In this regards also *Frosio/Mendis*, Monitoring and Filtering: European Reform or Global Trend?

357 DSM Directive, Recital 62.

Recitals narrow this down to those online services which play an important role on the market for online content by competing with other online content services, such as audio and video streaming services, for the same target groups. An assessment of this has to be made on a case-by-case basis.[358] A further partial restriction with regard to start-ups is made within the framework of Art. 17 para. 6 DSM Directive.

The starting point of the regulation is the clarification in Art. 17 para. 1 stipulating that the providers of such platforms themselves perform an act of communication to the public or an act of making available to the public within the meaning of the InfoSoc Directive (Art. 3) if the platform provides the public with access to works protected by copyright or other subject matters uploaded by its users. The service provider must therefore obtain the permission of the rights holders mentioned in Art. 3 para. 1 and 2 InfoSoc Directive for communication to the public or making publicly available.

Based on this finding, the essence of the new liability regime follows the conditions set by Art. 17 para. 3 DSM Directive. The liability privilege laid down in Art. 14 ECD therefore does not apply to the copyright-relevant actions of the users of the respective platform if they do not act commercially. In this respect, the Recitals[359] list those users whose activities are not for profit or whose activities on the platform do not generate significant revenues. In this case, platforms generally need to obtain the user rights granted by the respective rights holders in form of a licence agreement, or they are directly responsible for copyright infringements with the legal consequences provided for in the InfoSoc and Enforcement Directives.

However, the regulation offers a way out of direct liability. If, therefore, no licensing is possible for the activities of the users, the platform providers can resort to the envisaged alternative to the license agreements laid down in Art. 17 para. 4 in order to avoid direct liability. Art. 17 para. 4 DSM Directive provides for three conditions to be met cumulatively. Platforms must have made sufficient efforts to obtain authorisation from rights holders ("all efforts"), they must have made every effort to ensure that legally protected content is as inaccessible as possible ("in accordance with high industry standards of professional diligence"), and they must, as previously under Art. 14 of the ECD, remove content as soon as possible after becoming aware of it and prevent similar infringements of rights in respect of the work in the future (notice and takedown and staydown). As

---

358 DSM Directive, Recital 63.
359 DSM Directive, Recital 69.

mentioned, the reference to "content recognition techniques" as it appeared in the Commission's proposal for the DSM Directive was replaced. In this respect, Recital 66 speaks only of efforts to prevent the availability of unauthorised and other protected content recognised by the respective rights holders. In line with the principles of the ECD, the obligations laid down in the DSM Directive should not be induced to introduce a general monitoring obligation.

The requirement to prevent the availability of copyright protected content is also limited in two places. First, a proportionality clause in Art. 17 para. 5 determines the level of effort required, including the type, target group and size of the service and the works or other content uploaded by users, the availability of appropriate and effective means, and their cost to service providers. In turn, secondly, Art. 17 para. 6, according to which SMEs are exempted from obligations under certain conditions, must be cumulative. The exception applies in this respect to platforms that are less than three years old and have a turnover of less than EUR 10 million[360], which is why it can be referred to as a "startup-clause". These are now only obliged to seek authorisation and, as before, to remove any copyright infringing content after gaining knowledge. Those SMEs, which have more than 5 million monthly users, must at least prevent further uploads of this kind in the future. In addition, Art. 17 para. 9 contains further provisions according to which platforms are to provide their users with complaint mechanisms in the event that their content is incorrectly identified and treated as copyright infringement.

In addition, Art. 17 para. 7 clarifies that the justified use of copyright-protected content should remain protected within the framework of copyright barriers. In particular, with regard to the fundamental rights to freedom of expression and freedom of the arts enshrined in the CFR, a balance with intellectual property rights shall be found. To this end, the DSM Directive mentions quotations, criticisms, reviews, cartoons, parodies and persiflage as mandatory exceptions and restrictions. Service providers shall establish effective and expeditious complaint and redress procedures in the event of disputes concerning the blocking of access to and for removal of content in order to enable users to act within this framework.

By limiting the liability privileges established in the ECD and thus increasing the associated risk of direct liability to damages, the DSM Directive therefore not only places greater responsibility on platform providers in comparison with the previous liability framework but also goes one step

---

360 Calculated in accordance with Commission Recommendation 2003/361/EC.

further in comparison to other current regulations or regulatory undertakings, such as the German Network Enforcement Act (NetzDG)[361], which is already in force in Germany, or the Proposal of the European Commission for a Regulation for the Prevention of the Distribution of Terrorist Content Online[362], which do not rely on broad civil liability but on a system of sanctions. Under certain conditions, the functioning of the scheme de facto turns the fundamental principle of liability privilege under the ECD into a fundamental liability of intermediaries, albeit with exceptions.

2.4.5. Further Relevant Legislative Acts

2.4.5.1. Platform-to-Business Regulation

As part of its Communication Mid-Term Review on the implementation of the Digital Single Market Strategy[363], the Commission announced in May 2017 that it would take action to address unfair contract terms and unfair trading practices in relationships between platforms and companies. In particular, issues of dispute settlement, criteria for fair practices and transparency obligations should be clarified. The background was an inventory of platform-to-business trading practices, which indicated that some online platforms used trading practices that might discriminate against business users, for example by removing products or services from search results without adequate notice or even by favouring their own products or services.

The resulting Regulation on promoting fairness and transparency for business users of online intermediation services (Platform-to-Business Regulation, P2B Regulation)[364] came into force on 31 July 2019 and will

---

361 Network Enforcement Act (Netzwerkdurchsetzungsgesetz, NetzDG) of 1 September 2017, BGBl. I, p. 3352.
362 COM/2018/640 final, supra (fn. 220).
363 Communication from the Commission to the European Parliament, the Council, the European Economic and Social Committee and the Committee of the Regions, on the Mid-Term Review on the implementation of the Digital Single Market Strategy, A Connected Digital Single Market for All, COM(2017) 228 final.
364 Regulation (EU) 2019/1150 of the European Parliament and of the Council, of 20 June 2019, on promoting fairness and transparency for business users of online intermediation services, OJ L 186, 11.7.2019, pp. 57–79.

be applicable as of 12 July 2020.[365] It is intended to achieve a better balance between platforms and businesses. The scope of the Regulation covers online brokerage services and online search engines which, through their respective platforms, offer goods or services to consumers located in the European Union, such as online e-commerce marketplaces, collaborative marketplaces, online services for software applications or online services for social media. Not included are, inter alia, peer-to-peer online intermediation services without the participation of commercial users or pure business-to-business online intermediation services which are not offered to consumers.

Core elements of the Regulation are, in particular, the obligation to set up an internal system for handling complaints from commercial users and information and transparency obligations. These include the disclosure of the main determining parameters for the ranking of an online intermediation service and the reasons for the relative weighting of these parameters. In addition, it must be broken down which data collected on the platform may also be used by the participating companies and which remain reserved for the provider of the platform.

With regard to enforcement, the Regulation refers to the Member States, which should adopt measures that are effective, proportionate and dissuasive and ensure the implementation of the Regulation. Reference is made to existing enforcement systems; the Member States are explicitly not obliged to set up new enforcement bodies.[366]

2.4.5.2. Proposal for a Regulation on Preventing the Dissemination of Terrorist Content Online

In order to prevent the spread of terrorist online content, the EU Internet Forum was first launched in December 2015 on the basis of an "European Agenda on Security" in order to combat the misuse of the Internet by terrorist groups. Voluntary measures and partnerships between Member States and hosting services were aimed at reducing the accessibility of online terrorist content, for example by setting up a hash database to ensure

---

365 The provisions of the P2B Regulation relevant in the context of this study are reprinted in the Online Annex, available at www.nomos-shop.de/44382, II. E.
366 P2B Regulation, Recital 46.

that content is permanently and irrevocably removed.[367] Most recently, the Forum participants agreed on an EU crisis protocol for a coordinated and rapid response to confine the viral spread of terrorist and extremist violence content.[368]

Independently of these discussions, in autumn 2018 the European Commission presented a draft Regulation of the European Parliament and of the Council on preventing the dissemination of terrorist content online (TERREG)[369] with the aim of improving the effectiveness of the current measures for the detection, identification and removal of terrorist content on online platforms.[370] The Commission followed an approach similar to that already established in Germany by the NetzDG. The proposed rules are primarily aimed at hosting service providers offering services within the Union, irrespective of their location or size, and there would not be a threshold or exception for Small and Medium Enterprises (SME).[371] In order to ensure the removal of illegal terrorist content, the draft Regulation provides for the possibility of a removal order, which may be issued in form of administrative or judicial decisions by a competent authority in a Member State. Hosting service providers can be obliged to remove content or deactivate access to such content within a very short time. In addition, providers may also need to take proactive measures to automatically detect and remove terrorist material. Furthermore, the draft includes safeguards to ensure the protection of fundamental rights. It mentions in Recital 5 that the newly (proposed) rules would leave untouched the liability privilege of the ECD.

More specifically, the draft Regulation contains due diligence, reporting and information obligations, the possibility of a removal order and, where appropriate, the obligation to take proactive measures. However, the draft Regulation does not contain a civil liability approach but instead refers to a system of sanctions. Illegal terrorist content as defined in the proposal is information used to incite and glorify terrorist offences and to invite people to contribute to these offences and content which contains instructions for the commission of terrorist offences or for promoting participation in

---

367 European Commission – Press release, EU Internet Forum: a major step forward in curbing terrorist content on the internet, Brussels, 8 December 2016.
368 A Europe that protects – EU Crisis Protocol: responding to terrorist content online, October 2019.
369 COM/2018/640 final, supra (fn. 220).
370 The provisions of the TERREG proposal relevant in the context of this study are reprinted in the Online Annex, available at www.nomos-shop.de/44382, II. F.
371 Explanatory Memorandum, 3.2 Impact Assessment.

terrorist groups[372], thus following the definition of terrorist offences in Directive (EU) 2017/541.[373]

The provision in Art. 6 of the draft Regulation, which states that hosting service providers may, where appropriate, be required to take "proactive measures", i.e. the use of automatic detection techniques, to protect their services against the dissemination of terrorist content, is subject to discussions in the legislative process and relevant with regard to the liability framework for hosting service providers. However, according to the draft Regulation, as mentioned above this should be done explicitly in accordance with the ECD. Thus, no (proactive) measure should in itself result in the service provider losing the right to the exclusion of liability granted under certain conditions in Art. 14 of the ECD. Nor should a decision by national authorities to implement proportionate and concrete proactive measures in principle result in Member States imposing a general monitoring obligation under Art. 15 para. 1 of the ECD.[374] According to Art. 6 para. 2 of the draft Regulation, proactive measures in this sense include, for example, automated tools to prevent the re-uploading of content that has previously been removed or blocked, or to immediately detect and block terrorist content. Such measures shall be effective and proportionate, taking into account the risks posed by the content concerned, the fundamental rights of users and the fundamental importance of the freedom of expression and information. In addition, Art. 9 of the draft Regulation provides for further safeguards with regard to the application and implementation of proactive measures.

As an enforcement instrument, Art. 17 of the draft Regulation sets out possible sanctions to be developed by the Member States, which should in principle be effective, proportionate and dissuasive. Specifically, the draft Regulation will address systematic violations of distance orders, under which Member States are to ensure that financial sanctions of up to 4% of the hosting service providers' worldwide annual revenue of the past financial year can be imposed. Sanctions, proactive measures and monitoring are in principle subject to the jurisdiction of the Member State in which the hosting service provider's principal place of business is located in ac-

---

372 Explanatory Memorandum, 1.3 Summary of the proposed Regulation.
373 Directive (EU) 2017/541 of the European Parliament and of the Council of 15 March 2017 on combating terrorism and replacing Council Framework Decision 2002/475/JHA and amending Council Decision 2005/671/JHA, OJ L 88, 31.3.2017, pp. 6–21.
374 Explanatory Memorandum, 1.2 Consistency with existing EU legal framework in the policy area.

cordance with Art. 15 of the draft Regulation. Providers without a principal place of business in a Member State must appoint a legal representative whose location determines the jurisdiction.

2.5. EU Support, Coordination and Supplementary Measures

The area of support, coordination and supplementary measures at EU level includes various instruments which the European Commission uses either within the framework of its exercise of powers under Art. 2 para. 5 TFEU where the European Union lacks competence or to prepare legal acts for which it has competence under, for example, Art. 2 para. 2 TFEU. These (coordinating or preparatory) measures include, inter alia, the development of roadmaps showing how the Commission is planning to deal with an issue in the future, the setting up of working groups composed of experts and stakeholders and, finally, the development and issuing of recommendations which are adopted by the legislative bodies as non-binding instruments. In the area of regulation of online content, the Recommendations on the protection of minors and human dignity as well as two recent developments in the fields of hate speech and online disinformation are particularly relevant and will be presented below. Similar developments in the area of dealing with artificial intelligence will not be examined here, even though they play an important role in approaching challenges of the "digital world", as they do not directly relate to the area of content-related issues.

2.5.1. The Recommendations on the Protection of Minors and Human Dignity

First attempts to follow a horizontal approach across different types of content dissemination were made in 1998 with a Council Recommendation on the development of the competitiveness of the European audiovisual and information services industry by promoting national frameworks aimed at achieving a comparable and effective level of protection of minors and human dignity (1998 Recommendation).[375] The 1998 Recom-

---

375 Council Recommendation of 24 September 1998 on the development of the competitiveness of the European audiovisual and information services industry by promoting national frameworks aimed at achieving a comparable and effect-

mendation was based on the idea that the development of a competitive audiovisual and information service industry depends on the creation of a climate of confidence and hence on the protection of certain important general interests, such as the protection of minors and human dignity.[376] Therefore, the development of a common indicative framework at European level was considered being necessary, given the global character of the communication networks that needed to be dealt with. However, the importance of the subsidiary principle was stressed in light of the fact that the protection of minors is a culture-dependent issue for which the approach of each Member State is decisive.[377] Consequently, the 1998 Recommendation focussed on self-regulation by the industry and created guidelines for establishing a self-regulatory framework to protect minors on national level while addressing both Member States (to establish a (voluntary) national framework) as well as broadcasters and the respective industry (undertake research, promote cooperation, design codes of conduct, etc.). However, this framework was not to serve as replacement of or an alternative to the existing legal framework but rather to fulfil a supplementing function. The 1998 Recommendation was followed by several evaluation reports of the Commission concluding, inter alia, that it was applied quite heterogeneously and with differing degrees of commitment across the Member States, which was regarded to be possibly resulting from the cultural heterogeneity and varied development of the Internet use in the respective Member States.[378]

The 1998 Recommendation was further supplemented in 2006 by the Parliament and Council Recommendation on the protection of minors and human dignity and on the right of reply in relation to the competitiveness of the European audiovisual and on-line information services industry

---

ive level of protection of minors and human dignity, OJ L 270, 7.10.1998, pp. 48–55; cf. in detail: *Lievens*, Protecting Children in the Digital Era: The Use of Alternative Regulatory Instruments, pp. 103 et seq.

376 Cf. Recital 11 of 1998 Recommendation, supra (fn. 375).

377 Cf. Recital 16 and 18 of 1998 Recommendation, supra (fn. 375).

378 Cf., e.g., the 2001 Evaluation Report from the Commission to the Council and the European Parliament on the application of Council Recommendation of 24 September 1998 concerning the protection of minors and human dignity, COM/2001/0106 final, available at https://eur-lex.europa.eu/legal-content/SK/TXT/?uri=celex:52001DC0106.

(2006 Recommendation).[379] The output of the 2006 Recommendation can be split in three parts: firstly, guidelines for the Member States by establishing the necessary measures to ensure the protection of minors and human dignity, secondly, measures expected to be taken by the industry and, thirdly, activities that the Commission intended to tackle.[380]

With regard to the requirements to be satisfied by the Member States, it should be noted that, as already indicated in the Commission's second evaluation report from 2003[381] concerning the 1998 Recommendation, the 2006 Recommendation focuses more on aspects of co-regulation, although there is no concrete definition of that term. For instance, the Member States are encouraged to consider the introduction of measures in their domestic law or practice regarding the right of reply or equivalent remedies in relation to online media, to promote the take-up of technological developments (particularly regarding media literacy) in close cooperation with the parties concerned,[382] to promote a responsible attitude on the part of professionals, intermediaries and users of new communication media (in-

---

379 Recommendation of the European Parliament and of the Council of 20 December 2006 on the protection of minors and human dignity and on the right of reply in relation to the competitiveness of the European audiovisual and on-line information services industry, OJ L 378, 27.12.2006, pp. 72–77; cf. on this in detail *Lievens*, Protecting Children in the Digital Era: The Use of Alternative Regulatory Instruments, pp. 112 et seq.

380 For example information campaigns, installation of a European freephone number to assist Internet users by directing them to available complaint mechanisms and information resources or to explore the possibility of supporting the establishment of a generic second level domain name reserved for monitored sites committed to respecting minors, etc. The provisions of the 2006 Recommendation relevant in the context of this study are reprinted in the Online Annex, available at www.nomos-shop.de/44382, III. A.

381 Second Evaluation Report from the Commission to the Council and the European Parliament on the application of Council Recommendation of 24 September 1998 concerning the protection of minors and human dignity, COM/ 2003/0776 final, available at https://eur-lex.europa.eu/legal-content/en/ALL/?uri= CELEX%3A52003DC0776.

382 Annex II of the 2006 Recommendation outlines examples of possible actions naming: continuing education of teachers and trainers, in liaison with child protection associations, on using the Internet in the context of school education; introduction of specific Internet training aimed at children from a very early age, including sessions open to parents; an integrated educational approach forming part of school curricula and media literacy programmes, so as to provide information on using the Internet responsibly; organisation of national campaigns aimed at citizens, involving all communications media, to provide information on using the Internet responsibly; distribution of informa-

ter alia by drawing up a code of conduct in cooperation with professionals and regulatory authorities at national and Community level) and, finally, to promote measures to combat all illegal activities harmful to minors on the Internet and to make the Internet a much more secure medium, e.g. by adopting a quality label for service providers or by establishing appropriate means for the reporting of illegal and/or suspicious activities on the Internet.

Regarding the audiovisual and online information services industry, the 2006 Recommendation suggests developing positive measures for the benefit of minors, including initiatives to facilitate their wider access to audiovisual and online information services while avoiding potentially harmful content, for instance by means of filtering systems. Such measures, according to the 2006 Recommendation, could include harmonisation through cooperation between the regulatory, self-regulatory and co-regulatory bodies of the Member States and through the exchange of best practices, e.g. by using a system of common descriptive symbols or warning messages and by indicating the age category and/or which aspects of the content led to a certain age recommendation.[383] Furthermore, Member States were expected to develop measures to increase the use of content labelling systems for material distributed over the Internet and consider effective means of avoiding and combating discrimination.

The essence of the two Recommendations on the protection of minors and human dignity is threefold: Firstly, the need for special protection of minors and human dignity and the need for action in this respect was already recognised as early as 1998 with regard to the Internet and in particular by including the audiovisual and information society services industry in this process. Secondly, however, the European Commission saw the Member States as being responsible to take appropriate measures, inter alia, to take account of cultural specificities and different developments in

---

tion packs on possible risks of the Internet and the setting up of hotlines to which reports or complaints concerning harmful or illegal content could be addressed; adequate measures to establish or improve the performance of telephone hotlines.

383 Annex III of the 2006 Recommendation names examples of possible actions such as offering access to services specifically intended for children which are equipped with automatic filtering systems operated by access providers and mobile telephone operators; introducing incentives to provide a regularly updated description of the sites available; and posting banners on search engines drawing attention to the availability both of information about responsible use of the Internet and of telephone hotlines.

the digital environment of the respective state. Consequently, and because of their nature as non-binding acts, the Recommendations are weak in their wording (e.g. "encouraging" or "considering the introduction of measures") and merely provide a general framework, supplemented by proposals for more concrete examples of implementation. Thirdly, despite the non-binding and general wording, there are some aspects that are particularly emphasised for the creation of an appropriate regulatory environment: cooperation between the parties both in form of the states and the respective stakeholders, but also at international level and by involving the industry itself in the process.

2.5.2. The Actions Concerning the Tackling of Illegal Content Online

The cornerstone for countering illegal hate speech (online) was already laid with the 2008 Council Framework Decision on combating certain forms and expressions of racism and xenophobia by means of criminal law.[384] That Framework Decision provided for the approximation of laws and regulations of EU Member States on offences involving certain manifestations of racism and xenophobia. It was based on the obligation for Member States to introduce a criminal provision for certain serious manifestations of racism and xenophobia and make this type of crime punishable by effective, proportionate and dissuasive penalties. The Framework Decision detailed certain forms of conduct that fulfil the criteria to be regarded as criminal offences, inter alia, public incitement to violence or hatred directed against a group of persons or a member of such a group defined on the basis of race, colour, descent, religion or belief, or national or ethnic origin. The Member States had to ensure that such conduct is punishable by effective, proportionate and dissuasive penalties, which meant for a term of imprisonment of a maximum of at least one year, and, with regard to legal persons, the penalties had to consist of criminal or non-criminal fines and additionally other measures (e.g. exclusion from entitlement to public benefits or aid, temporary or permanent disqualification from practice or commercial activities, being placed under judicial supervision, etc.).

---

384 Council Framework Decision 2008/913/JHA of 28 November 2008 on combating certain forms and expressions of racism and xenophobia by means of criminal law, OJ L 328, 6.12.2008, pp. 55–58.

However, at that time the Internet sector did not play a prominent role in the Framework Decision. Rather "the commission of an act [...] by public dissemination or distribution of tracts, pictures or other material" (Art. 1 para. 1 lit. b Framework Decision) was covered in general. Yet, with the actual rise of hate speech in the online environment, this particular issue has become more and more prominent and has raised questions about how to combat it effectively.[385] Against that background, the Joint Statement issued by the extraordinary Justice and Home Affairs Council of 24 March 2016 on the terrorist attacks in Brussels underlined that "the Commission will intensify work with IT companies, notably in the EU Internet Forum, to counter terrorist propaganda and to develop by June 2016 a code of conduct against hate speech online"[386]. Subsequently, in May 2016, the Commission agreed with Facebook, Microsoft, Twitter and Google (YouTube) a "Code of conduct on countering illegal hate speech online" (in the following CCHSO)[387], which aimed to prevent and counter the spread of illegal hate speech online, to help users to notify illegal hate speech on social platforms and to improve the support by civil society as well as the coordination with national authorities.[388]

The CCHSO mainly addressed the problem that, although robust systems for the enforcement of criminal law sanctions against individual perpetrators of hate speech exist at national level, those systems need to be accompanied by effective measures in the online area, in particular with actions geared at ensuring that illegal hate speech online is expeditiously acted upon by online intermediaries and social media platforms, upon receipt of a valid notification, in an appropriate time-frame. Therefore, the signatories agreed, inter alia, to have in place clear and effective processes to review notifications regarding illegal hate speech on their services so they can remove or disable access to such content. In addition, they committed

---

385 Cf. for an overview and developments in CJEU case law *Belavusau*, in: Amsterdam Law Forum, 4(1), 2012, p. 20.

386 Joint statement of EU Ministers for Justice and Home Affairs and representatives of EU institutions on the terrorist attacks in Brussels on 22 March 2016, available at https://www.consilium.europa.eu/en/press/press-releases/2016/03/24/statement-on-terrorist-attacks-in-brussels-on-22-march/.

387 Available at https://ec.europa.eu/info/policies/justice-and-fundamental-rights/combatting-discrimination/racism-and-xenophobia/countering-illegal-hate-speech-online_en or http://ec.europa.eu/justice/fundamental-rights/files/hate_speech_code_of_conduct_en.pdf.

388 Cf. on the Code of Conduct in detail: *Quintel/Ullrich*, Self-Regulation of Fundamental Rights? The EU Code of Conduct on Hate Speech, Related Initiatives and Beyond.

to establishing rules or Community Guidelines clarifying that the promotion of incitement to violence and hateful conduct is prohibited on those platforms. Furthermore, they agreed to review the majority of users' notifications about alleged hate speech within 24 hours and to remove, if necessary, all those content assessed as being illegal. Further important points concerned the promise to further work on improving the feedback by the providers to users and being more transparent towards the general society by, inter alia, encouraging the provision of notices and flagging of content as described above. In this respect, the Commission sought to promote the adherence to the commitments set out in the CCHSO also to other relevant platforms and social media companies (in coordination with the Member States) and to assess the public commitments made on a regular basis.

In addition, in May 2016 the EU High-Level Group on combating racism, xenophobia and other forms of intolerance was set up to foster the further exchange and dissemination of best practices between national authorities and concrete discussions on how to fill existing gaps and better prevent and combat hate crime and hate speech. Since then, the High-Level Group serves also as platform for dedicated discussions on how to tackle specificities of particular forms of intolerance, also in light of the experience of civil society and communities. A sub-group on countering hate speech online deals with particular issues raised in the context of the CCHSO.

In the meantime, the Commission has issued the fourth evaluation on the EU Code of Conduct.[389] The Commission's assessment is generally positive: IT companies are now assessing 89% of the flagged content within 24 hours and 72% of the content deemed to be illegal hate speech is removed, compared to 40% and 28% respectively when the Code was first launched in 2016. Hence, from the perspective of the Commission, the CCHSO has been delivering continuous progress and contributed to the development of partnerships between civil society organisations, national authorities and signatory IT platforms on awareness raising and education activities. However, according to the Commission's assessment, the com-

---

389 European Commission, Factsheet February 2019, available at https://ec.europa.e u/info/sites/info/files/code_of_conduct factsheet_7_web.pdf

panies need to further improve their feedback to the users notifying content and to provide more transparency on notices and removals.[390]

Despite the Commission's positive evaluation, it should not be forgotten in this context that the CCHSO is non-binding and that the signatories only voluntarily committed to the arrangements negotiated under the Code of Conduct. Withdrawal of this agreement is unilaterally possible at any time. This also applies to the data provided by the providers involved, which form the basis of the Commission's evaluation reports. For this it is not clear what data needs to be provided, and the access to the data can be unilaterally restricted at any time. It is therefore only an instrument of self-regulation with the corresponding disadvantages that this entails.[391] It has, however, made it possible to demand, with public visibility, compliance with these minimum standards and create greater awareness for the question of hate speech vis-à-vis the predominantly US-based IT companies[392], to which access on the part of the EU generally has been difficult. Correspondingly, the CCHSO is "aimed at guiding their own activities as well as sharing best practices with other Internet companies, platforms and social media operators".[393] The monitoring obligation of the European Commission as well as the (voluntary) obligation of the signatories to provide information and transparency add some elements which go in the direction of a co-regulatory mechanism, although there is no such obligation laid down in a binding legislative act. These mechanisms help to promote the effective implementation of the agreed measures. The CCHSO nonetheless does not contain any enforcement mechanisms or sanctions outside the publication of the assessment and progress by the Commission, which can only be regarded, to some extent, as constituting "moral sanctions" potentially affecting the public image of the concerned companies.

---

390 Cf. on this https://ec.europa.eu/info/policies/justice-and-fundamental-rights/co mbatting-discrimination/racism-and-xenophobia/countering-illegal-hate-speech-online_en.

391 Cf. on this Chapter 4.2.2.2 in detail.

392 Between 2018 and early 2019, *Instagram*, *Google+*, *Snapchat*, *Dailymotion* and *jeuxvideo.com* joined the Code of conduct.

393 Cf. on this also the announcement of the Code of Conduct on illegal online hate speech, available at https://ec.europa.eu/commission/presscorner/detail/en/I P_16_1937.

Finally, in the context of illegal content, the Communication on Tackling Illegal Content Online[394] published by the Commission in 2017 has to be taken into account as well, which then led to the Commission Recommendation (EU) 2018/334 on measures to effectively tackle illegal content online (Recommendation on Tackling Illegal Content Online)[395].

The Communication on Illegal Content Online lays down a set of guidelines and principles for online platforms (in particular hosting services provided by these platforms in the sense of Art. 14 of the ECD) aiming to facilitate and intensify the implementation of good practices for preventing, detecting, removing and disabling access to illegal content so as to ensure the effective removal of illegal content, increased transparency and the protection of fundamental rights online. It also aims at providing clarifications to platforms on their liability when they take proactive steps to detect, remove or disable access to illegal content (the so-called "Good Samaritan" actions). The Communication states that online platforms should systematically enhance their cooperation with competent authorities in the Member States, while the latter should ensure that courts are able to effectively react to illegal content online, as well as facilitate stronger (cross-border) cooperation between authorities. In that regard, online platforms and law enforcement or other competent authorities should appoint effective points of contact in the EU and, where appropriate, define digital interfaces to facilitate their interaction. Furthermore, the Commission encourages transparency, close cooperation between online platforms and trusted flaggers as well as the establishment of easily accessible and user-friendly mechanisms that allow their users to notify content considered to be illegal, automatic re-upload filters and counter-notice procedures.

However, what is particularly relevant for this study are the Commission's remarks in this context on the liability of hosting providers. In accordance with Art. 14 ECD, online platforms must take down illegal content

---

394 Communication from the Commission to the European Parliament, the Council, the European Economic and Social Committee and the Committee of Regions, Tackling Illegal Content Online Towards an enhanced responsibility of online platforms, COM/2017/0555 final, available at https://eur-lex.europa.eu/legal-content/EN/TXT/?uri=CELEX%3A52017DC0555#footnote6.

395 Commission Recommendation (EU) 2018/334 of 1 March 2018 on measures to effectively tackle illegal content online, C/2018/1177, available at https://eur-lex.europa.eu/legal-content/GA/TXT/?uri=CELEX:32018H0334. The provisions of the Recommendation (EU) 2018/334 relevant in the context of this study are reprinted in the Online Annex, available at www.nomos-shop.de/44382, III. B.

expeditiously once they are made or become aware of its existence in order to be exempt from liability. The Commission is of the view that proactive measures taken by those online platforms to detect and remove illegal content which they host – including the use of automatic tools and tools meant to ensure that previously removed content is not re-uploaded – do not in and of themselves lead to a loss of the liability exemption. In particular, the taking of such measures need not imply that the online platform concerned plays an active role which would no longer allow it to benefit from that exemption. Whenever the taking of such measures leads to the online platform obtaining actual knowledge or awareness of illegal activities or illegal information, it needs to act expeditiously to remove or to disable access to the illegal information in question to satisfy the condition for the continued availability of that exemption.[396] Thus, according to the Communication, online platforms should do their utmost to proactively detect, identify and remove illegal content online; therefore it strongly encourages online platforms to use voluntary, proactive measures aimed at the detection and removal of illegal content and to step up cooperation and investment in, and use of, automatic detection technologies.

The subsequent Recommendation on Tackling Illegal Content Online, which takes up the descriptive approach from the Communication on Tackling Illegal Content Online in a somewhat streamlined form by transferring them in the form of more concrete rules, is particularly interesting with regard to two aspects: On the one hand, the first section contains a list of definitions that are strongly reminiscent of existing EU Directives. According to these definitions, for example, "hosting service provider" means "a provider of information society services consisting of the storage of information provided by the recipient of the service at his or her request, within the meaning of Art. 14 of Directive 2000/31/EC, irrespective of its place of establishment, which directs its activities to consumers residing in the Union", and "illegal content" means "any information which is not in compliance with Union law or the law of a Member State concerned". On the other hand, the Recommendation focusses on the cooperation between hosting providers and Member States (regarding, e.g., designated points of contact for matters relating to illegal content online and providing fast-track procedures to process notices submitted by competent authorities), (other) trusted flaggers (e.g. providing in a similar way fast-track procedures to process notices submitted by certified experts, publish-

---

396 Cf. Communication on Tackling Illegal Content Online, supra (fn. 394), para. 11.

ing clear and objective conditions for determining trusted flaggers) and other hosting service providers (e.g. by sharing experiences, technological solutions and best practices).

2.5.3. The Actions Concerning the Tackling of Online Disinformation

"Fake news" has gained increased attention in the media as well as in academic and political discussions, particularly in the context of the U.S. elections in 2016. The details about assumed targeted disinformation campaigns at that time have been dealt with elsewhere and therefore need not to be described in more detail in this study. However, they have been followed up by a number of political and regulatory activities at national and international level that require further consideration.[397]

On EU level, concrete measures tackling online disinformation started in 2017. A European Parliament resolution called on the European Commission to examine the current situation with regard to false reporting and to examine whether legislative measures could limit the dissemination of "fake news".[398] Subsequently, a High-Level Expert Group on Fake News and online disinformation (in the following HLEG), set up by the European Commission on 15 January 2018, consisting of 40 members (representatives of civil society, social media platforms and media organisations), began its work. The HLEG was to advise the Commission on the examination of that phenomenon, the roles and responsibilities of the relevant stakeholders and the international dimension, to take an inventory of the various positions and to issue recommendations. In March 2018, the HLEG handed over its report "A multi-dimensional approach to disinformation"[399] to the responsible Commissioner, in which the term "disinformation" was introduced for the first time ("The threat is disinformation, not 'fake news'"[400]), including forms of speech that fall outside illegal

---

397 In detail on this and the following as well as on developments on national level *Ukrow/Etteldorf*, „Fake News" als Rechtsproblem.

398 European Parliament resolution of 15 June 2017 on online platforms and the digital single market (2016/2276(INI)), available at http://www.europarl.europa.eu/doceo/document/TA-8-2017-0272_EN.html?redirect, para. 36.

399 Report of the independent High level Group on fake news and online disinformation, A multi-dimensional approach to disinformation, published on 30.4.2018, available at https://op.europa.eu/en/publication-detail/-/publication/6ef4df8b-4cea-11e8-be1d-01aa75ed71a1.

400 Ibid., p. 12.

forms of speech, notably defamation, hate speech or incitement to violence, but can nonetheless be harmful by transferring misleading or inaccurate information shared by people who do not recognise it as such. The report addressed all forms of false, inaccurate or misleading information designed, presented and promoted to intentionally cause public harm or for profit, and it recommended promoting media literacy to combat disinformation, developing tools to enable users and journalists to tackle disinformation, preserving the diversity and sustainability of European news media and continuing research on the impact of disinformation in Europe. In addition, the HLEG advocated a catalogue of principles to which online platforms and social networks should commit themselves.

On 9 November 2017, the Directorate-General for Communications Networks, Content and Technology presented its roadmap for the effective fight against "Fake News and online disinformation".[401] At the same time, a public consultation was launched. The roadmap stated that access to reliable information is a cornerstone of any functioning democracy and essential for the formation of the social (political) opinion. However, that opinion is increasingly threatened by the growing number of fake news and their distribution, especially on social media platforms. The Commission emphasises the danger posed by such false information aimed at undermining the functioning of political institutions or democratic decisions or by state-sponsored propaganda aimed at influencing elections or reducing confidence in democratic processes. While effective regulatory means supporting the fight against illegal content already exist at national and European level, there is a lack of such means for content that is not illegal per se but only "wrong".

Building on this assessment, the Commission published its communication "Tackling online disinformation: a European approach" in April 2018, which laid the foundations for further action.[402] The concept of disinformation coined by the HLEG was adopted but deviated from its definition, now being conceived as "false or misleading information that is created, presented and disseminated for economic gain or to intentionally deceive the public, and may cause public harm". The Commission considers

---

401 Communication on fake news and online misinformation, available at https://ec .europa.eu/info/law/better-regulation/initiatives/ares-2017-5489364.

402 Communication from the Commission to the European Parliament, the Council, the European Economic and Social Committee and the Committee of Regions, Tackling online disinformation: a European Approach, COM/2018/236 final, available at https://eur-lex.europa.eu/legal-content/EN/TXT/?uri=CELEX:5 2018DC0236.

economic, technological, political and ideological circumstances to be the cause of the dissemination of disinformation. This includes, for example, the rise of platforms in the media sector, which in turn influences the more "traditional" media to the extent that they (must) seek new ways to monetarise their content, and the creation of new, or the manipulation of existing, technologies in the field of social networks, which enable or at least facilitate the dissemination of disinformation. Against this background, the Commission concludes that the fight against disinformation can and will only be successful in the long term if it is accompanied by a clear political will to strengthen collective resilience and support democratic efforts and European values. There is no single solution to this problem, given the many challenges arising from the complexity of the problem. There is, however, a need for action, and any political reaction should be comprehensive, continuously assess the phenomenon of disinformation and adapt the political instruments in the light of its development, according to the Commission.

In particular, the Commission identifies four main points which it considers to be essential for addressing problems in a solution-oriented way: Firstly, transparency must be created regarding the origin of information and the way in which it is produced, sponsored and disseminated. Secondly, diversity of information must be promoted to enable citizens to make informed choices, based on critical considerations. Thirdly, the credibility of information or credible information itself must be promoted. Fourthly, the development of integrated and long-term solutions requires awareness raising, promotion of media literacy, broad stakeholder involvement and cooperation between public authorities, online platforms, advertisers, journalists and media groups.

Finally, after this long process of evaluations, representatives of online platforms, leading social networks[403], advertisers and advertising industry agreed together with the Commission on a self-regulatory Code of Practice to address the spread of online disinformation and fake news (in the following CPD).[404] The CPD set a wide range of commitments, from transparency in political advertising to the closure of fake accounts and the demonetisation of purveyors of disinformation within the framework of ex-

---

403   The companies involved were *Facebook, Google, Twitter* and *Mozilla*.
404   EU Code of Practice on Disinformation, available at https://ec.europa.eu/digital-single-market/en/news/code-practice-disinformation.

isting EU legislation and Member States law.[405] The CPD stated, in particular, that the ECD and particularly Art. 12–15 shall be considered in the context of any obligation of the Code which targets mere conduits, caching providers or hosting providers such as providers of network, search engines, browsers, online blogging platforms, online forums, video-sharing platforms or social media. It includes commitments regarding the scrutiny of ad placements, political advertising and issue-based advertising, the integrity of services and the empowering of both consumers and the research community. In this regard the CPD is even more detailed in comparison with the aforementioned CCHSO. Regarding the monitoring of effectiveness, the signatories commit to write a (further detailed) annual report of their work to counter disinformation. That report shall be issued in form of a publicly available report reviewable by a third party.

Although the CPD is, like the Code of Conduct, non-binding, it is more detailed in content than the CCHSO and contains stronger formulations and more concrete requirements. The mechanisms of co-regulation are also less pronounced here. Signatories commit to select an objective third party organisation (besides the Commission) to review the annual self-assessment reports submitted by the signatories and to evaluate the level of progress made against their commitments. It needs to be underlined that also in this respect neither the actual degree of commitment nor the possibility to monitor it is very clear. Both the compliance with the CPD requirements and the making available of the corresponding data by the companies in order for third parties to review the measures are merely voluntary and cannot be demanded by an authority or sanctioned in case of non-availability or non-compliance. The evaluation problems resulting from this have already been expressed by the ERGA in its report of the activities carried out to assist the Commission in the intermediate monitoring of the Code of Practice on Disinformation as follows: "The platforms were not in a position to meet a request from ERGA to provide access to the overall database of advertising, even on a limited basis, during

---

405 In particular the EU Charter of Fundamental Rights, the European Convention on Human Rights, Regulation (EU) 2016/679 on the protection of natural persons with regard to the processing of personal data and on the free movement of such data, Directive 2005/29/EC concerning unfair business-to-consumer commercial practices in the internal market, Directive 2006/114/EC concerning misleading and comparative advertising and the case law of the CJEU and ECHR on the proportionality of measures designed to limit access to and circulation of harmful content.

the monitoring period. This was a significant constraint on the monitoring process and emerging conclusions."[406]

The Code includes an annex identifying best practices that signatories commit to apply to implement the Code's provisions. These best practices bring together the approaches of stakeholders, as laid down in the various stakeholder policies, in a general approach. In the area of advertising policies, the stakeholders endeavour to tackle disinformation by pursuing "follow the money" approaches[407] and prevent bad actors from receiving remuneration.[408] In the field of political advertising, online platforms are developing solutions to increase transparency of such advertising and enable consumers to understand why they are seeing those ads. Platforms announced to develop tools so that civil society is able to better understand the political online advertising ecosystem.[409] Platforms seek to safeguard service integrity by applying policies which limit the abuse of their service by inauthentic users, for example by policies restricting impersonation on YouTube.[410] Finally platforms announced to provide users with information, tools and support to empower consumers in their online experience (including also redress and reporting systems) and committed to support the research community by providing data[411] and creating own research

---

406 ERGA, Report of the activities carried out to assist the European Commission in the intermediate monitoring of the Code of practice on disinformation, June 2019, available at http://erga-online.eu/wp-content/uploads/2019/06/ERGA-2019 -06_Report-intermediate-monitoring-Code-of-Practice-on-disinformation.pdf.

407 The follow-the-money approach in general is aiming to cut the revenue resulting from right infringements. The Commission has committed in its Communication on a strategy for the Digital Single Market to adopting a "follow the money" approach aiming to cut the revenue flows that drive commercial-scale IPR infringers into their activities. The approach seeks to create a Memorandum of Understanding where signatories put in place mechanisms to minimise the placing of online advertising on websites which infringe intellectual property rights.

408 Facebook, e.g., by reducing the distribution of economic incentives for false news and inauthentic content like clickbait and by informing people by giving them more context on the posts they see; cf. Facebook false news policy, available at https://www.facebook.com/communitystandards/false_news.

409 E.g. Googles' control systems for consumers to determine what advertisements they see; cf. Google ad settings, available at https://support.google.com/ads/answ er/2662856?hl=en-AU.

410 Cf. YouTube Policy on impersonation, available at https://support.google.com/y outube/answer/2801947?hl=en-GB.

411 For example Facebook's "Initiative to Help Scholars Assess Social Media's Impact on Elections"; more information at https://newsroom.fb.com/news/2018/04 /new-elections-initiative/.

initiatives. These aimed-at best practices should also provide solutions and ideas for smaller companies to combat disinformation.

Concerning the Code of Conduct, as a last point the action plan against disinformation that the Commission presented on 5 December 2018 should be mentioned.[412] In that plan, the Commission and the High Representative for Foreign Affairs and Security Policy propose concrete measures to combat disinformation. These include the establishment of an early warning system, the close monitoring of the implementation of the Code of Conduct and an increase in funding for those purposes. Moreover, the exchange of data between Member States is to be facilitated and additional funding for media literacy projects is to be made available.

---

412 European Commission contribution to the European Council Action Plan against Disinformation, 5.12.2018, available at https://ec.europa.eu/commission/sites/beta-political/files/eu-communication-disinformation-euco-05122018_en.pdf.

3. Detailed Analysis of the E-Commerce Directive

After the overview of relevant legislative acts and non-binding policy documents of relevance for online content dissemination, the following chapter takes a detailed look at the provisions of the ECD[413] and their interpretation by the CJEU.

3.1. Scope of Application

3.1.1. Territorial Scope

There are no explicit or specifically laid down rules on territorial scope in the ECD. Recital 58 specifically excludes any extraterritorial scope of this Directive. This means that content originating from information society service providers outside the EU that target EU customers does not fall within the scope of that Directive. Member States are therefore at liberty to take action according to their national law concerning content supplied from providers based outside the EU. However, the Directive reminds of the necessity to consider existing international rules, especially where discussions about the area covered by the Directive have been led in international organisations such as the World Trade Organization (WTO) and the Organisation for Economic Co-operation and Development (OECD).[414] The Recitals point out that any diverging rule could undermine the EU's negotiating position in such international fora.[415] This implies that Member States' action should not contrast with the non-discrimination principles laid down for example in WTO rules, such as most-favoured-nation or national-treatment principles.

The ECD is therefore solely concerned with regulating the activities of information society service providers within the single market. From the perspective of the legislative bodies of the EU, the country-of-origin principle constituted the best regulatory choice to protect internal market princi-

---

413 The provisions of the ECD relevant in the context of this study are reprinted in the Online Annex, available at www.nomos-shop.de/44382, II. A.
414 Recital 58 ECD.
415 Recital 59 ECD.

ples for the emerging Internet service sector at the time and to protect, by setting some principles and standards, against the threats of legislative forum shopping[416] and a fragmentation of rules[417].

This contrasts with other more recently passed EU acts and legislative proposals that deal with matters of the information society and digital content. The General Data Protection Regulation[418] and the proposed Regulation to prevent the dissemination of terrorist content online[419] extend to information society service providers from third countries that target EU residents. The AVMSD applies to VSP providers from third countries with a market attachment to the EU which can follow from a subsidiary or parent of the service provider established in the EU.[420]

3.1.2. Functional Scope

The functional scope of the ECD is set by the coordinated field of activities. According to Art. 2 lit. h ECD, the coordinated field consists of all legal requirements set by Member States that apply to information society service providers or information society services, without regard as to whether they are general or specific measures. More specifically, the coordinated field covers therefore requirements that are necessary for the taking-up and the pursuit of activities by a service provider. These are requirements relating to authorisation and qualifications, the behaviour of the service provider, the quality of content, provisions relating to advertisement, contracts and the liability of intermediary service providers. Art. 2 lit. h point (ii) provides important exemptions to the coordinated field, namely requirements that are applicable to goods as such, their delivery and to services which are not provided by electronic means. The meaning of this provision is further explained in Recital 21.

The scope of the coordinated field should be strictly limited to the online activities of service providers, such as online information, online ad-

---

416 Recital 57 ECD.
417 Recital 59 ECD.
418 Art. 3 para. 2 GDPR; cf. on this already Chapter 2.4.3.3.
419 Commission, European Parliament legislative resolution of 17 April 2019 on the proposal for a regulation of the European Parliament and of the Council on preventing the dissemination of terrorist content online (COM(2018)0640 – C8-0405/2018 – 2018/0331(COD)), Recital 10 (Amendment 13). Cf. on this already Chapter 2.4.5.2.
420 Recital 44 AVMSD.

vertising, online shopping, etc. This delineation is illustrated by a list of excluded requirements which relate to tangible goods, such as product labelling, safety, product liability or provisions relating to the transport of goods, including the distribution of medicinal products.

The EU may have been aware of the risk that measures set for online service providers inadvertently permeate to other areas beyond the scope of this online-related Directive. An example could be commercial services that just have an electronic component but are otherwise governed by provisions that may fall under a different category of competence according to the EU Treaties.[421]

This close circumscription of the coordinated field may indeed pose further challenges as business models of the platform economy diversify and converge. The pre-eminence of online marketplaces, the rise of sharing economy platforms, the expansion of social media into adjacent markets or the convergence of on- and offline markets are just some illustrations. For example, it may be increasingly confusing to regulate the online advertisement of products through the rules concerning e-commerce while making the requirements relating to the sale of the products subject to product regulation (as detailed in Recital 21).[422] In addition, a number of EU product laws today provide specific rules on the sales of products online, such as product labelling in sales over the Internet.[423]

The ECD also excludes from its scope the field of taxation, cartel law, data protection, activities of notaries, legal representations before courts as well as gambling activities, which includes lotteries and betting.[424]

3.1.3. Personal Scope of Application

The ECD aims to regulate certain aspects of information society services. It refers in Art. 2 lit. a to the definition of information society services as laid

---

421 A concrete example of such a blurring line is the case CJEU, judgement of 2.12.2010, C-108/09, *Ker-Optika v ÀNTSZ Del-dunántuli Regionális Intézete*. Another more general illustration of this phenomenon is the burring line of sharing economy platforms such as Uber and Airbnb; cf. on these cases below Chapter 3.3.7.3.

422 *Rowland/Kohl/Charlesworth*, Information Technology Law, p. 269.

423 Thus, for example, Art. 5 para. 1 lit. a of Regulation (EU) 2017/1369 of 4 July 2017 sets a framework for energy labelling and repeals Directive 2010/30/EU 2017, OJ L 198, 28.7.2017, pp. 1–23.

424 Art. 1 para. 5 ECD.

down in Art. 1 para. 2 lit. a of the Technical Standards and Regulation Directive.[425] According to this, an information society service needs to be provided "for remuneration, at a distance, by electronic means and at the individual request of a recipient of services".[426] Service providers are defined as any natural or legal person providing an information society service.[427] The ECD regulates the activities of these service providers in the coordinated field covered by the Directive. Information society service providers cover a wide field of actors in the digital economy, from Internet retailers and financial services to electronic libraries, file transfer services, and social media and online agencies of various sorts.[428]

The remit of the meaning of the criteria by remuneration, at a distance, by electronic means and at the individual request of a recipient has been interpreted by the CJEU in a number of cases, such as notably *Mediakabel*[429] and *Papasavvas*[430]. More recently, the CJEU was asked whether sharing economy platforms *Uber*[431] and *Airbnb*[432] could be regarded as information society services. These cases illustrate the growing diversity of online business models, which now disrupt regulated, "offline" sectors of the economy. The claim of these services to be regarded as information society services can arguably be attributed to an advantageous regulatory environment for these services in such circumstances, namely the country-of-origin principle and liability exemptions for intermediary service providers.

For *Uber*, using this favourable regime as a market access opener[433] for the EU has not been successful for now. *Uber* had claimed that the electronic component of its ride hiring business was the essential activity, a

---

425 Supra (fn. 203), Art. 1 para. 1 lit. b. Cf. already above at 2.4.1.1.

426 Art. 1 para. 2 lit. a of Directive (EU) 2015/1535; Recital 17 of the ECD repeats this definition.

427 Art. 2 lit. b ECD.

428 *Büllesbach (ed.)*, Concise European IT Law, pp. 696–698.

429 CJEU, judgement of 02.6.2005, C-89/04, *Mediakabel BV v Commissariaat voor de Media*, in which the CJEU interpreted the meaning of "service provided at the individual request of a recipient".

430 CJEU, judgement of 11.09.2014, C-291/13, *Sotiris Papasavvas v O Fileleftheros Dimosia Etairia Ltd, Takis Kounnafi, Giorgos Sertis*, in which it elucidated on the meaning of "for remuneration".

431 CJEU, judgement of 20.12.2017, C-434/15, *Asociación Profesional Élite Taxi v Uber Systems Spain SL*.

432 Opinion of Advocate General Szpunar, delivered on 30.4.2019, C-390/18, *YA, Airbnb Ireland UC, Hotelière Turenne SAS, Association pour un hébergement et un tourisme professionnel (AHTOP), Valhotel*.

433 *Hatzopoulos*, The Collaborative Economy and EU Law, pp. 31–32.

view that was not shared by the CJEU. *Airbnb*'s claim was similar to that of *Uber*. However, Advocate General Szpunar came to a different conclusion than for *Uber* by applying the methodology used in that latter case.[434] The criteria for qualifying the status of the service provider are whether the alleged information society service creates a new, stand-alone market and whether it exerts control over the transactions facilitated by the platform.

The rulings provide useful clarification on the concept of information society services and their applicability to new sharing economy platform models, especially where they provide composite (electronic and non-electronic) services.[435]

3.2. The Country-of-Origin Principle

3.2.1. Application

The activities of information society service providers are framed by the country-of-origin principle. Art. 3 para. 1 ECD obliges Member States to ensure that information society service providers which are established in their jurisdiction, the country of origin, comply with the rules of that Member State throughout the EU. In turn the internal market principle (non-discrimination principle) precludes Member States from restricting the freedom to provide these information society services established in another Member State on the basis of their domestic (destination) provisions.[436] As a consequence, the information society services covered by the ECD are subject to the rules of just one Member State: that of the country of origin or where the service provider is established. This relatively clear application of the country-of-origin principle has been attributed to the EU's strong objective to create a harmonised regulatory framework for the then emerging electronic commerce services within the EU.[437]

On the other hand, this strict country-of-origin-rule approach also has its impracticalities, for example when court decisions, such as information requests, need to be enforced against information society service providers,

---

434 Opinion of Advocate General Szpunar, delivered on 30.4.2019, C-390/18, *supra* (fn. 432), para. 55–78.

435 For a more detailed analysis: *Savin*, in: Journal of Internet Law 23(3), 2019, pp. 1, 16.

436 Art. 3 para. 1 and 2 ECD.

437 *Rowland/Kohl/Charlesworth*, Information Technology Law, pp. 268–269.

including online intermediaries. Member state authorities are required to direct their requests towards the EU jurisdiction where the entity has its seat of establishment, even if a branch or subsidiary entity may exist in their own country.[438] Likewise, requests for enforcing against a provider would need to be directed towards the authority of the origin Member State or the appropriate regional authority if the enforcement falls under regional competencies. High administrative burdens and a perceived lack of effectiveness in enforcement are drawbacks of this approach. It has therefore been argued that the country-of-origin principle in the ECD creates a conflict of law rule by virtue of pointing towards the law of place of establishment of the ISS provider.[439]

The country-of-origin approach applies to those activities of information society service providers which are covered by the coordinated field of the Directive.

3.2.2. Derogations

Member States have the right to restrict the free movement of information society services under certain conditions. Art. 3 para. 4 ECD creates derogations for situations where Member States deem it necessary[440] for reasons of public policy, public health, public security and consumer protection to apply stricter rules than those provided by the country of origin. The public policy justifications relate to criminal offences, including the protection of minors, the fight against incitement to hatred and violations of human dignity. Beyond the need for a legitimate aim, these measures need to be proportionate.[441]

Member States are held to coordinate with the origin Member States and first ask that state to apply the enforcement measures sought.[442] The destination Member State may only act if the origin Member State did not act on requests made or when the action taken was insufficient. The Com-

---

438 Administrative Court of Berlin, judgement of 20.7.2017, case 6 L 162.17, para. 33–39. In this case Berlin authorities were refused an order for disclosure of information made to the local subsidiary of *Airbnb* on the grounds that this request would need to be directed at the company's EU seat of establishment in Ireland.
439 *Büllesbach (ed.)*, Concise European IT Law, p. 306.
440 Art. 3 para. 4 lit. a point (i) ECD.
441 Art. 3 para. 4 lit. a point (iii) ECD.
442 Art. 3 para. 4 lit. b ECD.

mission will need to be notified of any derogative measures taken by a destination Member States. It is held to examine any derogative action with an option to request that a Member State stop these measures should they be deemed disproportionate.

The focus on cooperation and the very closely circumscribed conditions for derogations demonstrate the importance that the EU has attached to the country-of-origin principle as a regulatory model in this area. Indeed, the derogations appear to have been used rarely so far.[443] Others have argued that the complexity of the derogations in Art. 3 para. 4 leaves the door open to incision by substantive law at national and EU level.[444]

It may be of interest for regulatory cooperation that the ECD's country-of-origin rule (and with it the derogations of Art. 3 para. 4) has been perceived as being most effective when implemented as a rule of legislative and not adjudicative jurisdiction, i.e. a rule with public law and not conflict-of-laws characteristics.[445]

Nevertheless, the EU may have been aware of the incentive that a rigorously applied country-of-origin principle may provide for legislative forum shopping or circumvention of stricter legislation by individual Member States. Recital 57 recognises the right of a Member State to take measures against a service provider in another Member State if the choice of establishment was motivated by a desire to evade stricter legislation in the former.[446] However, it can also be argued that the acknowledgement of this risk in a Recital is secondary to the more explicit and elaborate provisions of Art. 3 para. 4 ECD and the cooperation requirements of authorities posited in Art. 19 ECD.

Almost twenty years later the EU legislator charged the newly established European Regulators Group for Audiovisual Media Services (ERGA) with reporting and passing non-binding recommendation on "measures addressing the circumvention of jurisdiction" of audiovisual media service and video-sharing platforms within the framework of the AVMSD.[447] Meanwhile it has introduced specific powers for Member States to go against media service providers having demonstrably registered in a Mem-

---

443 *Savin*, EU Internet Law, p. 59. The intention of these derogations was clarified in: CJEU, judgement of 25.10.2011, C-509/09 and C-161/10, *eDate Advertising GmbH v X and Olivier Martinez, Robert Martinez v MGN Limited*.

444 *Rowland/Kohl/Charlesworth*, Information Technology Law, p. 270.

445 *Savin*, EU Internet Law, p. 60.

446 Recital 57 ECD.

447 Recital 11 AVMSD.

ber State for the purposes of circumventing stricter regulation else-where.[448]

3.2.3. Exemptions to the Scope of Application

Art. 3 para. 3 ECD refers to a number of areas (specified in the Annex of the Directive) which are outside of the scope of the coordinated field and, therefore, the country-of-origin principle. These are amongst others intellectual property rights, electronic money transfers, contractual obligations concerning consumer contracts, real estate contracts and unsolicited mail. These areas have been exempted either due to policy preoccupations by Member States or because they are already covered by other EU instruments.[449]

3.3. *The Intermediary Liability Regime*

3.3.1. Historical Backdrop

The rising problem of illegal and harmful content on the Internet was first addressed by the EU as early as 1996.[450] In its first Communication on this matter, the Commission underlined that Member States remained responsible for applying their national laws to the Internet. However, the risk of diverging responses of national legislators and courts to the role and responsibilities of Internet intermediaries was clearly identified. It could eventually distort competition, hamper the free movement of services and lead to fragmentation of the internal market, the Commission indicated.

At that stage, the EU considered a common EU framework to "clarify the administrative rules and regulations which apply to access providers and host service providers"[451] as a policy option. This was proposed alongside with promoting industry self-regulation and encouraging Member States to cooperate and define minimum standards for criminal content.[452]

---

448 Art. 4 para. 3 lit. b AVMSD.
449 *Savin*, EU Internet Law, p. 58.
450 Commission, Communication from the Commission: Illegal and Harmful Content on the Internet, COM(96) 487 final, 16.10.1996, available at https://core.ac.uk/reader/5078710.
451 Ibid., p. 25.
452 Ibid., pp. 24–25.

The threat of legislative intervention, however, was not hidden in that document.

By late 1998, that "threat" came true in that the Commission had incorporated proposals for an intermediary liability framework into the draft ECD. Several reasons can be assumed. First, the still young intermediary sector did not manage to come up with its own, self-regulatory rules. Secondly, the first national jurisprudence on intermediary liability laid bare diverging interpretations of whether and how intermediaries should be made liable for third-party content.[453] Thirdly, the US had enacted two centrepieces of intermediary liability regulation: the Communications Decency Act 1996[454] and the Digital Millennium Copyright Act 1998[455] (DMCA).

3.3.2. The Approach Chosen by the EU

The EU opted for a broad horizontal framework that did not follow the sectorial approach favoured in the US. It nevertheless borrowed heavily from the US provisions. This is particularly visible in the categorisations and definitions of intermediaries and certain conditions that govern the exemptions from liability. The EU framework is generally considered stricter than that of the US[456] as it expands the more onerous conditions on liability exemptions that the US imposed on intermediaries for copyright violations in the DMCA across all content areas. At the same time, however, it is also less specific.[457] It does not provide any guidance on the process and format of notices and counter-notices, nor does it spell out any "Good Samaritan" protections[458] for those intermediary providers that choose to proactively identify and remove illegal content.

---

453   Three of the most known intermediary liability cases from the UK, Germany and France of that time shall be illustrative of this: *Godfrey v Demon Internet Limited* [1999] EWHC QB 240 (23 April, 1999); *CompuServe [1998]* AG München 8340 Ds 465 Js 173158/95, MMR 1998, 429; *UEJF and Licra v Yahoo! Inc and Yahoo France* (Tribunal de Grande Instance de Paris). Cf. also Recital 40 ECD.
454   Communications Decency Act 1996 (47 USC § 230).
455   Digital Millennium Copyright Act, supra (fn. 197).
456   See for example *Savin*, EU Internet Law, p. 148; *Rowland/Kohl/Charlesworth*, Information Technology Law, p. 93.
457   *Edwards*, The fall & rise of intermediary liability, p. 74.
458   47 USC § 230 section 230 lit. c.

An explanation could be seen in the broad internal market focus of the ECD which does not allow for specifications dependent on substantive "content" law. Secondly, the regulatory choice to approximate laws using a minimum harmonisation approach may have inhibited the EU from putting down more specific procedural detail. Thirdly, one of the *raison d'être* for the liability framework was economic. A broad shield from liabilities for third-party content and a focus on self-regulatory solutions were meant to promote innovation and growth in the Internet economy. Notwithstanding these arguments, the above omissions have been criticised as causing legal uncertainty and hindering the effective removal of infringing content.[459]

3.3.3. Categories of Specific Information Society Service Providers

The EU liability framework does not establish a general liability regime but a system of exemptions for certain activities[460] of those information society services that are classed as intermediary service providers.[461] That latter term is however not set out in the definitions in Art. 2 of the ECD nor in any other EU instrument. Instead, the EU defines intermediary service providers only in relation to the activities that are subject to the exemptions or specific liability rules.

The ECD defines three types of activities for intermediary service providers (cf. already Chapter 2.4.1.3.): "Mere conduit" (Art. 12), "Caching" (Art. 13) and "Hosting" (Art. 14). Art. 15 stipulates additional protections for all three activities. Similar to the DMCA in the US, the ECD introduces a graduated system of liability exemptions for these activities, according to the technical involvement of the intermediary's activity in the intermediation process.

---

459 *Edwards*, The fall & rise of intermediary liability, pp. 73–77.
460 *Baistrocchi*, in: Santa Clara High Technology Law Journal 19 (1), 2003, pp. 111, 117–118.
461 Section 4 ECD.

Directive 2000/31/EC
Art. 12 Mere conduit
1. Where an information society service is provided that consists of the transmission in a communication network of information provided by a recipient of the service, or the provision of access to a communication network, Member States shall ensure that the service provider is not liable for the information transmitted, on condition that the provider: (a) does not initiate the transmission; (b) does not select the receiver of the transmission; and (c) does not select or modify the information contained in the transmission. 2. The acts of transmission and of provision of access referred to in paragraph 1 include the automatic, intermediate and transient storage of the information transmitted in so far as this takes place for the sole purpose of carrying out the transmission in the communication network, and provided that the information is not stored for any period longer than is reasonably necessary for the transmission. 3. This Art. shall not affect the possibility for a court or administrative authority, in accordance with Member States' legal systems, of requiring the service provider to terminate or prevent an infringement
Art. 13 Caching
1. Where an information society service is provided that consists of the transmission in a communication network of information provided by a recipient of the service, Member States shall ensure that the service provider is not liable for the automatic, intermediate and temporary storage of that information, performed for the sole purpose of making more efficient the information's onward transmission to other recipients of the service upon their request, on condition that: (a) the provider does not modify the information; (b) the provider complies with conditions on access to the information; (c) the provider complies with rules regarding the updating of the information, specified in a manner widely recognised and used by industry; (d) the provider does not interfere with the lawful use of technology, widely recognised and used by industry, to obtain data on the use of the information; and (e) the provider acts expeditiously to remove or to disable access to the information it has stored upon obtaining actual knowledge of the fact that the information at the initial source of the transmission has been removed from the network, or access to it has been disabled, or that a court or an administrative authority has ordered such removal or disablement. 2. This Art. shall not affect the possibility for a court or administrative authority, in accordance with Member States' legal systems, of requiring the service provider to terminate or prevent an infringement.

Art. 14
Hosting
1. Where an information society service is provided that consists of the storage of information provided by a recipient of the service, Member States shall ensure that the service provider is not liable for the information stored at the request of a recipient of the service, on condition that: (a) the provider does not have actual knowledge of illegal activity or information and, as regards claims for damages, is not aware of facts or circumstances from which the illegal activity or information is apparent; or (b) the provider, upon obtaining such knowledge or awareness, acts expeditiously to remove or to disable access to the information. 2. Paragraph 1 shall not apply when the recipient of the service is acting under the authority or the control of the provider. 3. This Art. shall not affect the possibility for a court or administrative authority, in accordance with Member States' legal systems, of requiring the service provider to terminate or prevent an infringement, nor does it affect the possibility for Member States of establishing procedures governing the removal or disabling of access to information.

Art. 15
No general obligation to monitor
1. Member States shall not impose a general obligation on providers, when providing the services covered by Art. 12, 13 and 14, to monitor the information which they transmit or store, nor a general obligation actively to seek facts or circumstances indicating illegal activity. 2. Member States may establish obligations for information society service providers promptly to inform the competent public authorities of alleged illegal activities undertaken or information provided by recipients of their service or obligations to communicate to the competent authorities, at their request, information enabling the identification of recipients of their service with whom they have storage agreements.

The common trait and therefore the defining element of all three types of intermediary service providers is that they process information that is provided by a recipient of the service or by a third party. It is therefore clear that the intermediary liability framework laid down in Art. 12–14 does not deal with scenarios where the information service provider is the originator of the content. The Commission underlined this also in its first application report of the ECD of 2003.[462] This distinction was later on clarified and confirmed by the CJEU ruling in *Papasavvas*.[463] All other conditions stated in Art. 12–15 relate to the availability of the exemption from liability

---

462 Commission, First Report on the Application of Directive 2000/31/EC of the European Parliament and of the Council of 8 June 2000 on Certain Legal Aspects of Information Society Services, in Particular Electronic Commerce, in the Internal Market, (2003) COM(2003) 702 final 12.

463 CJEU, judgement of 11.09.2014, C-291/13, supra (fn. 430).

for the information provided by the recipient of the service. This system of exemptions is also referred to as limitations, immunities or privileges.

The overarching condition for the application of the content liability immunity for all three activities is that they are "of a mere technical, automatic and passive nature, which implies that the information society service provider has neither knowledge of nor control over the information which is transmitted or stored".[464] The reference to knowledge and control implies that truly neutral and passive intermediaries would be immune from any kind of secondary liability, be it vicarious or contributory liability. In many legal systems, vicarious liability is normally allocated to third parties that have control over the actions and behaviour of another party. Contributory liability applies to those agents that have knowledge of infringing acts and are in a position to interfere.[465]

3.3.4. The Three Types of Specific Intermediary Service Activities

3.3.4.1. "Mere Conduits" According to Art. 12 ECD

Mere conduits transmit information through a communication network or provide access to such a network. The passivity of the mere conduit is defined through three conditions, the fulfilment of which qualifies for a full exemption from liability for the content transmitted. The conduit must not 1) initiate the transmission, 2) select the receiver of the transmission and 3) select or modify the information that is contained in the transmission. Art. 12 para. 2 clarifies that this includes transient storage where this happens solely as part of the transmission process and where the information is not kept longer than needed for the act of transmission. These exemptions do not prevent Member States' courts or authorities to issue orders for the termination or prevention of an infringement.[466]

When the ECD was drafted, "mere conduits" were mainly Internet access providers that provided customers with a connection to the wired Internet, using ISDN or (A)DSL dial-up connections. Since then, the variety of mere conduits has diversified in line with new Internet access technologies and the omnipresence of the Internet. Mere conduits today may also

---

464 Recital 42 ECD.
465 For a more detailed treatment of the subject: *Burk*, in: Philosophy & Technology 24(4), 2011, p. 437.
466 Directive 2000/31/EC (ECD), Art. 12 (3).

be mobile telecommunication service providers, Wi-Fi network access operators or various hotspot providers. These services are run by a huge variety of businesses and institutions from shops[467] or restaurants, transportation companies and hospitals to public authorities and universities.

In general, the proliferation of access providers has not led to more ambiguity over the availability of the protections offered by Art. 12 para. 1 ECD. By contrast, mere conduits have been very much in the focus of courts and authorities to help stop and prevent illegal activities and access to illegal content, according to the possibilities offered by Art. 12 para. 3 ECD. Internet access providers sit at a crucial junction of the Internet connection, which makes them an obvious target of enforcement. Consequently, mere conduits have been in the focus of legal disputes when it comes to the scope and breadth of injunctions for removal of, and prevention of access to, illegal content, especially in the context of the limitations imposed by Art. 15. This issue is one of the major controversial discussion points of the liability framework under the ECD[468] and will be dealt with further below.

3.3.4.2. Caching According to Art. 13 ECD

This provision protects providers from being held liable for cached content on their services.[469] In order to benefit from exemptions of liability of cached content, the intermediary service provider must meet five conditions. These five conditions essentially say that the provider must not interfere with the cached content beyond what is technically necessary and required by industry standards. It includes an obligation to remove or prevent unauthorised content once the provider has gained knowledge that a court or authority has removed that content. In practice, this Article has rarely been in the focus of legal disputes or controversy.

---

467 CJEU, judgement of 15.9.2016, C-484/14, *Tobias Mc Fadden v Sony Music Entertainment Germany GmbH*, para. 43.

468 Commission, Online Services, Including e-Commerce, in the Single Market, A Coherent Framework to Boost Confidence in the Digital Single Market of e-Commerce and Other Online Services, Accompanying the Document, SEC(2011) 1641 final 25.

469 *Lodder/Murray*, EU Regulation of E-Commerce: A Commentary, p. 45.

3.3.4.3. Hosting According to Art. 14 ECD

Art. 14 provides immunities from content liability for all those intermediary service providers that store information provided by a recipient of the service.[470] That recipient is also referred to as third party. The difference to the mere conduit and caching provisions is that the storage or "hosting" of information by these intermediaries is the actual service. It is therefore not transient. Moreover, its duration is determined by the recipient of the service. Normally the recipient of the service needs to rely on an Internet access provider (mere conduit) to access the hosting service in the first place.[471]

The more comprehensive involvement of information hosts in the intermediation process raises the bar for a full exemption from liability. At least one of the following two conditions has to be met, as they are laid down in more detail in Art. 14:

a) the provider does not have actual knowledge of an illegal activity or information on its service or the illegality was not apparent to him; or
b) the provider acted expeditiously by removing or disabling access to the information as soon as he obtained knowledge as in the previous condition.

Actual knowledge implies criminal and civil liabilities while awareness of facts and circumstances only implies civil liability.[472] Art. 14 para. 2 clarifies that the hosting services provider may not avail itself of any liability exemptions if it exercises control over the party that requests the storage of the information. Art. 14 para. 1 and 2 address the two main conditions for secondary liability: knowledge and control. As is the case for mere conduits and caching activities, courts and authorities are able to impose injunctions to terminate or prevent infringements. In addition, Member States may also impose procedures on hosting services on how illegal information needs to be removed or made inaccessible.[473]

Today's intermediary landscape is completely different to what it looked like at the turn of the millennium, when Internet access providers, news-

---

470 Cf. on the scope of Art. 14 ECD in particular *van Hoboken/Quintas/Poort*, Hosting intermediary services and illegal content.
471 *Büllesbach (ed.)*, Concise European IT Law, p. 331.
472 *Rowland/Kohl/Charlesworth*, Information Technology Law, p. 86; *Lodder/Murray*, EU Regulation of E-Commerce: A Commentary, p. 50.
473 Art. 14 para. 3 ECD.

rooms and the first search engines made up the bulk of Internet intermediaries. Since then e-commerce marketplaces, social media networks, user-generated content platforms and cloud services have appeared, and most of them have been classified as neutral hosts under Art. 14 making them profit from the liability privilege. This change was initiated by the Web 2.0 which allowed for new ways of user interaction and the sharing of content on the Internet. The subsequent rise of Internet intermediaries as key players in global markets and as gatekeepers to information has changed the legal, moral and technical assumptions that underpinned the ECD's liability immunities of the late 1990s. This will be discussed further below.

3.3.4.4. No General Monitoring Obligations According to Art. 15 ECD

Art. 15 para. 1 ECD provides a limitation to Member States' possibilities to oblige intermediary service providers to terminate or prevent infringements. The prohibition of requiring intermediary service providers to monitor the information they transmit or store or to actively search for indications of illegal activity is a necessary limitation if the neutral role of these actors were to serve as a meaningful basis for an exemption from liability. The fear was that any obligation to monitor Internet traffic in a general manner would lead to actual knowledge and a level of control that could invalidate any immunity.

There was also a real concern that any more onerous requirement to monitor the increasing amount of Internet traffic would hamper the development of the young Internet sector.[474] In addition there was a concern that a general monitoring requirement would conflict with the fundamental right to privacy.[475] The interplay between this prohibition and the possibility of courts and authorities to ask for injunction to prevent specific infringements[476] is another aspect of contention of the liability framework of the ECD.[477] On a legal level the debate centred on what the scope of a specific preventive injunction could be that fulfils the criteria of proportionality while being effective.[478] On a purely technical level the dividing

---

474 *Savin*, EU Internet Law, pp. 161–162.

475 *Büllesbach (ed.)*, Concise European IT Law, p. 333.

476 As provided for in Recital 47 ECD.

477 Commission, SEC(2011) 1641 final, supra (fn. 468), para. 47–51.

478 CJEU, judgement of 12.7.2011, C-324/09, *L'Oréal (UK) Ltd v eBay International AG, eBay Europe SARL, eBay (UK) Ltd and others*, para. 141; judgement of 3.10.2019, C-18/18, *Eva Glawischnig-Piesczek v Facebook Ireland Limited*.

line between an injunction targeted at preventing the occurrence of a particular type of violation and the requirement that the entire traffic of the site be monitored has been a subject to intense debate.[479]

Art. 15 para. 2 ECD specifies two obligations for information society providers. Firstly, Member States may establish obligations that public authorities be informed of illegal activities. Secondly, service providers may be obliged to inform authorities of the identity of third parties with whom they have service agreements. However, the latter requirement has been relativised in an early related CJEU judgement in *Promusicae*. The CJEU stipulated that Member States have to balance contradicting fundamental rights of property protection and privacy rights when they decide about a framework in which communication of personal data of users to rights holders would be foreseen.[480]

3.3.5. Delineation between National and EU Responsibilities

The ECD follows a minimum harmonisation approach. This means that in line with the principle of subsidiarity[481] it will only act in areas where it has no exclusive competence if the objectives of the measure can be better achieved through intervention at Union level.[482] Meanwhile the country-of-origin principle allocates the supervisory authority to the Member State where an information society service provider is established.[483] This also extends to the intermediary service providers.

The Directive left it to Member States to define procedures for the removal of, and disabling of access to, illegal information and activity by hosting providers. They are also known as notice-and-takedown procedures.[484] The Directive encourages self-regulatory measures such as voluntary agreements between stakeholders or codes of conduct.[485] The Commission's 2012 evaluation of the ECD found that only a few Member States had either managed to initiate the creation of voluntary agreements

---

479 *Nolte/Wimmers*, in: GRUR 16(1), 2014), pp. 16, 21–23; *Valcke/Kuczerawy/Ombelet*, Did the Romans Get it Right? What Delfi, Google, eBay, and UPC TeleKabel Wien Have in Common, p. 11.
480 CJEU, *Promusicae v Telefónica*, supra (fn. 135).
481 Recital 6 ECD.
482 Art. 5 para. 3 TEU.
483 Recital 22 ECD.
484 Art. 14 para. 3 ECD.
485 Recital 40 ECD.

on notice and takedown or enacted laws to that respect.[486] Where legislations or codes of conduct existed, they did not consistently cover the entire intermediary sector or only applied to certain content areas, such as copyright, child pornography or terrorist content. As a result, a fragmented picture of notice-and-takedown processes emerged, which, according to the stakeholder consultation by the Commission, created legal uncertainty and an obstacle to the Digital Single Market.[487]

The Directive's broad horizontal focus also means that it does not intervene in Member States' provisions in specific content areas. The definition of what is illegal under national law may therefore differ from one Member State to another. For example, defamation is regulated under Member State laws. This is also the case for exceptions and limitations to the reproduction right in EU copyright, which are optional.[488]

While Art. 12–14 give some guidance as to the applicability of criminal and civil sanctions, their applicability is without prejudice to sanctions or remedies according to national law. This means that the breach of intermediary service provider obligations may have different legal consequences depending on the Member State. For example, the approach to contributory liability is determined by Member States' legal traditions, and consequently the kind of sanctions that can be expected by intermediary service providers for the same violation may differ.[489]

3.3.6. Illegal Content – Challenges to EU Intermediary Liability Exemptions

The Commission was obliged by the Directive to re-examine the provisions of the intermediary liability framework with a view to adapt them if needed.[490] The first review of the ECD of 2003 however found that practical experience of the application of Art. 12–14 was still very limited. No court ruling had been issued that originated from cases after the enactment of the ECD.[491] Likewise it found no reason to intervene with legislation in the notice-and-takedown procedures. Four years later the Commission

---

486 Commission, SEC(2011) 1641 final, supra (fn. 468), para. 40–43.
487 Commission, SEC(2011) 1641 final, supra (fn. 468), para. 43.
488 Cf. Chapter 2.4.4.
489 *Verbiest/Spindler/Riccio*, Study on the Liability of Internet Intermediaries, pp. 34–35.
490 Art. 21 para. 2 ECD.
491 Cf. Commission report on the Application of the ECD, supra (fn. 462), p. 13.

commissioned two studies that dealt with the implementation and impact of the ECD. While one study dealt with the economic imact of the ECD,[492] the other specifically focused on the intermediary liability regime and the interpretation of its provisions by EU Member States and national courts.[493]

This latter study noted diverging interpretations on the liability provisions for host providers by courts. It specifically pointed to unclarity over the term "actual knowledge" in connection with illegal activity and information in Art. 14, para. 1 ECD.[494] Secondly, it noted the variety of injunctions issued against intermediaries. It pointed to an uncertainty and a potential conflict between preventive injunctions against specific infringements, also called staydown orders, and the prohibition to impose general monitoring obligations.[495] The availability of the liability exemptions to intermediaries seemed to be a less prominent issue. However, the report advocated vigilance regarding the emergence of Web 2.0 intermediaries and the potential for conflicting interpretations over the availability of Art. 14 for hosting activities.[496]

The 2012 evaluation of a public consultation on the application of the ECD found a more substantial need for clarification of the intermediary liability framework.[497] In addition to the problems mentioned in the 2007 study, the report now stated that courts had increasingly divergent views on the scope of activities covered by Art. 12–15 of the ECD. Apart from the longer standing problems with the liability of search engines, the report indicated that new Web 2.0 intermediaries, such as video-sharing platforms, e-commerce marketplaces and social networks, had caused substantial legal uncertainty. Yet in its ensuing evaluation of the E-commerce Action Plan the Commission followed the majority of stakeholders and did not undertake to reform the liability provisions of the ECD.[498]

---

492 *Nielsen and others*, Study on the Economic Impact of the Electronic Commerce Directive.

493 *Verbiest/Spindler/Riccio*, Study on the Liability of Internet Intermediaries.

494 *Verbiest/Spindler/Riccio*, Study on the Liability of Internet Intermediaries, pp. 36–47.

495 *Verbiest/Spindler/Riccio*, Study on the Liability of Internet Intermediaries, pp. 50–52.

496 *Verbiest/Spindler/Riccio*, Study on the Liability of Internet Intermediaries, pp. 102–104.

497 Commission, SEC(2011) 1641 final, supra (fn. 468), para. 24–26.

498 Commission staff working document E-commerce Action plan 2012–2015, SWD(2013) 153 final, available at https://ec.europa.eu/information_society/new

By 2016 the EU noted that the availability of illegal and harmful content had become an even more noticeable problem, especially as online platforms occupied an ever more important position in the daily lives of people. However, although acknowledging persisting concerns with regards to the responsibilities of online platforms, it vowed to "maintain the existing intermediary liability regime while implementing a sectorial, problem-driven approach to regulation".[499] The focus would be on reforming provisions regarding the liabilities of intermediaries through a legislative review of copyright and audiovisual media services. This sectorial approach was confirmed by a Communication and a Recommendation to tackle illegal content online, which both called for more responsibilities of online platforms.[500] These initiatives engendered a number of separate sectorial legislative initiatives aimed at addressing the responsibilities of intermediaries, particularly hosting services, without however opening the ECD-framework laid down in Art. 12–15. These initiatives will be discussed in more detail below (cf. also above Chapter 2.4.1).

3.3.7. EU Intermediary Liability Framework – How the CJEU Has Dealt with the Challenges

3.3.7.1. Challenge : The Question of Neutrality of Hosts

In the first five years after of the ECD, there was relatively little controversy over the availability of the liability immunities under Art. 12–15. Initially, the activity of search engines posed a problem to courts in the EU. However, this controversy was settled in the CJEU ruling in *Google France v Luis Vuitton*. The CJEU found that an Internet referencing service provider (i.e. search engine) could avail itself of the immunities provided through Art. 14 for hosting activities if it did not play an active role in the hosting process.[501] It proved, however, much more controversial to find criteria to determine when more interactive Web 2.0 intermediary service providers, or online platforms, acted in a "mere technical, automatic and

---

sroom/image/document/2017-4/130423_report-ecommerce-action-plan_en_4207
3.pdf, p. 17.

499 Communication on Online Platforms and the Digital Single Market Opportunities and Challenges for Europe, COM/2016/0288 final, pp. 7–9.

500 Cf. on this already in detail Chapter 2.5.3.

501 CJEU, judgement of 23.3.2010, joint cases C-236/08 to C-238/08, *Google France, Google Inc v Louis Vuitton Malletier*, para. 143.

passive" role, i.e. did not play an active role. The premise of their neutral character was increasingly unclear and hence interpreted differently by courts. A number of rulings during the first decade of the new millennium show diverging understandings by, for example, Belgian, French, German, Italian and UK national courts on the activities of e-commerce market-places, user-generated content platforms or search engines.[502]

The first two rulings at CJEU level that attempted to clarify this situation were *Google France v Luis Vuitton*[503] and *L'Oréal v Ebay*.[504] Both cases were brought by French trademark owners who alleged amongst others that Google and eBay's activities went beyond a mere passive and technical role of information society service providers. As a result, both claimants charged Google and eBay, respectively, with being directly liable for violating their trademark rights.

In *Google France v Luis Vuitton* the rights holders sought to establish the existence of actual knowledge and control by the fact that Google assisted clients using the AdWords service in drafting the commercial message next to the advertising link and in suggesting keyword combinations that improved the display of their adverts. The adverts in question appeared as "sponsored links" to websites that sold imitations of the rights holders' trademark-protected luxury goods. The CJEU found that a search engine's matching activity of users requests with keywords stored by advertisers and the subsequent display of results did not constitute an active role. However, the drafting of the advertising message which accompanied sponsored links and the selection of advertising keywords connected to this display may indicate such an active role.[505]

In *L'Oréal v Ebay*, which a UK court had referred to the CJEU, L'Oréal wanted to establish eBay's active role through the assistance it provided to sellers in optimising or promoting the display of certain listings. These listings, however, referred to products that violated the trademark rights of L'Oréal. Similar to *Google France*, the CJEU found in *L'Oréal v Ebay* that storage of an offer, setting the terms of service, providing general information to customers and getting remunerated are neutral components of an online marketplace's activity. By contrast, providing assistance to the seller,

---

502 Commission, SEC(2011) 1641 final, supra (fn. 468), para. 26–30; *Waisman/ Hevia*, in: International review of industrial property and copyright law 42(7), 2011, pp. 785 et seq.; *Bertolini/Franceschelli/Pollicino*, Analysis of ISP Regulation under Italian Law, pp. 156–163.
503 CJEU, *Google France v Louis Vuitton*, supra (fn. 501).
504 CJEU, *L'Oréal v eBay*, supra (fn. 478).
505 CJEU, *Google France v Louis Vuitton*, supra (fn. 501), para. 115–119.

such as optimising the display and promoting offers means active involvement and hence forfeiture of the liability exemption.[506] In both cases, the CJEU referred the matter back to the national courts so that they apply these criteria to the concrete facts and circumstances on a case-by-case basis.

These rulings, however, did not appear to have brought the clarity sought. National courts have continued to this day to come to diverging results and classifications of the role of hosting services providers. Prompted by the CJEU, they assessed the role of hosting services according to the criteria laid down by the EU court, but they developed their own methodologies in doing so. This is hardly surprising, given the vast variety of hosting services, different legal traditions and varying degrees of understanding of intermediaries' operations and business models.

In other rulings following these two key judgements, the CJEU had no trouble in allocating the Art. 14 hosting defence to social networking services, such as in *Netlog* (*SABAM v Netlog*[507]) and, very recently, *Facebook*[508]. Although in the latter case the Advocate General simply stated in his Opinion that, "irrespective of the doubts that one might have in that regard"[509], the referring court found that it was common ground that Facebook is a host provider and, by implication, a neutral actor. It is clear that the CJEU sticks to its line by letting national courts elucidate on this issue.

Lastly, the CJEU confirmed its "hands-off approach" in the *SNB-REACT* case by referring the question of whether Internet registries and registrars are neutral intermediary service providers that could qualify for the liability exemptions of the ECD back to the national court.[510] In this case, REACT, an industry association which defends the rights of trademark owners, brought a challenge against an IP address rental and registration service which had registered 38,000 IP addresses and domains that violated the trademark rights of its members.

Despite these rulings the concept of the neutral ("mere technical, automatic and passive") host remains unclear in its application at national lev-

---

506 CJEU, *L'Oréal v eBay*, supra (fn. 478), para. 115–117.
507 CJEU, judgement of 16.2.2012, C-360/10, *Belgische Vereniging van Auteurs, Componisten en Uitgevers CVBA (SABAM) v Netlog NV*, para. 27.
508 CJEU judgement *Eva Glawischnig-Piesczek v Facebook Ireland Limited*, supra (fn. 478), para. 22. Cf. further analysis below Chapter 3.3.7.3.4.
509 Opinion of Advocate General Szpunar on *Eva Glawischnig-Piesczek v Facebook Ireland Limited*, delivered on 4.6.2019, C-18/18, para. 30.
510 CJEU, judgement of 7.8.2018, C-521/17, *Coöperatieve Vereniging SNB-REACT U.A. v Deepak Mehta*, para. 47–52.

el.[511] Two current referrals which are pending in front of the CJEU are testimony to this. Both referrals come from copyright owners and seek guidance on the availability of the hosting defence (Art. 14) to the activities of video-sharing platform YouTube. In both cases the claimants had repeatedly notified to YouTube content that infringed their copyright and eventually asked the video-sharing platform to prevent notified content from reappearing (staydown requests). They also claimed that the activities of YouTube went beyond that of a passive host, namely by offering users to search, flag and comment on content, by deriving advertising and licencing revenues, by recommending content to users and by sorting and ranking content. The cases referred by the German and Austrian Supreme courts are still pending.[512]

One solution that has been brought forward in response to the difficulties in deciding whether Art. 14 is available to new Web 2.0 intermediaries is the creation of additional categories of intermediary service providers in the ECD.[513] The risk is that this may be overrun rather quickly by market developments, potentially even before such changes are enacted. In addition, this approach could risk steering away from the technology-neutral focus of the ECD. Others have argued to scrap the distinction between neutral and active hosts altogether,[514] because this assessment is very complex and requires deep technical and operational understanding of the concrete hosting context at hand. It also diverts from the fact that most Web 2.0 intermediaries today profit immensely from the data and information generated by user activity. Claims of being a neutral host sit uncomfortably with the intrusive nature of many of these platforms and the mas-

---

511 Commission, Synopsis Report on the Public Consultation on the Regulatory Environment for Platforms, Online Intermediaries and the Collaborative Economy, available at https://ec.europa.eu/digital-single-market/en/news/synopsis-report-contributions-public-consultation-regulatory-environment-data-and-cloud, pp. 15–16.

512 Request for a preliminary ruling from the Bundesgerichtshof (Germany) lodged on 6 November 2018, *LF v Google LLC, YouTube Inc, YouTube LLC, Google Germany GmbH* (Case C-682/18); Request for a preliminary ruling from Oberster Gerichtshof (Austria) lodged on 1 July 2019, *Puls 4 TV GmbH & Co KG v YouTube LLC and Google Austria GmbH* (C-500/19).

513 Synopsis Report of the Commission, supra (fn. 511), p. 16.

514 *Martens*, An Economic Policy Perspective on Online Platforms, pp. 34–35; *Ullrich*, in: International Journal of Law and Information Technology 26(3), 2018, p. 226, 242.

sive benefits generated from exploiting big data.[515] This way of thinking is also expressed in an early preparatory document of the Commission services concerning a possible future "Digital Services Act", according to which the distinction between active and passive hosts could be given up in the future.[516]

3.3.7.2. Challenge 2: Actual Knowledge

Once intermediary service providers are found to act in a mere technical and passive way, they can avail themselves of the liability exemptions if they do not have actual knowledge of the illegal activity/information or if they remove it expeditiously once they have obtained that knowledge. This requirement is specific to caching and hosting activities[517] and not relevant for the liability for mere conduits.[518] In addition, hosting providers are not allowed to be aware of facts and circumstances from which illegal activity is apparent.[519]

Knowledge is a precondition for finding contributory liability. However, early reports have shown that Member States had implemented these requirements differently into their national law.[520] Even where they followed a literal transposition of the Directive's text, courts had come up with differing interpretations.[521] The consensus that has arisen through national and EU rulings is that there are three ways in which an intermediary service provider can gain that actual knowledge. First, a court order, secondly a notice by an allegedly damaged party and third through awareness over illegal activity and content.

---

515 *Zuboff*, The Age of Surveillance Capitalism: The Fight for a Human Future at the New Frontier of Power, para. 2051; *Naughton*, Platform Power and Responsibility in the Attention Economy, pp. 388–389; *Friedmann*, in: Journal of Intellectual Property Law and Practice 9(2), 2014, pp. 148, 150.

516 Cf. the leaked document confirming that DSM Steering Group is engaged in drafting a Digital Services Act that would serve as a basis for a REFIT of the ECD and establish new rules on platforms, available at https://cdn.netzpolitik.or g/wp-upload/2019/07/Digital-Services-Act-note-DG-Connect-June-2019.pdf.

517 Art. 14 para. 1 lit. a and b ECD, and Art. 13 para. 1 lit. e ECD, respectively.

518 CJEU, *McFadden v Sony*, supra (fn. 467), para. 63–65.

519 Art. 14 para. 1 lit. a ECD.

520 *Verbiest/Spindler/Riccio*, Study on the Liability of Internet Intermediaries, pp. 34–47.

521 Commission, SEC(2011) 1641 final, supra (fn. 468), para. 32–36.

On the second point, under receipt of a notice, the intermediary would need to decide on the veracity of the claim and then remove the information expeditiously in order to qualify for the liability exemption. However, since the ECD did not provide any procedural requirements for notice and takedown, the understanding over what constitutes actual knowledge following a notice has differed across the EU. The CJEU has so far not been called up to give guidance on this issue. The Commission is currently reviewing whether there is a need for EU-wide notice-and-takedown processes.[522]

Awareness of illegal activity has been another ambiguous concept. If a provider truly is a passive host, it is unclear how it should become aware of illegal activity or information on its servers. This matter was first addressed by the CJEU in *L'Oreal v Ebay*. The CJEU stated that a sufficiently precise and substantiated notice could result in such awareness.[523] Secondly, a hosting provider could lose its immunity if it did not act on indications of illegal activity that it should have become aware of as a diligent economic operator. This includes voluntary proactive investigative activity by the intermediary.[524] This was the first time that the CJEU referred to duties of hosting providers that go beyond barely reactive responses to notifications. Diligent economic operator principles come close to duties of care, which are optional for Member States to impose on hosting providers,[525] and to principles of corporate responsibility.

Under current EU law this may, however, deter any "Good Samaritan" activity because it does not protect the intermediary explicitly in case of error when actively searching for illegal content or having procedures in place. Unlike the US,[526] the EU has not provided such a protection in its legislation. It has also been argued that this ruling may create a conflict with Art. 15 of the ECD, which prohibits the imposition of general monitoring duties. The fear is that it may force intermediaries to monitor for illegal activity in order to act as a diligent economic operator.[527] It is true that the broad and monolithic prohibition of Art. 15 may be perceived as standing in the way of diligent economic operator principles. However,

---

522 COM(2017) 555 final (supra fn. 394), p. 4.
523 CJEU, *L'Oréal v eBay*, supra (fn. 478), para. 122.
524 CJEU, *L'Oréal v eBay*, supra (fn. 478), para. 120, 122.
525 Recital 48 ECD.
526 47 USC § 230 s. 230 (c).
527 *Savin*, EU Internet Law, p. 161.

this is not the only possible interpretation, as will be shown in the discussion of the problem in the next section.

There is still a lack of clarity on this approach, as the CJEU has not elaborated further on the diligent economic operator principle in any of the following cases dealing with intermediary liability. The ruling seems to have made an impact however: in the new DSM Directive, efforts of content-sharing service providers to prevent the availability of unauthorised works are to be assessed according to diligent operator principles.[528] The ruling is also used as an argument by the Commission in its Communication on Tackling Illegal Content Online for encouraging the use of proactive measures to detect illegal content.[529]

3.3.7.3. Challenge 3: Preventive Injunctions and Duties of Care

From an early point onwards, Member States have taken the opportunity provided in the ECD to impose on intermediary service providers injunctions to terminate and prevent infringements.[530] Courts and authorities have tried to impose so-called staydown orders, which seek to ensure that information successfully blocked once would not be reposted. Secondly, authorities and courts also sought to order intermediary service providers to prevent similar or even all sorts of infringements in the future.

Very quickly these cases were countered by intermediaries who claimed that this imposed *de facto* obligations to monitor information on a general basis and would therefore contradict Art. 15 ECD. It was initially argued that staydown orders necessitated general monitoring, since in order to detect a re-upload the intermediary would be required to monitor the entirety of its traffic. The counter argument was that staydown orders were specific to the information already notified and therefore did not require general but only a closely circumscribed monitoring, which was therefore au-

---

528 Cf. Recital 66 of DSM Directive.
529 COM(2017) 555 final (supra fn. 394), para. 11–13. In addition it has been used as guidance to complement provisions for traders that are online marketplaces in the Unfair Commercial Practices Directive: Guidance on the Implementation/Application of Directive 2005/29/EC on Unfair Commercial Practices SWD(2016) 163, pp. 123–127.
530 Art. 12 para. 3, Art. 13 para. 2 and Art. 14 para. 3 ECD.

thorised under ECD.[531] The same was eventually argued for the prevention of similar infringements.[532]

A large part of the confusion in this debate centres around the definition of the term "monitoring", which is left aside by the ECD. The fact that prevention and filtering techniques have become more effective and less intrusive has also played into this debate.[533]

3.3.7.3.1. L'Oréal v Ebay (C-324/09)

The CJEU addressed this problem first in *L'Oréal v Ebay*. It confirmed that an injunction must not result in the monitoring of all data in order to prevent any future intellectual property infringements. This would be irreconcilable with the ECD and the IP Enforcement Directive[534]. Notwithstanding these limitations, any measures taken had to be effective and proportionate. Therefore, if the hosting provider did not act on its own initiative to prevent infringements of the same kind by the same seller, it could be ordered by a court to do so.[535] With this the CJEU defined specific preventive orders as acceptable where they were aimed at preventing the same kind of infringement by the same originator (seller). In addition, an online market place may be ordered to make it easier to identify its customer-sellers in order to give damaged persons a right to an effective remedy, while balancing it with other rights as laid down in *Promusicae*.[536]

---

531 Recital 47 ECD.
532 For a discussion over the years: *Verbiest/Spindler/Riccio*, Study on the Liability of Internet Intermediaries, pp. 50–52; Commission, SEC(2011) 1641 final, supra (fn. 468), para. 25–26; Synopsis Report of the Commission, supra (fn. 511), pp. 18–19.
533 *Angelopoulos*, European Intermediary Liability in Copyright. A Tort-Based Analysis, pp. 473–474; *Edwards/Veale*, in: Duke Law & Technology Review 16(1), 2017/18, pp. 18, 82.
534 Art. 3 of Directive 2004/84/EC; CJEU, *L'Oréal v eBay*, supra (fn. 478), para. 139.
535 CJEU, *L'Oréal v eBay*, supra (fn. 478), para. 141.
536 CJEU, *L'Oréal v eBay*, supra (fn. 478), para. 142–143.

3.3.7.3.2. Scarlet Extended (C-70/10) & Netlog (C-360/10)

Two important subsequent cases in this matter were brought by the Belgian music authors and rights holder association (SABAM) against an Internet access provider (Scarlet Extended) and an Internet host (the social networking site Netlog).[537]

In both cases SABAM tried to impose an obligation that these intermediaries prevent the unauthorised making available of works in its repertoire through the services of these intermediaries. In *Scarlet Extended* the Internet access provider was asked to filter any peer-to-peer traffic of its subscribers through which works for which SABAM collected the copyright licence were shared. In *Netlog*, the association required that social network users be prevented to share any works that were under the license of SABAM. Both orders would have resulted in the intermediaries monitoring the entire traffic on their systems indiscriminately. Both requests were struck down by the CJEU as disproportionate and irreconcilable with the freedom to conduct business, the right to protection of personal data and the freedom to receive or impart information and in violation with the general monitoring prohibition of Art. 15 para. 1 of the ECD.[538]

In *L'Oréal v Ebay* the CJEU defined the acceptable scope of a specific preventive injunction in the light of the general monitoring prohibition on the one hand and the duties of intermediaries to prevent infringing activities[539] on the other. The two cases of *SABAM* provided guidance on the balancing acts involved in broader and indiscriminate preventive injunctions.

3.3.7.3.3. McFadden (C-484/14)

The *McFadden* case dealt with the acceptable scope of preventive measures by another type of provider, a mere conduit which was offering a public Wi-Fi network. This case shed some light on the acceptable preventive measures an Internet access provider could be expected to take to deter infringing activity, in this case copyright violations, by users of its (free) service.

---

537 CJEU, judgement of 24.11.2011, C-70/10, *Scarlet Extended SA v Société belge des auteurs, compositeurs et éditeurs SCRL (SABAM)*.
538 Ibid., para. 53; CJEU,*SABAM*, supra (fn. 507), para. 51.
539 Recitals 40, 45 ECD.

The CJEU had to choose between three measures suggested by the referring court: the filtering of the entire traffic, the disconnection of the network connection and password protection of the Wi-Fi network. The court decided that only the third measure was proportionate. Requiring from a Wi-Fi network provider that its users sign up to the service by revealing their identity was deemed a proportionate means of deterring unauthorised use of the network.[540] This ruling confirmed that preventive measures such as customer identification are adequate obligations that could be imposed on intermediaries as part of a duty of care, at least were intellectual property protection is concerned.[541]

3.3.7.3.4. Eva Glawischnig-Piesczek v Facebook Ireland (C-18/18)

The jurisprudence on the scope of preventive activity filtering was further refined and extended in the recent *Facebook* case.[542] The CJEU was asked whether the social network could be obliged to suppress repeated instances of defamatory comments made against the Austrian politician Eva Glawischnig-Piesczek. The case dates back to 2016 when the former member of the Austrian Parliament and spokeswoman of a party was confronted with insulting and defaming comments on her Facebook page, following an Article she had written about the refugee situation in Austria. That comment, which was publicly accessible to all users, also contained a photo of the politician posted by the commenting user. Facebook declined to follow Glawischnig-Piesczek's request to remove the comments and photograph of her. The politician finally succeeded in a prohibitory injunction, in which it asked Facebook to cease and desist from disseminating any photographs of her that showed accompanying text identical or equivalent to the original insulting comments.

Both parties went through successive appeals stages and arrived at the Austrian Supreme Court (Oberster Gerichtshof). That court was asked to whether it was proportionate to place an order against a social network that extended to preventing identical statements or those with an equivalent meaning to the original harmful comments. The Supreme Court, aware of the EU law ramifications at stake, turned to the CJEU for guid-

---

540 CJEU, *McFadden v. Sony*, supra (fn. 467), para. 90–98.
541 *Ullrich*, in: International Journal of Law and Information Technology 26(3), 2018, p. 226, 243–244.
542 CJEU, *Eva Glawischnig-Piesczek v Facebook Ireland Limited*, supra (fn. 478).

ance, essentially requiring clarification on the scope of a staydown order: could it include the same comments and extend to equivalent comments? What was the limit of the prohibition on general monitoring obligations imposed by Art. 15 of the ECD? This case can be seen as a major chance for clarifying the acceptable scope of preventive obligations of social networks classified as hosting providers under the ECD. In other words, they provided the CJEU with an opportunity to shed light on when a specific prevention duty was turning into a disproportionate, general monitoring obligation.

The CJEU ruled that Facebook could be obliged to accept a staydown order for identical comments made by any user of the network against the politician in question. In addition, it could be asked to prevent equivalent defamatory comments from the same user, provided the difference in the content did not require Facebook to engage in an independent assessment. The comments would have to be made inaccessible for all users within the EU, while leaving it open to the Member State to decide on whether this duty could be extended globally in the context of the applicable international law.

The ruling has been interpreted as an endorsement of automatic filtering techniques as means of qualifying for the immunities of Art. 14 of the ECD.[543] The Court stated that, in the light of the availability of automated search tools and technologies, the staydown obligation would only extend to equivalent content for which the service provider would not need to make an independent assessment.[544] This is also supposed to affirm the purely technical, passive and automatic character of the activity. However, it also shows the problems of not having any "Good Samaritan" protections in place. The intermediary's preventive activity is limited to the strict necessary extent if it wants to protect its "neutral" status. The Advocate General had usefully distinguished in his opinion on this case between preventing infringements in intellectual property, as laid down in *L'Oréal v Ebay*, and in defamation cases.[545] The implication in this case is that the

---

543 *Keller*, Filtering Facebook: Why Internet Users and EU Policymakers Should Worry about the Advocate General's Opinion in Glawischnig-Piesczek' (*Inforrm's Blog*, 7 September 2019) https://inforrm.org/2019/09/08/filtering-facebook-why-internet-users-and-eu-policymakers-should-worry-about-the-advocate-generals-opinion-in-glawischnig-piesczek-daphne-keller/.

544 CJEU, *Eva Glawischnig-Piesczek v Facebook Ireland Limited*, supra (fn. 478), para. 46.

545 Opinion of Advocate General Szpunar on *Eva Glawischnig-Piesczek v Facebook Ireland Limited*, supra (fn. 509) para. 68–69.

use of automatic filtering tools for preventing the same and equivalent infringements in defamation cases is classed as a specific prevention obligation, which is incompliant with Art. 15 ECD.[546] This seems to be in line with the recent endorsement of the EU lawmakers for the use of automated filtering technology by Internet intermediaries in order to prevent specific infringements and illegal activity[547], at least as long as the general monitoring prohibition is in place.

However, one of the potential problems is the broad horizontal focus of the ECD. As shown above, the scope of preventive or more far-reaching duty of care obligations may depend on the violations at stake. The balancing act required may lead to varying outcomes depending on whether IP rights, personality rights such as defamation, public security or other interests are at stake. The scope of preventive duties may therefore vary depending on whether hate speech, copyright breaches, defamatory comments, counterfeit sales, child pornography or illegal or unauthorised products are at stake. A larger Internet host may have to deal with all or some of these issues at the same time and would need to adjust its responsibilities to the type of content involved.

3.3.7.4. Other Intermediary-Related Case Law

There are a number of other cases which are usually evoked when talking about intermediary liability law but have not been analysed here so far. *Pirate Bay*, *GSMedia* and *Telekabel*[548] all concern copyright breaches that are facilitated by the use of intermediaries (Internet access providers or hosting services). In all three cases the Advocate Generals evoked the enforcement options against intermediaries that are available for rights holders under the liability provisions of the ECD.[549] They did so alongside considering the options offered by the InfoSoc and IP Enforcement Directives

---

546 CJEU, *Eva Glawischnig-Piesczek v Facebook Ireland Limited*, supra (fn. 478) para. 45–47.

547 COM(2017) 555 final, supra (fn. 394), pp. 14–15.

548 CJEU, judgement of 14.6.2017, C-610/15, *Stichting Brein v Ziggo BV and XS4All Internet BV*.

549 Opinion of Advocate General Szpunar, delivered on 8.2.2017, C-610/15, *Stichting Brein v Ziggo BV and XS4All Internet BV*, para. 67, 60, 83; Opinion of Advocate General Wathelet, delivered on 7.4.2016, C-160/15, *GS Media BV v Sanoma Media Netherlands BV, Playboy Enterprises International Inc, Britt Geertruida Dekker*, para. 86; Opinion of Advocate General Cruz Villalón, delivered on

(IPRED)[550] to issue injunctions against intermediaries for facilitating IP rights violations. In all three cases the Court's judgement entirely sidelined the reasoning of the Advocate Generals on the ECD and instead focussed exclusively on applying the remedies offered by the InfoSoc Directive and IPRED. This may have been a precursor to the provisions in Art. 17 of the Copyright Directive: the Court was preoccupied with clarifying first whether these intermediaries could be charged for primary copyright breach. The implication is that a finding of primary liability would automatically exclude protections and remedies available under the ECD.[551] If an intermediary was found to engage directly in acts of communication to the public, this would remove the foundation of the liability exemptions which protect passive hosts that have no editorial control or influence over the content they host.

3.3.8. Defining a "Duty-of-Care" Standard

3.3.8.1. The Reasoning behind New Responsibilities for Internet Intermediaries

In recent years, the call for a review of the current liability immunities towards enhanced duties of care for information hosts (under Art. 14) have become more frequent and vocal. One argument is that the broad and far-reaching liability protections stem from a time when these actors needed to be protected from legal uncertainty and liabilities. Primary or more readily available secondary liability for content could have hampered the emerging Internet and commercial activity therein. It would have put an undue burden on these intermediaries to monitor, filter and arbitrate information posted, especially when technology was less advanced.

These circumstances have changed. Today Internet intermediaries are more than just normal economic actors. Some of them have become powerful corporate actors with far-reaching control over both content and the infrastructure of the Internet. The control over content and infrastructure has conferred on them gatekeeping powers which would call for en-

---

26.11.2013, C-314/12, *UPC Telekabel Wien GmbH v Constantin Film Verleih GmbH, Wega Filmproduktionsgesellschaft mbH*, para. 52, 77, 78.

550 Art. 8 para. 3 InfoSoc Directive; Art. 11 IPRED.

551 For a more detailed review: *Rosati*, in: European Intellectual Property Review 39(12), 2017, p. 737, 737 et seq.

hanced responsibilities. In addition, the increasing amount of data shared via these intermediaries is exploited and monetised in unprecedented ways. This further questions the merely technical, automatic and passive character of the activities of intermediaries, which is, however, the preconditional criterion for the far-reaching immunities they currently enjoy.[552]

In line with the emergence of powerful Web 2.0 platforms, there have been increasingly calls for enhanced responsibilities alongside so-called duties of care to be imposed on Internet intermediaries. The rationale is that increased powers also justify increased responsibilities. There is a tendency away from the traditional liability framework towards responsibility. The justifications are both of a moral and economic nature.[553] In essence they see new obligations according to the model of corporate responsibility imposed on the intermediaries. A number of theories and suggestions that explore these enhanced responsibilities use the doctrine of duty of care as an underlying concept. Duty of care is common to many legal systems. In tort law it is defined as "a legal obligation imposed on an individual to avid foreseeable harm to others by taking reasonable care".[554] As a framework that defines a standard of responsibility, it lends itself notably to more complex economic and socio-economic contexts that require factual and technical expertise. This is especially the case where pure verification on legal merits is fraught with difficulties.[555] The scope of duty of care obligations often comprises procedural aspects, such as decision-making procedures or risk management.[556] A failure to observe duties of care can lead to liabilities that can be compared to those resulting from negligence and may result in criminal or civil penalties depending on the type of harm caused.

---

552 These books give more detail on the power and influence of intermediaries within the internet and daily life in general: *Moore/Tambini (eds.)*, Digital Dominance – The Power of Google, Amazon, Facebook, and Apple; *Wagner*, Global Free Expression – Governing the Boundaries of Internet Content; *Zuboff*, The Age of Surveillance Capitalism: The Fight for a Human Future at the New Frontier of Power.

553 *Taddeo/Floridi*, in: Science and Engineering Ethics 22(6), 2016, p. 1575; *Helberger/Pierson/Poell*, in: The Information Society 34(1), 2018, p. 1; *Valcke/Kuczerawy/Ombelet*, Did the Romans Get it Right? What Delfi, Google, eBay, and UPC TeleKabel Wien Have in Common.

554 *Waisman/Hevia*, in: International review of industrial property and copyright law 42(7), 2011, p. 785, 790.

555 *Hofmann*, Delegation, Discretion and the Duty of Care in the Case Law of the Court of Justice of the European Union.

556 *Rhee*, in: Notre Dame Law Review 88(3), 2013, p. 1138, 1147–1150.

3.3.8.2. Proposals for a "Duty of Care"-Approach

The idea of using the duty-of-care principle for obliging online platforms to participate in more proactive infringement prevention is not new. Several authors have by now explored it. In essence these proposals look at allocating responsibilities to platforms that result in a) them taking *ex ante* account of the risks that exist on their systems with regards to illegal content and activity, b) deploying measures to address these risks, c) ensuring that risk assessment and risk responses are conducted in a transparent way. Some of the more substantial proposal in this area shall be briefly portrayed below.

Helman and Parchomovsky[557] and *Verbiest, Spindler and Riccio*[558] have developed the idea of technology-based safe harbours, where duty of care is tied to the use of state-of-the-art filtering and prevention technology used by intermediaries. Both suggest co-regulatory solutions, namely technical standardisation, to create statutory oversight over the development and use of these technologies. *Helman and Parchomovsky* have developed a proposal specific to the prevention of copyright violations on Internet platforms. *Verbiest, Spindler and Riccio* propose the EU New Approach towards standardisation as a (co-)regulatory model. Intermediaries would be required to use that preventive filtering technology against repeat infringements, which has been mandated through technical standards. The aim is to ensure a level playing field between intermediaries and transparency over the content-management decisions, such as filtering algorithms. The application of the New Approach and technical standards to the platform economy have also been taken up by *Busch.*[559] He showcases his solution through the development of an ISO standard for online reviews.[560]

Valcke et al. look at (self-regulatory) codes of ethics as for example drawn up by press associations or journalism councils as a possible model for a duty-of-care standard. These standards would be used by courts as a yardstick when adjudicating on content liability disputes involving ISPs.[561]

---

557 *Helman/Parchomovsky*, in: Columbia Law Review 111(6), 2011, p. 1194, 1225.
558 *Verbiest/Spindler/Riccio*, Study on the Liability of Internet Intermediaries, pp. 19–23.
559 *Busch*, in: Journal of European Consumer and Market Law 6(6), 2017, p. 227.
560 Technical Committee ISO/TC 290, ISO 20488:2018, Online consumer reviews – Principles and requirements for their collection, moderation and publication, available at https://www.iso.org/standard/68193.html.
561 *Valcke/Kuczerawy/Ombelet*, Did the Romans Get it Right? What Delfi, Google, eBay, and UPC TeleKabel Wien Have in Common.

Waismann et al. have proposed a flexible standard of duty care for search engines, which is based on reasonableness. That reasonableness would be dependent on scope, cost, harm and impact on fundamental rights.[562] *Woods and Perrin*[563] have so far made the most detailed proposal for a statutory duty of care, which is at the heart of a recent UK Government White Paper to deal with the harms caused by illegal and unacceptable content on social media.[564] This proposal ties the preventive and reactive activities by intermediaries to the *ex ante* definition of key harms that content on these platforms causes to society. They base their approach on the theory that today's social media platforms are public spaces and therefore have special responsibilities to protect users who enter these spaces. Parallels to this regulatory approach can be found in EU health and safety, environmental protection and data protection regulation, amongst others. The proposal is, however, open about whether self- or co-regulation should be used to implement their solution.

Ullrich[565] has proposed a duty of care standard along a technical compliance framework that obliges platforms to deploy a risk-based approach towards the identification and removal of illegal content, similar to approaches used in fraud detection. The conceptual framework follows that of *Woods/Perrin, Verbiest/Spindler/Riccio* and *Busch*. The definition of public interests that platforms need to safeguard (equivalent to the definition of harms) is translated into essential technical and procedural requirements that these platforms need to fulfil as responsible actors. Compliance with these essential requirements could be achieved through a technical standard. Meeting this standard would be considered as a safe harbour from liability. The regulatory model relies on co-regulation and takes the New Approach as a blueprint. Enforcement could either be achieved through national regulators or other cooperative forms of regulatory work on EU level.

What most of these standards have in common is that the traditional distinction between active and neutral hosts would become obsolete or at

---

562 *Waisman/Hevia*, in: International Review of Industrial Property and Copyright Law 42(7), 2011, p. 785.

563 *Perrin/Woods*, Reducing Harm in Social Media through a Duty of Care; *Woods*, in: InterMEDIA 46(4), 2018/19, p. 17, 17 et seq.

564 Great Britain and Media and Sport Department for Culture, Online Harms White Paper, 2019, available at https://www.gov.uk/government/consultations/online-harms-white-paper/online-harms-white-paper.

565 *Ullrich*, in: International Journal of Law and Information Technology 26(3), 2018, p. 226, 226 et seq.

least less important. Instead, emphasis is put on enhanced responsibilities that are proportionate to the involvement in the intermediation process and the risk exposure to illegal activity. The proposals take account of the type of content, the corporate power and the essential functionality that these intermediaries occupy in people's everyday life. However, it should be stated that there are also views that the current intermediary framework is fit for purpose and does not need to be changed.[566] Commentators point out that a further "responsibilisation" of intermediaries might lead to more opaque private speech regulation on the Internet.[567]

3.3.8.3. Illegal Content, Technical Standards and the New Approach

Most of the above proposals focus on establishing responsibility and transparency on the content management decisions taken by online platforms. The idea is that public oversight is established over how the commercial interest in content and data exploration is reconciled with the protection of public interests and fundamental rights.

One solution could be the mandating of European standards bodies to create a technical standard for duty of care regarding the various types of illegal and infringing content. Possible models could be existing principles applied in IT Security (ISO 27000), Occupational Health and Safety (ISO 45001), product standards or even transaction risk monitoring in anti-money laundering.[568] Such a standard would lay down the technical and procedural requirements for ensuring that online hosts prevent and remove illegal content in line with the public interest. These public interest principles would be set out in sector-specific legislation. Compliance with such technical standards would provide proof of conformity with an acceptable level of duty of care and immunity from content liability.

The abovementioned methodology already exists within the EU: the New Approach is a tried and trusted regulatory solution, in which indus-

---

566 For example: *Savin*, EU Internet Law, p. 173; and *EDRi*, Open Letter on Intermediary Liability Protections in the Digital Single Market, 28 April 2015, available at https://edri.org/open-letter-on-intermediary-liability-protections-in-the-digital-single-market/.

567 *Belli/Sappa*, in: JIPITEC 8, 2017, p. 183; *Frosio*, in: Northwestern University Law Review 112, 2017, p. 20.

568 Cf., e.g., *Perrin/Woods*, Reducing Harm in Social Media through a Duty of Care; *Ullrich*, in: International Journal of Law and Information Technology 26(3), 2018, p. 226.

try-led standardisation is a key component and could potentially be adapted to the problem at hand.[569] It has been considered one of the success stories of European integration.[570] Meanwhile, the EU has continuously reformed its standardisation policy and committed to expand it to the Digital Single Market.[571] Standards could be adopted on a sectorial level to different types of platforms and content, eventually covering the entire ISP sector. Platforms would need to overhaul their risk management activities, making legal compliance a core element of their commercial risk management. The regulator would have authority to review the content (risk) management choices and processes of these platforms and test whether public interest criteria are being respected.

Co-regulation also means that the process of standard creation would be managed by industry, but regulators would be involved in this process and oversee whether the public interest criteria are being adequately reflected in the standard design and implementation. This would entail the review of and involvement in major decisions, from algorithm design of infringement detection and removal systems to procedural arrangements for notice and takedown or statutory reporting. Duty of care is, therefore, not only focussed on preventive actions. A holistic system would also ensure that procedural rights are being observed. It would prescribe formal notice and takedown as well as automated takedown procedural requirements, such as for example the content of notifications, processing times, information requirements to users and counter claim procedures. The standard would also prescribe regular and harmonised statutory reporting by platforms to the public and to regulatory authorities, with some information only being accessible to the regulator.

3.3.8.4. Duty of Care for Internet Intermediaries in the EU Framework

Recital 48 of the ECD gives Member States the option to impose reasonable duties of care on intermediary service providers in order to detect and

---

569 *Quintel/Ullrich*, Self-Regulation of Fundamental Rights? The EU Code of Conduct on Hate Speech, Related Initiatives and Beyond, pp. 18–19.

570 *Van Gestel/Micklitz*, in: Common Market Law Review 50(1), 2013, p. 145, 156–157.

571 Commission Communication on ICT Standardisation Priorities for the Digital Single Market, COM(2016) 176 final, available at https://ec.europa.eu/digital-sin gle-market/en/news/communication-ict-standardisation-priorities-digital-single-market.

prevent certain illegal activities. It is not clear whether Member States have made concrete use of these provisions. Courts in EU Member States have, however, since the start of the ECD made use of the duty-of-care doctrines in their national laws when adjucating on content liability questions regarding intermediaries.[572]

The first calls for more formalised duties of care to be imposed on intermediaries have arisen out of public consultations.[573] They have mainly been voiced by holders of intellectual property rights and parties interested in the protection of children's rights, product safety or combating hate speech. However, the consultations also show that stakeholders have a different understanding of the scope of duties of care. Intermediaries themselves tend to limit duty of care to the fulfilment of notice-and-takedown obligations and purely voluntary engagements. Other parties tend to extend this to proactive mechanisms of identifying and preventing harms and violations, which could be imposed as obligations.[574]

The Commission has so far referred sparingly to duty of care in its policy documents, although a 2017 European Parliament study has taken up this concept.[575] Nevertheless, the repeated intention to encourage and mandate more proactive measures that platforms should take to fight illegal content can be seen as a readiness to consider that platforms may step up their responsibilities in the fight against illegal content. This shines clearly through in the 2016 Communication on Platforms in the Digital Single Market, where the Commission vows to encourage more proactive, voluntary measures by platforms to fight illegal content and to review the need for formal notice-and-takedown procedures.[576]

---

572 *Verbiest/Spindler/Riccio*, Study on the Liability of Internet Intermediaries, pp. 58–61, 100.

573 Cf. Commission, Summary of the Results of the Public Consultation on the Future of Electronic Commerce in the Internal Market and the Implementation of the Directive on Electronic Commerce (2000/31/EC), available at https://ec.euro pa.eu/information_society/newsroom/image/document/2017-4/consultation_su mmary_report_en_2010_42070.pdf; Synopsis Report of the Commission, supra (fn. 511), p. 19; as well as the Commissions' Summary of Responses to the Public Consultation on the Evaluation and Modernisation of the Legal Framework for IPR Enforcement, 2016, available at http://ec.europa.eu/DocsRoom/docume nts/18661, pp. 36–39, 50–52.

574 Synopsis Report of the Commission, supra (fn. 511), pp. 19–20; Summary Report IFPR enforcement, ibid., p. 44.

575 *Sartor*, Providers Liability: From the eCommerce Directive to the future.

576 COM(2016) 288 final, supra (fn. 499), p. 9; *Helberger/Pierson/Poell*, in: The Information Society 34(1), 2018, p. 1, 11.

Both the 2017 Communication and the subsequent Recommendation one year later (cf. also above Chapter 2.5.3) aim at clarifying the role of intermediary service providers at tackling illegal content. There is a stronger commitment towards encouraging platforms to take more proactive responsibilities. However, any binding and mandatory measures on proactively identifying illegal content and being involved in its prevention do not seem to be part of overarching horizontal efforts. Rather, the Commission hinted at making this kind of activities binding through sectoral legislation, such as harmful and illegal content in audiovisual media services or for copyright violations.[577] Meanwhile, in the Recommendation online service providers are held to act in proportionate and diligent manner when it comes to identifying and removing illegal content.[578] Here, too, a stronger emphasis on proactive measures to be taken by intermediaries is noticeable.[579] Still, so far the Commission initiatives are limited to non-binding commitments at a horizontal level.

3.3.9. Intermediary Liability Provisions in Sectoral Legislation

As exposed above (Chapter 2.4), there are numerous legislative acts of the EU that deal with some form of responsibility of service providers for content disseminated by them, irrespective of whether it was created by the provider itself. The provisions introduced there are reviewed in the following in order to compare them with the approach taken by the ECD on liability and are supplemented by some further examples of provisions outside of the Digital Single Market context.

3.3.9.1. Sectoral Provisions in Digital Single Market Acts

3.3.9.1.1. Audiovisual Media Services Directive

The Commission had announced an update of the AVMSD as part of its Digital Single Market strategy in 2016. The revised AVMSD was one element of its sectoral, problem-driven approach aimed at putting new provi-

---

577 COM(2017) 555 final, supra (fn. 394), p. 12.
578 Commission Recommendation on measures to effectively tackle illegal content online, supra (fn. 395), Recitals 17, 27.
579 Ibid., para. 18, 36, 37.

sions in place to protect minors from harmful and illegal content on VSPs. For that purpose, VSPs had to be brought within the scope of the updated AVMSD. However, VSPs are habitually qualified as intermediary service providers and therefore subject to the liability immunities of the ECD. The new AVMSD therefore needed to impose new obligations on these VSPs to deal with illegal and harmful content that respect the framework of the ECD's Art. 14 and 15. Indeed, Art. 28a and 28b, which create new provisions applicable to VSPs, ensure that the measures imposed apply without prejudice to the liability provisions of the ECD.[580]

VSPs are held to protect minors from specific content and fulfil other requirements applying to commercial communications. In addition, Member States are obliged to ensure that VSPs take appropriate measures that shall be "determined in light of the nature of the content in question, the harm it may cause, the characteristics of the category of persons to be protected as well as the rights and legitimate interests at stake, including those of the video-sharing platform providers and the users having created or uploaded the content as well as the general public interest"[581].

These obligations impose a de facto duty of care on VSPs. Having to gauge protective measures to the content in question, the harms, and the user rights and interests at stake does require an *ex ante* risk assessment. Following that assessment, the VSP would then need to take preventive measures that target the risks they have identified. The legal text proposes some of these measures that VSPs would be expected to take. These include flagging and reporting mechanisms, age verification systems, content rating or parental control systems.[582] Member States need to ensure that these measures are being applied by VSPs.[583] On a practical level this means national regulators should be in a position to judge on the adequacy of the risk assessment and the proportionality of the risk responses developed by VSPs.

Despite these comprehensive provisions, the limitations imposed by the general monitoring prohibition of Art. 15 ECD remain in place. The text warns against measures put in place by platforms leading to "ex-ante control measures and upload filters".[584] This is supposed to warrant against any indiscriminate filtering and content suppression by platforms. In prac-

---

580 Art. 28a para. 5, Art. 28b para. 1 and 3, Recital 48 AVMSD.
581 Art. 28b para. 3 sentence 1 AVMSD.
582 Art. 28b para. 3 sentence 7 AVMSD.
583 Art. 28b para. 3 sentence 2 AVMSD.
584 Art. 28b para. 3 sentence 2 AVMSD.

tical terms, a proper risk assessment by the VSP and subsequent focus on the specific risks in the context of the harms identified by Art. 28b para. 1 AVMSD should not result in general monitoring. The support of co-regulatory measures (along self-regulation)[585] fits within the Digital Single Market framework. It would be an opportunity for the European Regulators Group for Audiovisual Media Services (ERGA) to drive the creation of industry standards around the abovementioned measures prescribed by the AVMSD.[586]

Overall Art. 28a and 28b constitute a comprehensive substantiation at sectorial level of the conditions VSPs need to meet before they can avail themselves of the immunities offered by the ECD. Critical points are that regulators will need to be careful not to impose measures that stray into conflict with Art. 15 ECD and that the AVMSD covers only VSPs in its extended scope. If the same content and harms are found on other types of intermediary service providers, a different regulatory scheme may apply. This may lead to unnecessary legal fragmentation. Therefore, it is important to clarify at least what determines an essential functionality of a service which then in turn allows that service – e.g. a social media service – to be qualified as VSP if that functionality is the sharing of videos. Insofar the Commission guidelines that will be issued in this respect will have an important impact.[587]

3.3.9.1.2. DSM Directive

The recently passed DSM Directive supplements the ECD liability provisions. The newly defined category of online content-sharing service provider clearly targets profit-making user-generated content platforms (including VSPs) and peer-to-peer networks that are in direct competition with online streaming services for audio and video content.[588]

---

585 Art. 28b para. 2 sentence 4 AVMSD, Recitals 49, 58.
586 Art. 30 AVMSD.
587 Cf. further on this *Cole*, Guiding Principles in establishing the Guidelines for Implementation of Article 13 (6) AVMSD; *Weinand*, Implementing the EU Audiovisual Media Services Directive, pp. 666 et seq.
588 Art. 2 para. 6 and Recital 62 DSM Directive: not-for-profit online encyclopedias, not-for-profit educational and scientific repositories, open source software-developing-and-sharing platforms, online marketplaces and business-to-business cloud services are explicitly excluded from the definition.

In contrast to the revised AVMSD, the new DSM Directive interferes directly with the availability of the liability immunities in the ECD. It denies any content-sharing service provider that gives the public access to copyright-protected works uploaded by its users the immunities offered in Art. 14 para. 1 ECD.[589] According to the interpretation of EU copyright law, these providers engage in direct acts of publication or reproduction and would therefore incur primary liability for copyright breaches. This appears to be in line with recent case law of the EU, such as for example in *Pirate Bay*[590].

As a result, the bulk of user-generated content platforms, such as YouTube, Dailymotion and arguably also Facebook, which had been at the centre of copyright holders' discontent, would find themselves outside the safe-harbour protections for these kinds of activities. One could stop the analysis here since the intermediary immunities of the ECD are not any longer available for these platforms. Nevertheless, a review of the measures online-content-sharing providers need to take in order to avoid primary liability for copyright violations shall still be of interest.

Art. 17 para. 1 DSM Directive obliges these intermediaries to obtain the authorisation of the rights holders for copyright-protected content, for example by concluding licensing agreements. Where an authorisation was not available, the provider would need to prove that they have made best efforts to obtain such an authorisation, prevent the availability of unlicensed content according to professional diligence standards and remove it expeditiously upon reception of a notice.[591] This provision requires content-sharing providers to act essentially as diligent operators.

The providers' efforts shall be judged by taking into account its size and business model as well as the cost and availability of suitable means to prevent unlicensed content.[592] It has been argued that these measures *de facto* impose automated filtering systems (upload filters) on providers due to the sheer amount of content hosted by these platforms.[593] If that is true, than the measures go beyond the wide-reaching proactive obligations which the legal framework would likely have prevented to impose under the current

---

589 Art. 17 para. 1 DSM Directive.
590 CJEU, judgement of 25.4.2017, C-527/15, *Stichting Brein v Jack Frederik Wullems*; *Rosati*, in: European Intellectual Property Review 39(12), 2017, p. 737, 737 et seq.
591 Art. 17 para. 4 DSM Directive.
592 Art. 17 para. 5 DSM Directive.
593 *Henrich*, Nach der Abstimmung ist (fast) vor der Umsetzung; cf. already Chapter 2.4.4.2.

Art. 15 ECD. Still, one could argue that in the AVMSD the legislating bodies of the EU found an acceptable way around this.

The AVMSD and the DSM Directive represent two possible avenues of development for the future of intermediary service provider liability. The AVMSD way would see the current liability immunities being upheld. Their availability would, however, be more tightly regulated and subject to more prescriptive proactive and reactive obligations along *de facto* duty-of-care responsibilities. The alternative way, pursued by the DSM Directive, would see those intermediary service providers whose activities affect the substantive law of the content or the offers in question to be primarily liable. As a result, they would fall outside the scope of the safe harbours of the ECD for this kind of violations. The risk would be that one and the same intermediary may be subject to different liability provisions – possibly for the same kind of content if that content is subject to different rights violations.

3.3.9.2. Other Rules Complementing the ECD Liability Provisions

3.3.9.2.1. InfoSoc and Enforcement Directive

Art. 8 para. 3 of the InfoSoc Directive gives rights holders the ability to apply for injunctions against intermediaries used by a third party to infringe copyright or related rights. This is supported by the IPRED, which in Art. 9 para. 1 provides for the availability of provisional and final injunctions against intermediaries as per the InfoSoc Directive. Both pieces of legislation apply without prejudice to the liability provisions of the ECD.[594] These early provisions merely supplement the ECD in that they specify the kind of sanctions that are available against intermediaries in case of intellectual property violations (cf. also above Chapter 3.3.7.3).[595]

---

594 Recital 16 InfoSoc Directive; Art. 2 para. 3 lit. a IPRED.
595 See on copyright related aspects also *Nordemann*, Liability of Online Service Providers for Copyrighted Content.

3.3.9.2.2. 2016 Guidance Note to the Unfair Commercial Practices Directive

A number of sectorial regulations have recently tried to take account of the fact that online platforms or intermediary service providers host an increasing variety of content. While the Unfair Commercial Practices Directive itself offers no link to the ECD, the Commission's 2016 Guidance note clarifies in detail the interface between obligations on online marketplaces that act as traders and the liability immunities under Art. 14 para. 1 ECD.[596]

Online platforms or marketplaces may qualify as traders according to Art. 2 lit. b of the Directive when they charge a commission on transactions between suppliers and users, offer additional paid services or derive revenue from targeted advertising. They would engage in business-to-consumer commercial practices if their actions are directly connected to promotion, sale or supply of products to consumers.[597] If a platform fulfils these conditions, and the assumption in the document is that most online marketplaces today would, they are subject to professional diligence requirements (also referred to as a standard of special skills and care) towards consumers.[598] These duties are complementary to the exemptions established under Art. 14 ECD.[599] The document cites Art. 1 para. 3 of the ECD, which states that the latter applies without prejudice to the level of protection of public health and consumer interests.[600] It therefore argues that online platforms that are considered as traders and that do not fulfil their

---

596 Commission staff working document, Guidance on the implementation/application of Directive 2005/29/EC, accompanying the document Communication from the Commission on a comprehensive approach to stimulating cross-border e-Commerce for Europe's citizens and businesses, SWD/2016/0163 final, https://eur-lex.europa.eu/legal-content/EN/TXT/?uri=CELEX%3A52016SC0163, pp. 121–129.

597 Directive 2005/29/EC of the European Parliament and of the Council of 11 May 2005 concerning unfair business-to-consumer commercial practices in the internal market and amending Council Directive 84/450/EEC, Directives 97/7/EC, 98/27/EC and 2002/65/EC of the European Parliament and of the Council and Regulation (EC) No 2006/2004 of the European Parliament and of the Council ('Unfair Commercial Practices Directive'), OJ L 149, 11.6.2005, pp. 22–39; Commission, Unfair Commercial Practices Directive Guidance, supra (fn. 596), p. 122.

598 Art. 2 lit. h Directive 2005/29/EC.

599 Commission, Unfair Commercial Practices Directive Guidance, supra. (fn. 596), p. 123.

600 Ibid., p. 126.

professional due diligence requirements would not be able to invoke the liability immunities of the ECD. The professional diligence requirements would consist of enabling relevant third parties to comply with EU consumer and marketing law. Examples given are "enabling relevant third party traders to clearly indicate that they act, vis-à-vis the platform users, as traders" and "designing their web-structure in a way that enables third party traders to present information to platform users in compliance with EU marketing and consumer law".[601] Unfair practices would include any misleading information provided on the characteristics of the product that influence the decision to buy[602] or omissions that the consumer needs to make an informed purchase decision.[603]

If enforced, these provisions would follow the regulatory avenue taken by the DSM Directive. Intermediary service providers acting as traders would need to meet first the professional diligence requirements of EU consumer law. This would make the protections of the ECD for online marketplaces practically obsolete.

3.3.9.2.3. Regulation on Market Surveillance and Compliance of Products

In 2017, the Commission published a notice on the market surveillance of products sold online.[604] The document noted the increasing challenges of protecting consumer health and safety posed by the rise in e-commerce and a sale of non-compliant and unsafe products. The fight against unsafe and non-compliant non-food and food products via online marketplaces is part of the Commission's horizontal strategy to tackle illegal information online.[605]

This Regulation does not provide any new responsibilities on online platforms relating to the sale of products by third party sellers. However it establishes a link between the rise in e-commerce and complex global supply chain and problems in enforcing product safety rules.[606] While uphold-

---

601 Ibid.
602 Art. 6 para. 1 lit. a, b and f of Directive 2005/29/EC.
603 Art. 7 of Directive 2005/29/EC.
604 Commission Notice on the market surveillance of products sold online, C/2017/5200, OJ C 250, 1.8.2017, pp. 1–19.
605 COM(2017) 555 final, supra (fn. 394), p. 3.
606 Recital 13 of Regulation (EU) 2019/1020 of the European Parliament and of the Council of 20 June 2019 on market surveillance and compliance of products

ing the liability framework of Art. 12–15 ECD[607], it imposes on information society service providers an obligation to cooperate with market surveillance authorities in specific cases in order to eliminate the risks posed by products offered online.[608] It also gives market surveillance authorities powers to restrict access to "online interfaces" with non-compliant or illegal product offers.[609] An online interface is a website operated by an economic operator or on behalf of it,[610] e.g. by an online marketplace.[611]

The Regulation stops short of including information society service providers in the list of economic operators with supply chain responsibilities for product safety and consumer protection. At least the preparatory documents during the drafting phase of the Regulation show that some Member States wanted to include online platforms in the list of economic operators and asked for stronger enforcement tools against online platforms.[612] The regulation does, however, include so-called fulfilment service providers as a new type of economic operators.[613] These companies help pure e-commerce sellers to store and ship products to customers. They are enablers of e-commerce. The political will to allocate responsibilities to these new logistics platforms is a sign of how difficult it has been in the past for market surveillance authorities to enforce product safety rules within the thriving activity of online marketplaces. Many of these companies have contributed to the boom of sellers from outside the EU who market products directly to European customers.[614] It is interesting to note

---

and amending Directive 2004/42/EC and Regulations (EC) No 765/2008 and (EU) No 305/2011, OJ L 169, 25.6.2019, pp. 1–44.

607 Recital 16, Art. 1 para. 4 Regulation (EU) 2019/1020 (Goods Package).

608 Art. 7 para. 2 Regulation (EU) 2019/1020 (Goods Package).

609 Recital 41, Art. 14 para. 3 lit. k point (ii) of Regulation (EU) 2019/1020 (Goods Package).

610 Art. 3 para. 15 of Regulation (EU) 2019/1020 (Goods Package).

611 For more detail: *Ullrich*, in: Maastricht Journal of European and Comparative Law 26(4), 2019, p. 558.

612 Commission Staff Working Document – Impact Assessment – Proposal for a Regulation of the European Parliament and of the Council Laying down Rules and Procedures for Compliance with and Enforcement of Union Harmonisation Legislation on Products – SWD(2017) 466 final – Part 2/4 447; *Technopolis Group*, Ex-post evaluation of the application of the market surveillance provisions of Regulation (EC) No 765/2008.

613 Art. 3 para. 11 and 13, Recital 13 of Regulation (EU) 2019/1020 (Goods Package).

614 *Ullrich*, in: Maastricht Journal of European and Comparative Law 26(4), 2019, p. 558, 570–572.

that it will be relevant to understand how in the future companies that have reduced responsibilities as an information society service reconcile this with the enhanced product compliance responsibilities they might have as fulfilment service providers.

3.3.9.2.4. Directive on Combating Terrorism

The Directive (EU) 2017/541 on combating terrorism has a special provision that requires Member States to ensure the prompt removal of any online (and offline) content that constitutes a terrorist offence.[615] The Directive states that any efforts to remove or block access to content which constitutes a terrorist offence should be without prejudice to the ECD. It repeats the prohibitions to require service providers to generally monitor information or proactively seek facts that would indicate illegal activity (Art. 15 para. 1 ECD). It also repeats the hosting service immunities established in Art. 14 para. 1 lit. a ECD which relate to a lack of knowledge.[616] This Directive has a purely complementary and clarifying character with regard to the remedies available against intermediary service providers in the fight against terrorist content online.

3.3.9.2.5. Proposal for a Regulation on Preventing the Dissemination of Terrorist Content Online

The Commission proposed this Regulation in September 2018 in order to tackle the threat of terrorist content online (cf. more detailed above Chapter 2.4.5.2). The proposal is targeted specifically at hosting service providers in order to mitigate the use of their service for spreading terrorist offences.[617] It is currently in the EU legislative process and it will need to be seen how it evolves during the mandate of the new Commission when

---

615 Art. 3 para. 1 lit. a and Art. 5 of Directive (EU) 2017/541 of the European Parliament and of the Council of 15 March 2017 on combating terrorism and replacing Council Framework Decision 2002/475/JHA and amending Council Decision 2005/671/JHA, OJ L 88, 31.3.2017, pp. 6–21.
616 Ibid., Recital 23.
617 Cf. on the relationship between the proposal and the ECD also *Barata*, New EU Proposal on the Prevention of Terrorist Content Online – An Important Mutation of the E-Commerce Intermediaries' Regime.

trilogue negotiations potentially will start. Its initially proposed text[618] has been significantly amended by the European Parliament. This analysis will focus on the latest version of the text[619] where it concerns the liability provisions of the ECD.

It should be noted that the proposal focusses on the *prevention* of the dissemination of terrorist content through hosting providers. It therefore touches on the core of the debate on what intermediary service providers can be asked to do proactively without losing their immunities. The Parliament amendment upholds and reaffirms the protections of the ECD immunities for intermediary service providers, where the Commission's proposal had originally sought to mandate broader proactive measures for hosting providers.[620] In particular a controversial exception that would for the first time have given the authorities the option to override the prohibition to impose general monitoring duties on hosts (Art. 15 ECD) has been deleted.[621] Meanwhile a passage that obliges hosting providers to act with duty of care regarding the prevention of terrorist content has remained in, although in significantly changed form.[622] The duty of care consists of hosting providers protecting users in a "diligent, proportionate and non-discriminatory manner" from terrorist content, while upholding the provisions of Art. 14 and 15 ECD. In addition, it now provides a useful reference to the revised AVMSD by stating that video-sharing service providers would be bound by Art. 28b of that Directive.[623]

Art. 6, originally named "proactive measures", is now called "specific measures". In fact, any of the 33 references to proactive measures in the Commission's proposal has been either deleted or replaced by the Parliament. Since the proposal is aimed at the prevention of terrorist content, this might have been considered redundant. However, as becomes clear through the amended version of Art. 6, one of the main objectives of the Parliament was to ensure that hosting providers would not be incited to engage in unduly broad preventive monitoring activities that could lead to conflict with Art. 15 para. 1 ECD. For example, the amended proposal now

---

618 COM/2018/640, supra. (fn. 369).
619 European Parliament legislative resolution of 17 April 2019 on the proposal for a regulation of the European Parliament and of the Council on preventing the dissemination of terrorist content online TA/2019/0421, available at https://eur-l ex.europa.eu/legal-content/EN/TXT/?uri=EP:P8_TA(2019)0421.
620 Ibid., Recital 9.
621 Ibid., Recital 9.
622 Ibid., Art. 3.
623 Ibid., Art. 3 para. 2b.

allows Member States to ask those hosting providers who had received a substantial number of removal orders from authorities to put in place specific measures. These measures must not impose a general monitoring obligation or the use of automated tools.[624] Nevertheless, the fact that hosting providers still need to weigh the use of specific measures "in light of the risk and level of exposure to terrorist content" and of fundamental rights means that they are asked to engage in an *ex ante* risk assessment and balancing exercise which is characteristic of a duty of care.[625]

The proposal also obliges hosting providers to issue transparency reports on any removals and the use of automated tools. The Parliament has amended these obligations by requiring hosting providers to include more detail and data than original proposed by the Commission.[626] Again reporting obligations are an essential part of a duty of care. Art. 9–11 establish additional duties on hosting providers on content that has been taken down. These are: mechanisms on the adequacy and proportionality of automated tools, effective complaints, counter claim and information procedures for removed content.

As the proposal stands now – and, as mentioned, this is only the Parliament's position which will be subject to compromise negotiations once the Council has concluded a General Approach –, it already formalises, substantiates and steps up procedures that hosting services will need to comply with in the fight against illegal terrorist content in order to avail themselves of the immunities offered under the ECD. It therefore follows the route taken in the new AVMSD.

3.3.9.2.6. General Data Protection Regulation

The GDPR does not contain any specific provisions that regulate the activities of Internet intermediaries. It merely mentions that it does apply without prejudice to the ECD, in particular with the liability rules of intermediaries in Art. 12–15 ECD.[627] This suggests that the GDPR and ECD are to be considered as complementary. The practical consequences of this ar-

---

624 Ibid., Art. 6 para. 4.
625 Ibid., Art. 6 para. 1.
626 Ibid., Art. 8.
627 Recital 21, Art. 2 para. 4 GDPR, supra (fn. 20); cf. on the relationship between GDPR and ECD also *de Gregorio*, The e-Commerce Directive and GDPR: Towards Convergence of Legal Regimes in the Algorithmic Society?

rangement are, however, far from clear due to open language in both acts. The ECD itself states in Art. 1 para. 5 lit. b that it "shall not apply to questions relating to information society services covered by Directives 95/46/EC and 97/66/EC" (the data protection and privacy in telecommunication rules at the time: cf. in detail already Chapter 2.4.3). Suffice to state here that so far conflicts between data protection and intermediary liability rules have only developed gradually. On a conceptual level, one could argue that both provisions barely touch one another.[628] The GDPR is about the protection of privacy of data subjects. However, Internet intermediaries are involved also with considering data protection aspects when they action "right-to-be-forgotten" requests or notice-and-takedown or information requests from authorities. But these activities concern the actions of the intermediary in the course of exercising its obligations under content liability rules. Whether the intermediary executes these obligations in compliance with GDPR or not does not change the extent of the liability over the third-party content itself.

The case may be different where the breach of data and privacy protection rules are at the heart of content uploaded by a user, such as the right-to-be-forgotten or videos depicting persons that did not consent to being shown. If an intermediary was notified of this and failed to act, then the infringing activity would relate to breaches of data protection rules and the intermediary could be held (primarily) liable for that.[629] The CJEU attempted to outline that delineation in the *Google Spain* ruling.[630]

3.3.9.2.7. Platform-to-Business Regulation

The EU passed the Regulation promoting fairness for business users of online intermediation services[631] in June 2019 to address the problem of imbalances in bargaining power in the interactions between business users and online platforms.[632] The Regulation targets e-commerce market places, including collaborative platforms, app stores, social media services

---

628 For a detailed discussion of the interplay between the ECD's intermediary liability rules and the GDPR see: *Keller*, in: Berkeley Technology Law Journal 33(1), 2018, p. 287, 354.
629 Ibid., p. 359.
630 CJEU, *Google Spain v AEPD*, supra (fn. 79), para. 38
631 Regulation (EU) 2019/1150, supra (fn. 364).
632 Ibid., Recital 2.

and online search engines (cf. already Chapter 2.4.5.1 in detail).[633] While no reference exists to the ECD, the regulation clearly identifies these services as information society service providers according to Directive 2015/1535.[634] Although restricted to commercial users of platforms, the regulation makes provisions that can be of interest in the debate over the liability immunities for hosting providers under the ECD. Search engines, for example, will need to disclose the parameters used for ranking results and provide detail on any possibilities that exist for users to influence rankings.[635]

Other online intermediation services need to disclose differential treatment given to those users which they control directly.[636] This would include details on access given to data for users which are controlled by the intermediation service, internal pricing information relating to rankings, setting or technical services or functionalities.[637] Furthermore, online intermediation services need to give business users details on what access they have to general and personal data provided by the user or generated by the user on the platform.[638] The transfer of data through third parties also needs to be disclosed and the purpose explained, with the possibility for the business user to opt out from this activity.[639]

The motivations for this Regulation and its provisions really throw further doubt on the adequacy and timeliness of the current liability immunities of the ECD, which rest on the mere technical, automatic and passive nature of the activities of intermediary service providers. It can be argued that any online intermediation service provider that would, under this Regulation, disclose differential treatment and far-reaching accesses to, and

---

633 Ibid., Recitals 6, 11, Art. 1 para. 2.
634 Ibid., Art. 2 para. 2 lit. a; Directive (EU) 2015/1535 of the European Parliament and of the Council of 9 September 2015 laying down a procedure for the provision of information in the field of technical regulations and of rules on Information Society services, OJ L 241, 17.9.2015, pp. 1–15.
635 Regulation (EU) 2019/1150, supra (fn. 364), Art. 5.
636 Ibid., Art. 7. A typical example would be differences in display or ranking of a product sold by Amazon as opposed to the same product sold on the Amazon marketplace by a third party seller. Cf. Commission, press release of 17.7.2019, Antitrust: Commission opens investigation into possible anti-competitive conduct of Amazon, available at https://ec.europa.eu/commission/presscorner/detail/en/ip_19_4291.
637 Art. 7 of Regulation (EU) 2019/1150, supra (fn. 364).
638 Ibid., Art. 9.
639 Ibid., Art. 9 para. 2 lit. d.

exploitation of, user data[640] can hardly claim to be a passive host under the ECD. A future Digital Services Act by the EU should take note of this Regulation when redrafting the liability conditions for intermediary service providers.

---

640 Which is part of the business model of Web 2.0 platforms.

4. Towards a Future Regulatory Framework for Online Content

In this section the findings of the study above are reflected in view of a possible future re-orientation of the EU regulatory framework applicable to providers disseminating online content. The problems and new approaches displayed above will be summarised in order to understand which avenues could be explored taking into consideration some framework conditions.

4.1. Lessons Learnt

4.1.1. Difficulties in the Application of the ECD

The unabated occurrence and rise of illegal content and activity promulgated through platforms which are ISS and therefore fall under the scope of the ECD have thrown doubts on whether liability protections that were conceived in a different technological and socio-economic context still can be valid today. In particular, the study highlighted three key issues in this regard. The principal idea for setting up a liability framework granting privileges to intermediaries was based on the idea that they fulfil the condition of neutrality. The study has shown that this starting point cannot be upheld as a rule any longer and poses problems in that it contradicts the approach of having more active platforms when it comes to monitoring for illegal content. A further problematic area has been to determine the exact meaning of the notion "actual knowledge" which is a requirement for the liability privilege being lost by a service provider in connection with illegal content. This is especially true as there is until today an absence of any more formalised notice requirements from which actual knowledge could "automatically" be derived, as well as an unclarity of the protection for "Good Samaritan" efforts by intermediaries. A final problem that has surfaced clearly in the case law concerning the interpretation of the ECD is the technological tension between Art. 14 and 15 ECD, which, on the one hand, allow for specific infringement prevention injunctions against service providers but prohibit, on the other hand, general monitoring obligations by these.

The application of the ECD and the national transpositions of it over the last nearly two decades have brought to the fore further problems. The Directive was based on the country-of-origin principle and thereby the approach that there would be one Member State that uses its jurisdiction power where necessary vis-à-vis established providers on their territory. From the outset the ECD was framed in a way that exceptional derogations from the country-of-origin principle were possible, as there was an assumption that there should be a backstop in case of problems concerning certain overarching goals and enforcement measures. However, the procedure, which resembles exceptional derogation procedures of the AVMSD, turned out to be complex, burdensome and lengthy and has therefore been rarely used irrespective of the fact that Member States or their competent authorities have in the past been pointing out enforcement shortcomings. Therefore, this procedure alone has not proven to be a sufficient approach to reconcile legitimate protection interests with the fundamental principle of country-of-origin.

A final issue that has been creating difficulties in the application of the ECD is that beyond its limited number of substantial provisions already the categorisation of specific information society services to which the liability regime applies in different levels has turned out to be no longer reflective of the reality of intermediaries fulfilling these and combined functions today. The definitions or categories of service provider functions have also not been so clear that there would not have been disputes about the application to certain specific types of providers, which is obvious from even very recent case law.

4.1.2. New Actors, New Approaches and New Regulatory Models

One of the results of the difficulty in applying merely the definition of information society services which dates back to 1998 and only having a limited amount of specific subcategories established in the ECD is a differentiation of definitions to different types of (sometimes new) actors in different legislative acts. This is especially clear in several of the legislative acts of the Digital Single Market strategy of the Juncker Commission. Not only did the AVMSD introduce the notion of video-sharing platform providers, the DSM Directive addresses for an important part of the Directive online content-sharing service providers, the P2B Regulation establishes rules for certain online intermediary services and the proposed TERREG concerns hosting service providers but addresses these in a new manner. These are illustrative examples showing that there is no clarity any longer about the categories of providers active in the online environment; thus it has obviously been difficult to formulate even some horizontally designed provisions in a way that they target all online providers. An important challenge lies therefore in the consistency of regulatory approaches in the online environment, already in defining the scope of application also with a view to other existing legislative acts or attempting at finding a new horizontally applicable categorisation.

New solutions to the problems mentioned above see a move away from liability immunities to formulating explicit responsibilities for these new online platforms. In its case law the CJEU has tried to come up with some concepts such as that of the diligent economic operator. One answer would see the creation of duties of care being imposed on online platforms in the fight against illegal content. Duties of care could take account of the increasingly active role of platforms in the management and dissemination of third-party content. Specific preventive duties, following a risk-based approach, would be tied to clearly defined reactive obligations of notice and takedown and transparency reporting. Beyond the case law of the court, some new legislative acts of the EU have explicitly taken a new approach to liability of online actors even if the corresponding act explains that the ECD privileges shall remain untouched. In the revised AVMSD, for example, video-sharing platform providers are now within the scope of application, but the obligations imposed on them are subject to leaving in place the liability exemptions of the ECD. However, the obligations imposed on these service providers actually necessitate that the platforms take a much more active role in that they have to help in achieving the goal that its users comply with applicable rules concerning content dissemination. Having to undertake ex ante risk assessments and depending on the outcome concerning the potential for harm, the provider then has to implement also preventive measures. Failure to do so will result in an assumption that the platform is not complying with its obligations.

For some legislative acts there is even an explicit departure from the ECD liability regime, even though in those cases only for specific contexts in which already the CJEU jurisprudence indicated that a primary liability by the platform provider is conceivable. This is the case concerning intellectual property rights, and the DSM Directive introduces a significant obligation for online content-sharing service providers and thereby does not any longer just refer to the liability provisions of the ECD but instead acknowledges that these platforms are taking an active role in the communication to the public of certain content and therefore can be addressed also as being primarily liable. The DSM Directive creates an exception to the safe-harbour exemptions for host service providers under the ECD and requires an active role of the platform providers to obtain authorisation for the dissemination of copyrighted content. If they cannot achieve that, they have to take measures to prevent the availability of the concerned content. Irrespective of clauses limiting the liability for certain platforms and making it conditional, this is a clear change in approach to the role of platforms in EU legislation. As has been shown, this new approach can also lead to different types of liability of one provider for the same content if the content violates not only copyright but also other rights.

It is not only the DSM Directive that has an impact on the liability rules of the ECD; there are a number of other EU legislative acts that create increased duty-of-care expectations or other obligations vis-à-vis certain online service providers, namely certain types of platforms. These are expected to comply with professional due diligence requirements in light of achieving a sufficient consumer protection level. Even though the platforms concerned are not mainly dealing with dissemination of online content, it is a strong indicator of how generally the liability exemptions of the ECD are being limited again by other sectorial legislation. In some cases the new approach even entails an explicit expectation that the measures to be taken by platforms are also preventive in nature: for certain types of content there will be the need to prevent upload of content if the platform has been repeatedly used for dissemination of such illegal content.

The new legislative and policy approaches also concern a new or reinforced role of still relatively new regulatory models. In light of the difficulties of enforcement not least due to uncertainties about the role of service providers and the cross-border dimension, regulatory approaches try to include the industry and other sector players in the "regulation" of the services that are provided. The instrument with which this shall be pursued is typically a co-regulatory framework which is suggested in several legislative acts towards the Member States as a way to move forward in the implementation of that act. Most notably, the revised AVMSD refers to such models in a separate provision. The goal is to first encourage the addressees of regulatory measures to be active and to push secondly for the development of industry standards. If such self-regulatory approaches bring promising results, they have the advantage of being more direct and having a less infringing nature on fundamental rights. However, experiences so far hint more towards co-regulatory approaches which give some external monitoring body also a role when self-regulatory codes of conduct are created. In addition, the possibility of action by regulatory authorities in case of non-compliance with self-set rules is necessary (cf. also below).

In this context it is also noteworthy that recent regulatory instruments rely on the use of certain technical solutions or standards by the providers in order for them to show compliance with the obligations. Even though the national transposition phase of the DSM Directive is still ongoing, it seems clear that the obligations of Art. 17 DSM Directive will only be reachable if technical solutions are implemented.

4.1.3. Margin for Member States in Implementation: the Example of GDPR

The GDPR is an interesting example to illustrate the margin that Member States retain when implementing EU law. Although it is a Regulation and shows a strong degree of harmonisation in its detailed regulatory provisions, which typically leaves Member States little margin in implementation, it will be shown that for specific elements of the Regulation this is not the case. Compared to this, the AVMSD, for example, shows a lower degree of harmonisation which, although it increased over time (cf. on this Chapter 2.4.2.1), continues to focus on the definition of minimum standards. In particular, it allows Member States (generally) to subject media service providers under their jurisdiction to stricter rules. Such a provision in a general formulation would not work in a Regulation seeking the degree of legal harmonisation as in the case of the GDPR.

The principles relating to the processing of personal data laid down in Art. 5 GDPR do not provide for derogations or room for interpretation for Member States. This means that the principles of lawfulness, fairness, transparency, purpose limitation, data minimisation, accuracy, storage limitation, integrity, confidentially and accountability apply in all Member States. National implementation must not contradict these principles. According to Art. 23 para. 1 GDPR, Member States can deviate from these principles, the information obligations laid down in the GDPR for processors and the rights of data subjects, but only if the derogation respects the essence of the fundamental rights and freedoms and if this is a necessary and proportionate measure in a democratic society to safeguard several public interests mentioned in this Article specifically (e.g. national security or the enforcement of civil law claims). Art. 23 para. 2 GDPR defines the minimum content to which such rules must correspond (e.g. the national provisions shall contain specific provisions at least as to the purposes of the processing, the scope of the restrictions introduced, the safeguards to prevent abuse or unlawful access or transfer, etc.). It thus provides a national margin in implementation within certain limits. The lawfulness of processing standard is also largely harmonised. It contains however limited possibilities for Member States to be more specific: in particular, and this is relevant in the context of this study, in the area of data processing for journalistic purposes, but also with regard to data processing for the fulfilment of contracts or a public task (Art. 6 para. 1 lit. b) and e) GDPR) and, furthermore, as far as genetic data, biometric data or data concerning health is concerned.

In this context, the structure of supervision is also interesting, particularly with regard to the independence of the national supervisory authorities.[641] Although the setting up of supervisory authorities is in principle under the responsibility of Member States, in particular to preserve national specificities in relation to existing supervisory structures (including in the case of federal states with multiple layers of authorities in charge) and the competence of supervision, the GDPR contains specific provisions to ensure the independence of these regulators. This is mainly due to the fact that the independence of supervision is based on fundamental rights[642], the protection of which the GDPR aims to guarantee. Therefore, Member States should in particular provide that the members of national supervisory authorities are appointed by means of a transparent procedure and that they act with integrity, refrain from any action that is incompatible with their duties. Moreover, the supervisory authority should have its own staff and be provided with the financial and human resources, premises and the infrastructure necessary for the effective performance of its tasks. It should also have a separate, public annual budget.[643] This considerably limits the institutional autonomy of the Member States in assigning a competent authority for the application of the GDP rules.[644] The CJEU has already clarified with regard to the predecessor Directive that independence of supervisory authorities is an essential element of data protection law because of the fundamental rights dimension. A broad interpretation of this term is also compatible with the competences of the EU and does not violate the

---

641 Cf. on this in detail already Chapter 2.4.3.4.
642 CJEU, judgement of 9.3.2010, C-518/07, *European Commission v Federal Republic of Germany*, para. 21 et seq.
643 Cf. Recitals 120 and 121.
644 On the general question, whether and to what extent (secondary) Union law may contain requirements for the organisation of the Member States' authorities, cf. *Stöger*, in: ZöR 65(2), 2010, p. 247, 247 et seq.

principles of conferral of powers, subsidiarity and proportionality.[645] The legal restriction of the Member States' margin in implementation is therefore justified for the case of GDPR.

However, there is one area of substantive rules in the GDPR for which the details are not harmonised. This concerns specific processing situations listed in Chapter 9 GDPR. Such situations include in particular data processing for journalistic purposes (as already described in detail in Chapter 2.4.3.1.), but also for the purposes of academic, artistic or literary expression (Art. 85 GDPR), in the context of employment (Art. 88 GDPR) or relating to processing for archiving purposes in the public interest, scientific or historical research purposes, or statistical purposes (Art. 89 GDPR). These provisions highlight legal areas that are not subject to a blanket and unconditional application of the principles and competencies on which the GDPR relies but rather give Member States the possibility to apply their framework in achieving the obligatory goal.

Above all, the latter underlines that the degree of harmonisation depends on the balancing between the goals pursued by harmonisation and the interference in Member States' competences. The higher the weight to be given to an objective at Union level (e.g. fundamental rights guarantees or the independence of supervisory authorities), the stronger the argument for harmonisation. By contrast, the more a regulation interferes in Member States' competences (e.g. in media regulation as detailed in Art. 85 GDPR), the more restraint is required with regards to harmonisation. The more an objective is shaped by national interests (e.g. Art. 23 para. 1 GDPR), the stronger the need is for a national margin in implementation.

4.1.4. Institutional Dimension of Enforcement on National and EU level: the Example of the GDPR

As described in detail above (Chapter 2.4.3.5), the GDPR has established differentiated cooperation and consistency mechanisms for cross-border cooperation between competent national data protection authorities. At the "top" of this structure sits the EDPB, which has the powers both to give directions in the application of GDPR rules and to make final decisions. The EDPB can make binding decisions on disputes between competent data protection authorities from different Member States in a dispute resolution procedure in accordance with Art. 65 GDPR and, under certain

---

645 CJEU, *European Commission v Germany*, supra (fn. 642), para. 46 et seq.

circumstances, also in disregard of the assessment of the lead supervisory authority in the respective case. Although the EDPB has no means of enforcing its rights or sanctions, the binding nature of the decision can nevertheless significantly interfere with the powers of the lead supervisory authority.

4.1.4.1. The European Data Protection Board Compared to Other Sectors

Compared to other cooperation institutions established at EU level that are set up to improve the uniform and efficient application of EU rules by cross-border cooperation, these powers are considerable. For example, in the audiovisual sector, ERGA is also composed of representatives of the competent national regulatory bodies. It also has the task of providing technical expertise to the Commission, facilitating exchange and cooperation between regulators and delivering opinions at the request of the Commission, which has now been detailed in the revised AVMSD in Art. 30b. While the task of ensuring a coherent national implementation of the European requirements is the responsibility of the Commission within the framework of the AVMSD (Art. 30b para. 3 lit. a AVMSD), and ERGA only advises it in this respect (Art. 2 lit. a Commission Decision on establishing the ERGA[646]), that task is expressly assigned to the EDPB within the framework of GDPR (Art. 70 para. 1 GDPR). Accordingly, ERGA has no powers to make binding decisions vis-à-vis its members or the Member States. However, the Commission does have such binding regulatory powers: according to Art. 2 para. 5c, Art. 3 para. 2 and 3 AVMSD, the Commission can make binding decisions about the competence of a regulatory body and on the compatibility of measures taken in deviation from the country-of-origin principle with EU law. ERGA itself, by contrast, is limited to taking a position as part of this procedure. Such decision-making powers of the Commission are, in turn, unknown in the GDPR (besides the decision-making powers within the framework of adequacy decisions for the transfer of data to third countries).

Similar to ERGA, the Body of European Regulators for Electronic Communications (BEREC) is also essentially responsible for providing support,

---

646 Commission Decision of 3.2.2014 on establishing the European Regulators Group for Audiovisual Media Services, C(2014) 462 final, available at https://ec. europa.eu/digital-single-market/en/news/commission-decision-establishing-euro pean-regulators-group-audiovisual-media-services.

advice and opinions.[647] The nature of involvement of this group of regulators, which comprises a Board of Regulators (composed of one member
from each Member State) and working groups, depends on the type of procedure. Regarding the resolution of cross-border disputes arising under the
European Electronic Communications Code (EECC)[648] between undertakings in different Member States, Art. 27 para. 2 and 3 EECC, for example,
provide for an involvement of BEREC. Where the dispute affects trade between Member States, the competent national regulatory authority or authorities shall notify the dispute to BEREC in order to bring about a
consistent resolution of the dispute, in accordance with the objectives set
out in Art. 3 EECC. In this scenario, BEREC shall issue an opinion inviting
the national regulatory authority or authorities concerned to take specific
action in order to resolve the dispute or to refrain from action.

However, any obligations imposed on an undertaking by the national
regulatory authority as part of the resolution of the dispute shall (inter
alia) only take the *utmost* account of the opinion adopted by BEREC
(Art. 27 para. 5 EECC). This does not imply any power of last resort. In the
context of the procedure for consolidating the internal market for electronic communications (Art. 32 EECC), the EECC provides on the other hand
for another distribution of tasks than, for example, the abovementioned
EECC rules on the resolution of cross-border conflicts or the rules laid
down by the AVMSD or the GDPR. Art. 32 para. 1 EECC states that
"[n]ational regulatory authorities shall contribute to the development of
the internal market by working with each other and with the Commission
and BEREC, in a transparent manner, in order to ensure the consistent application, in all Member States, of this Directive". The Directive therefore
considers that ensuring a coherent application of the Directive is a common task for the parties concerned. However, and without going into detail regarding the respective rules of the EECC, in order to enhance
consistent regulatory practice across the Union, the Commission may require the national regulatory authority to withdraw certain of its draft
measures, where BEREC shares the Commission's serious doubts as to the

---

647 Cf. Art. 4 of Regulation (EU) 2018/1971 of the European Parliament and of the
     Council of 11 December 2018 establishing the Body of European Regulators for
     Electronic Communications (BEREC) and the Agency for Support for BEREC
     (BEREC Office), amending Regulation (EU) 2015/2120 and repealing Regu-
     lation (EC) No 1211/2009, OJ L 321, 17.12.2018, pp. 1–35.
648 Directive (EU) 2018/1972 of the European Parliament and of the Council of
     11 December 2018 establishing the European Electronic Communications Code
     (Recast), OJ L 321, 17.12.2018, pp. 36–214.

compatibility of the draft measure with EU law and in particular with the regulatory objectives of this Directive.[649] Therefore, although the involvement of BEREC is essential for making a decision, the power to take the actual decision lies with the Commission.

4.1.4.2. Essential Factors for Institutional Organisation

These differences in the distribution of competences and tasks to regulatory authorities on cooperation structures can be attributed to the diversity of the regulatory subject matters and to their relation to the levels of harmonisation, legislative competence, the marketplace principle and the limits that result from the regulatory area concerned. These factors make the institutional arrangement of the GDPR meaningful and, to a certain degree, even necessary. However, as will be shown, these factors find their limits in the media privilege principle. Therefore, this aspect needs to be considered when thinking about whether such structures of the GDPR could be transferred to other areas in the domain of online content dissemination.

As already described in Chapter 4.1.3, the GDPR achieves a high level of harmonisation if compared to other EU provisions in the online context such as the AVMSD, both with regard to the applicable law itself and its enforcement. Against this background, it seems consistent that the EDPB is granted final decision-making powers where the law of the Member States has been harmonised and where a cross-border situation is concerned. The extensive harmonisation of data processing principles, (partially) harmonised legal bases for processing and the largely uniform granting of rights for data subjects are factors that enable the EDPB to base its (binding) opinions and decisions on a set of rules that are already compulsory in all Member States. It therefore does not need to consider the national implementations in the 28 Member States. This makes it also easier to decide on cross-border issues. On the other hand, the AVMSD, for example, limits itself to granting the ERGA powers to deliver opinions. This ensures that national interests and particularities with regard to media law are taken into account and that the Commission's decisions are limited to the examination of compatibility with EU law. It would therefore be difficult to conceive a cooperation structure like ERGA in this context in a way that it would resemble the EDPB, not only considering that the Member

---

649 Cf. on this also Recitals 154 and 201 EEC.

States are even given deviation possibilities from the country-of-origin principle but also because of the differing task as far as cross-border issues are concerned.[650]

The powers of the EDPB end where the harmonisation remit of the GDPR ends: according to Art. 70 para. 1 GDPR, "[t]he EDPB shall ensure the consistent application of this Regulation". Regarding the dispute resolution by the EDPB, the GDPR stipulates in Art. 65 para. 1 that, "[i]n order to ensure the correct and consistent application of this Regulation in individual cases, the Board shall adopt a binding decision [...]". The GDPR recognises therefore in principle that there are areas in data protection law which do not necessitate a "consistent application". The advantages of the simplified decision-making through the powers conferred to the EDPB for areas falling under a standardised legal basis do not work for these specific scenarios. That applies in particular to the media privilege in Art. 85 GDPR, where the implementation is left to the Member States, allowing, in particular, to provide for deviations from the cooperation and consistency mechanisms determined in Chapter 7 GDPR.

This, in turn, is consistent insofar as the question of the scope of the powers of a supranational "body of the Union with own legal personality" (Art. 68 para. 1 GDPR) also involves questions of competencies between Member States and the EU. For the area of data protection, a legal basis establishing competence of the EU is laid down in Art. 16 TFEU. It states that the EU shall create the rules relating to the protection of individuals with regard to the processing of personal data by Union institutions, bodies, offices and agencies, and by the Member States when carrying out activities which fall within the scope of Union law. Compliance with these rules shall be subject to the control of independent authorities. Regarding the rules relating to the free movement of data, Art. 16 para. 2 TFEU in that sense is a *lex specialis* rule compared to the general internal market provision of Art. 114 TFEU. This allows for the economic integration of data protection into the EU legal framework.[651] However, the administrative and economic focus of this provision does not allow the adaption of rules in other areas per se. This addresses in particular the regulatory areas that are excluded from the GDPR framework by Art. 85 et seq. As the EU has no explicit and comprehensive competence for regulating the media

---

650 This explicitly does not concern the question whether the ERGA could possibly be granted powers in relation to individual areas of AVMSD regulation or in relation to other regulatory matters.

651 *Kingreen*, in: Calliess/Ruffert, Art. 16 TFEU para. 4, 7.

and its function and influence during the process of public opinion making as such (cf. Chapter 2.3.2.1), GDPR cannot reach out into this areas. Even the allocation of powers to a supranational institution at EU level can therefore only be based on the distribution of competencies. This applies even if, as in the case of the EDPB, the institution is essentially composed of Member State authorities.

A further factor for the institutional arrangement in the framework of GDPR is the market location principle (cf. Chapter 2.4.3.3), which excludes, at least for the harmonised area, the application of the country-of-origin principle by Member States. Due to the far-reaching harmonisation achieved by the GDPR, which requires relatively uniform rules to be observed in the Member States, the application of the market location principle is, on the one hand, less restrictive for data processors in the Member States. Compared to this, the introduction of the market location principle in less harmonised areas, such as in the context of the new AVMSD requirements for VSPs, would be difficult to implement, especially for providers, as Member States are given a wide scope of action, especially with regard to mechanisms of self- and co-regulation. On the other hand, third-country entities can also be addressed by the EU legal framework of the GDPR, whereas, if the country-of-origin principle was to apply at EU level, it would depend on whether individual Member States had enacted regulations at national level that would allow access to such third-country data controllers or processors. Therefore, the EDPB has been given the task of issuing guidelines and issuing binding opinions or making binding decisions in order to avoid such diversity. For example, the question of "jurisdiction" is decisive for the assessment of which supervisory authority is responsible. For the questions of the (substantive) legality of processing it depends alone on the "market location", whereby the EDPB can then refer to the rules of the GDPR in evaluating the case.

4.1.4.3. The Setup between National DPAs and Their Cooperation on EU Level

Finally, the question of the delimitation of the scope of application of a regulatory area also plays a decisive role in institutional design. Economic operators which target their offers to the EU must adhere to the requirements set on EU level[652], as has been explicitly laid down in GDPR. Thus, for example, service providers must adhere to the information obligations of the GDPR when processing customer data on the basis of a contract and protect the rights of those concerned. They are subject to the supervision of a data protection authority of the respective Member State to which they direct their offer. The process for determining a lead supervisory authority facilitates those cases where a provider has targeted several Member States and would therefore be subject to different competent supervisory authorities. This shifts multiple regulatory engagements from the entrepreneur (the processor) to the area of supranational cooperation between the authorities. The far-reaching powers of the EDPB and the consistency mechanisms fit in well with these closely circumscribed cases. The data protection authorities of which the EDPB is composed can contribute their expertise and thus facilitate an easier and unified application of the law. This, however, reaches its limits where sector-specific data protection law is concerned. The media privilege or its national implementation can serve again as an example for this. Here the limits of binding decision-making powers at EU level can be illustrated particularly well by the – here simplified – example of the highly complex implementation of the media privilege in Germany:

Due to its federal nature, Germany is divided into 16 federal states (*Länder*) with legislative powers. Media law lies within the competence of the federal state legislators, whereby there are typically separate laws for private broadcasters, public broadcasters, the press, online media (so-called *Telemedien*) and, in some cases, other forms of media. The implementation of the "media privilege" has therefore led to more than 50 different individual regulatory arrangements for the media law sector in Germany. In this example, the differences in the supervision of data processing for journalistic purposes shall be highlighted.[653] In many federal states, the supervision of private broadcasting under data protection law has been delegat-

---

652 An approach which, by the way, is also followed by the Recommendation on Tackling Illegal Content Online (supra, fn. 395) when it defines a hosting service provider "irrespective of its place of establishment, which directs its activities to consumers residing in the Union".

653 For a detailed overview on this and the following, and for references to the respective laws: Institute of European Media Law, synopsis on the planned changes in national legislation to implement the 21st Amending Treaty to the Interstate Broadcasting Treaty and the GDPR, available at https://emr-sb.de/syn opse-art-85-dsgvo/; further explanations and analysis by *Ory*, in: UFITA 82(1), 2018, p. 131.

ed to the Länder regulators appointed to supervise the media in terms of content (related to the national transposition of AVMSD). This was done in view of the fact that these authorities are more closely involved in issues relating to media law (and freedom) and that supervision should be unified.[654] In other federal states, the media authorities are only obliged to monitor the area of journalistic data processing, whereby the general data protection authorities are responsible for the other types of processing. In the remaining other Länder, the general data protection authorities supervise the data processing of private broadcasters as a whole, including the journalistic data processing. The supervision of journalistic data processing in public broadcasting, on the other hand, lies with "broadcasting data protection officers" (*Rundfunkdatenschutzbeauftragte*) within the broadcasters themselves, in order to ensure that public broadcasters are not under the influence of the state by giving state authorities control powers. For the press, in turn, the federal states have predominantly opted to delegate the supervision to the German Press Council (*Deutscher Presserat*), an institution of self-regulation. Thus, in addition to the already existing 16 general state data protection authorities and the Federal Commissioner for Data Protection at the federal level, a large number of supervisory institutions are also being set up. In order to ensure that media law concerns are generally taken into account in the supervision of data protection and vice versa, cooperation mechanisms are regularly introduced into the federal state laws at the national level in order to provide for cooperation between, for example, state media authorities and data protection authorities. At EU level, there is a lack of such cooperation requirements. It is therefore necessary to rely on Member States' national implementations that they provide for cooperation mechanisms between authorities that are specific to the area and therefore closer to the subject matter.

How important media-specific considerations can also be in the context of harmonised data protection law has been shown by the *Google Spain* ruling of the CJEU[655]. It is true that the EDPB would not be authorised within the scope of application of the GDPR to make exclusive press-specific decisions. There are specific cases when in addition to the regular interests to be considered in data protection law – which are economic or public interests on the side of the processors and personal rights on the side of the

---

654 Cf. for example the Parliament of the Saarland, explanatory memorandum on the amendment of the Saarland Media Act, printed papers 16/277, available at https://www.landtag-saar.de/file.ashx?FileName=Gs16_0277.pdf, p. 30.
655 CJEU, *Google Spain SL v AEPD*, supra (fn. 79).

data subjects –also interests of the media are concerned. This is often the case in scenarios where data subjects are content creators on platforms. In such situations it would make sense to have a media regulator or a supervisory authority with that background to shape the decision. However, such an assignment is not guaranteed per se by the GDPR, which is geared to competences of the supervisory authorities in data protection matters including on EU level the EDPB.

4.1.5. Application to the ECD of Interim Findings Relating to the GDPR to the ECD

The analysis of the margin of implementation has resulted in two main conclusions: On the one hand, maximum harmonisation leads to greater legal certainty for both legal users and regulators. This applies in particular to cross-border situations, which benefit from the widest possible harmonisation of the criteria for assessment. Furthermore, this applies in particular to the establishment of standards which address matters in shared competence and where the rules of the Member States were very diverse. Contrary to this, on the other hand, harmonisation reaches its limits where matters are concerned which lie predominantly within the regulatory competence of the Member States.

The ECD contains a number of provisions which would be suitable for a high level of harmonisation, such as the information requirements for ISS. With regard to the liability rules, which are the focus of this study, however, such a generalising conclusion is not easily possible. On the one hand, this study has shown that the current design of these rules poses a great challenge to addressees and regulators against the background of the changing media landscape. The boundaries between pure intermediaries and content providers are blurred, which is why the question needs to be answered in a differentiated manner. In principle, maximum harmonisation should be achieved as far as possible. The ECD already operates in the digital environment, and its scope of application therefore naturally concerns cross-border issues. On the other hand, however, a harmonisation approach that is as broad as possible should not ignore the fact that the blurring of the boundaries between pure intermediaries and content providers has also led to a blurring of the boundaries between pure electronic commerce and media. This may call for a differentiated approach, not least in the light of fundamental rights (cf. Chapter 2.1.3) and the allocation of competences (cf. Chapter 2.3.2). Although the EU legislator is not barred to regulate media content entirely, it must take account of cultural policy concerns on the part of the Member States (cf. Chapter 2.3.1). The framework conditions presented in the context of this study and demanded in the process of evaluation could be implemented by a restrictive harmonisation approach by way of sectorial exceptions. This would in a way resemble the approach chosen by GDPR for the media privilege. If one would pursue this direction too far, however, the identified deficits of the current regulatory framework under ECD would continue due to wide areas being uncovered. Media and cultural policy interests of the Member States should be taken into account by establishing as far-reaching a regulatory approach on EU level as possible while at the same time leaving the assessment of cases relevant to media law to the national regulatory authorities. Due to the proximity and expertise of the regulators already established in the field of media supervision, these would also be a suitable contact point for monitoring and enforcement in the context of ECD.

The latter point is also linked to the question of institutional structure. The analysis in this context first and foremost emphasised that cooperation between both the Member States and the regulators of the different Member States is of essential importance and requires a foundation in EU law. This is all the more true in the context of the ECD, which already in its current approach mainly concerns cross-border cases in the (digital) internal market. The specification in Art. 19 ECD, which is limited to general requirements without the establishment of concrete procedures, does not seem sufficient for these purposes. In addition, the concrete shaping of the institutional component – in addition to the degree of harmonisation and legislative competence already mentioned – depends on factors such as the intended scope of application (in particular the country-of-origin principle or market location principle; for more details see Chapter 4.3.2) and the delimitation of the regulatory area. The more binding competences, in particular enforcement or final decision powers, are granted to the institution(s) outside or above national regulatory authorities, the narrower these factors have to be defined; the more convergent the legal material, the more difficult it is to implement a supranational regulatory structure at EU level such as in the case of GDPR with the EDPB.

In this respect, the ECD in its current form is more similar to the model of the AVMSD, especially with regard to the country-of-origin principle and the cautious harmonisation approach. In particular, it places the assessment of measures taken by a Member State against providers in another Member State with regard to their compatibility with Union law with the Commission (Art. 3 para. 6 ECD). It is therefore not set up like the

GDPR, which confers less power to the Commission, but boosts the powers of the regulatory body. It is to be assumed that, as regards the ECD, the position of the Commission will essentially remain unchanged in the future due to its proximity to the subject matter and other competences in the area of the internal market. Beside this, there is another factor which opposes the transfer of the institutional model of the GDPR or comparable models to the regulatory scope of the ECD. The ECD is not as narrowly confined to a specific area as the GDPR but takes a horizontal approach – and in that sense can be regarded as a "convergent legal basis" – that spreads across many other areas, which may each need specific institutional considerations. This is shown not only by the diversity of the addressees but also by the exemptions from the current scope of application. In this context, it would be preferable to have an institutional structure in the sense of enhanced and procedurally regulated cooperation between national regulators (e.g. in existing models such as BEREC or ERGA) in conjunction with more differentiated rules on law enforcement.

4.2. Important Considerations

In this section, before discussing possible avenues to pursue in the future, some important elements that should be considered in any reform discussion concerning the regulatory framework for online content dissemination are presented. They are elements that relate to the fundamental rights framework, in which the regulation of content dissemination takes place, and will also allow to consider alternative regulatory approaches.

4.2.1. Value-based Approach Necessitates Effective Enforcement

On the one hand, this study has shown that the dissemination of online content addresses a number of fundamental rights issues worthy of protection, which particularly applies to content harmful to minors and illegal content. The fundamental rights from both the ECHR and the CFR as well as from national constitutional provisions must be respected by the Union and its Member States in their actions, in particular when considering legislative activities. This results not only in rights positions granted to individuals against overstepping into their protected realm by state action but also – especially as far as human dignity is concerned – in positive protection obligations for these rights by the States. Such positive obligations to act concern the EU to a much lesser extent, especially since the CFR explicitly does not establish any new competences for the EU, but they are highly relevant for the Member States. They must ensure that any interferences found which are incompatible with fundamental rights can be dealt with effectively. For the regulatory authorities, this means that they must take all means at their disposal – either directly from the fundamental rights or through other legal provisions which protect these fundamental rights – to remedy and actively counteract any impairment.

The study has further shown that the EU, and thus also its Member States which have committed themselves by being members of the EU, are based on certain values and objectives which must be taken into account in their actions. One of these values is respect for human dignity and human rights, which in turn incorporates the aforementioned fundamental rights considerations into the EU's system of values. These values should not only be understood in the sense of general principles without any specific meaning or significance, but their observance is actually a prerequisite for accession to the EU and their non-compliance can lead to sanctions vis-à-vis the respective Member State in the procedure according to Art. 7 TEU. If there is a situation in the EU where these values are disregarded, then the EU and its Member States are called upon to take action. The EU can still only act within its framework of competence. Concerning illegal or harmful content online that is freely available and very harmful to minors, this observation does not necessarily mean that the EU itself or the Member States have to take specific action against specific content. They do, however, have to work towards establishing appropriate and effective systems that provide the right means for regulators or law enforcement authorities. This is reflective of the fundamental rights obligation of the regulatory authorities to use all means at their disposal to deal with interferences: if these means prove to be ineffective and unsuitable for the protection of fundamental rights after they have been taken, this can in turn result in a duty on the part of the legislature (depending on the distribution of competences) which results from the values and fundamental rights.

This finding is emphasised by the Union's objectives. These are enshrined in the TEU, including inter alia the creation of an internal market, and set out what the EU must achieve in legislative and coordinating terms. They basically lay down an "EU programme", which must also be completed by coordinated policies of the Member States in the context of the exercise of the limited powers by the EU institutions and in the relevant thematic and legal areas. This can also result in standstill obligations for the Member States, which prohibit them from counteracting the inte-

gration more closely defined by the EU's goals. It follows from the impera-
tive of loyalty to the EU that the Union, if it has seized a competence and
has comprehensively regulated a matter, is also obliged to shape this matter in such a way that the Member States in turn have the actual possibility
of fulfilling their obligations under the system of values and fundamental
rights. The effect of this can be the need for legislative action: if the national regulatory authorities have taken all means at their disposal to fulfil
their obligations under the fundamental rights framework, and if the
Member States have also taken all steps possible within their scope of competence to establish an effective system, but this turns out to be not sufficient to counter violations of fundamental rights or values, then the result
might be that the EU is obliged to take action.

In the context of the study and taking into consideration that there are
difficulties in the application of the ECD, this has another consequence.
Should there be no legislative clarification in the near future, competent
authorities will have to apply existing rules also to cross-border dissemination of content in a more proactive manner even if it may not seem clear
from the outset whether a provider targeted by them may be able to claim
a liability exemption. In light of the need for an efficient protection of fundamental rights and values, inactivity is no option. This means that even
difficulties in achieving an effective enforcement of rules cannot justify
that competent authorities do not at least attempt at reaching a most value-
respecting situation. More pragmatically spoken, this will also be a result
from the wider acknowledgement in policy and society that there are problems in the context of online content dissemination which need to be addressed by more concrete action.

4.2.2. Involvement of Industry through Self- and Co-regulatory Measures

As has been explained in detail in Chapter 2 and 3 of this study, the
question of regulating dissemination of online content is part of a complex
regulatory system involving many different legislative acts. This also results
from the fact that a large number of different stakeholders are involved in
the development, production, distribution, exploitation and marketing of
such content. The three main categories are users, content providers/
producers and distributors/platforms, which in turn are split into a number of different types of actors – much more diverse in the digital environment than in the analogue environment. While legislation and regulation
in relation to traditional content providers such as broadcasters has grown

in parallel to the technological progress, it is lagging behind against the rapid and steady development of the Internet and its intermediaries. The regulatory space has increased tremendously due to the borderless nature of the digital world, as has the technical expertise needed to create effective, appropriate and enforceable rules. For these reasons, the involvement of various stakeholders in regulatory approaches has become much more important. Below, the regulatory models of self- and co-regulation will be addressed. These approaches are said to have a number of advantages, which will be examined. Already existing and potential instruments of self- and co-regulation will also be discussed.

4.2.2.1. Defining Self- and Co-regulation

In the EU context, self-regulation has been defined as "the possibility for economic operators, the social partners, non-governmental organisations or associations to adopt amongst themselves and for themselves common guidelines at European level (particularly codes of practice or sectorial agreements)".[656] Co-regulation has been defined as a "mechanism whereby an [EU] legislative act entrusts the attainment of the objectives defined by the legislative authority to parties which are recognized in the field (such as economic operators, the social partners, non-governmental organisations, or associations)".[657] The term "regulated self-regulation" can also be found.

However, there is no uniform use of these terms or a universally valid definition at European or international level. Furthermore, the systems of self- and co-regulation differ widely in the Member States, both in terms of their design and their intensity.[658] The status given to self- and co-regulation regularly varies and may in particular depend on the extent to which a national regulatory framework exists in the area affected by self- or co-regulation. In the context of this study, the finding of a definition is not necessary. It shall suffice to clarify in this context that co-regulation depends on the interaction between a regulator and the regulated entity. While industry is still charged with creating a framework of rules and standards to which it is bound, for co-regulation to work there must be certain

---

656 Interinstitutional Agreement on Better Law-Making, 2003, OJ C 321, para. 22.
657 Ibid., para. 18.
658 *Cappello (ed.)*, Self- and Co-regulation in the new AVMSD, IRIS Special 2019-2.

review, monitoring[659] and approval mechanisms, which are overseen by regulatory authorities or quasi-regulatory bodies.[660] Breaking the rules or standards by the industry would incur legally enforceable sanctions, specified in law or administrative rules, by these bodies. Self-regulation, on the other hand, regularly takes place without external monitoring mechanisms (by outside institutions set up and operated and staffed by the regulated bodies themselves) and generally does not provide for sanctions.[661]

4.2.2.2. Advantages and Disadvantages of Self- and Co-regulation

The advantages of self-regulation and co-regulation as a more "softer law" approach are illustrated when comparing to some of the disadvantages of so-called "hard law" in the form of legislation as far as it concerns the online sector. Due to partly lengthy legislative mechanisms and procedures, it is not readily accessible to rapid adaptations due to changing market conditions or technical and societal change. If unsuitable principles are first enshrined in law or if suitable principles lose their suitability in the course of time due to external influences, tying to hard legal foundations can hinder innovation and reactive response to these changes.[662] Furthermore, there are hurdles to law enforcement, especially against foreign providers, as described in this study, for example because providers are difficult for the regulatory authorities to grasp or costly procedures have to be followed. In this context, it is worth to consider the risk of "forum shopping", which makes certain States more attractive as host countries due to a perceived lighter regulatory framework, against the background of the country-of-origin principle, which is laid down in hard legislation. Above all, online providers are not dependent on a particular location to make content accessible to any local public.[663]

Rules established through self-regulation and co-regulation may be attractive in this context for several reasons: they are not narrowly dependent on legislative processes and can be regularly adapted by the stakeholders involved. They can also be evaluated at regular intervals, allowing a rela-

---

659 *Schulz/Held*, Regulated Self-regulation as a Form of Modern Government, p. 63.
660 *Marsden*, European Law, Regulatory Governance and Legitimacy in Cyberspace, pp. 61–63.
661 Ibid., pp. 63, 227
662 Cf. *Finck*, in: LSE Law, Society and Economy Working Papers (15/2017), p. 7.
663 Cf. on this and the complex of self- and co-regulation online at whole: *Cappello (ed.)*, Self- and Co-regulation in the new AVMSD, IRIS Special 2019-2.

tively timely reaction to latest technologies and emerging problems. The latter is also one of the main arguments frequently put forward for self-regulation by the respective industry stakeholders, in particular platform providers: information asymmetry. In fact, the emergence of self-regulatory systems on the Internet appears to be a logical response to the challenges of traditional regulation with this new medium. For one, it is in the nature of this rapidly evolving area that the legislative bodies do not always have the necessary technical knowledge of the functioning of the systems concerned and of the (side) effects that a particular regulation may cause. This in conjunction with the sheer amount of content and business models has led to a "capability challenge" on the side of regulators with regards to designing effective regulation and enforcing it.[664] Secondly, the expansion of the Internet and the cross-cutting nature of content and business models call for international, cross-sectorial and innovative solutions,[665] which – given the relatively short history of the Internet and its rapid rise – have not yet emerged. Thirdly, cultural and legal traditions in Europe have been conducive to collaborative forms of regulation especially in new, emerging economic sectors and industries.[666]

In this regard, the Commission argued in its 2016 Communication on Online Platforms[667] that traditional top-down legislation reaches its limits in the platform economy and that therefore self- and co-regulatory measures are likely to stay or become even more important for that economy's future governance. In addition, it can be argued in line with Recital 13 AVMSD[668] that the mechanisms of self- and co-regulation may lead to a more effective enforcement of rules because they have been developed with the support of the regulatory subjects. In these scenarios, willingness to comply with regulatory requirements is in principle higher overall. Fi-

---

664 *Freeman*, in: Italian Antitrust Review 2(1), 2015, p. 75, 80.

665 *Cohen*, in: Theoretical Inquiries in Law, 17(2), 2016, p. 369, 375–387

666 *Marsden*, European Law, Regulatory Governance and Legitimacy in Cyberspace, pp. 67–70; *Senden et al.*, Mapping Self- and Co-regulation. Approaches in the EU Context.

667 Communication on Online Platforms and the Digital Single Market Opportunities and Challenges for Europe, COM/2016/0288 final, available at https://eur-le x.europa.eu/legal-content/EN/TXT/?uri=CELEX:52016DC0288#footnoteref21.

668 Recital 13 states: "Experience has shown that both self- and co-regulatory instruments, implemented in accordance with the different legal traditions of the Member States, can play an important role in delivering a high level of consumer protection. Measures aimed at achieving general public interest objectives in the emerging audiovisual media services sector are more effective if they are taken with the active support of the service providers themselves".

nally, it should also be pointed out that self- and co-regulatory arrangements can be more easily applied to specific and more closely circumscribed regulatory areas than legislative measures. The latter are bound to achieving a certain objective (e.g. combating hate speech or discrimination) and do not necessarily focus on regulating a certain area (e.g. obligations of platforms in the online sector). Co- and self-regulation make it easier to differentiate the targets of regulatory measures: on the one hand, only those categories or types of providers are involved in the regulatory design process that are actually affected by a particular problem or objective. On the other hand, it also facilitates the definition of regulatory addressees or categories that have to comply with certain specifications. This is particularly relevant in the area of intermediaries if one considers the large variety of platforms which each may have a completely different orientation (e.g. search engines and social networks).

In its Opinion on Self-regulation and Co-regulation in the Community legislative framework, the European Economic and Social Committee has summarised the advantages of these forms of regulation as follows: (1) they tend to promulgate comparatively new and innovative norms which announce and reflect eras of change and are often harbingers of legal progression in areas where binding rules are non-existent or insufficiently developed; (2) they are assumed to improve the substantive quality of decisions and policy making by incorporating new information obtained from the different participants; (3) they increase learning processes among the participants and in this way generate new knowledge; (4) they can strengthen the orientation of private action on the common good and on the basic values of society as well as the integration of public values into decisions; (5) they are supposed to resolve, contain or reduce conflict among competing interests and the actors involved; (6) they achieve cost-effectiveness and (7) they increase compliance with regulation via greater commitment to and support for the implementation of decisions.[669]

However, besides the fact that this enumeration shows an ideal model situation but typically is not reflective for all self- and co-regulatory measures, such mechanisms are also linked with risks and challenges related to their implementation and enforcement. For example, in its Resolution of

---

669 Opinion of the European Economic and Social Committee on Self-regulation and co-regulation in the Community legislative framework (own-initiative opinion) (2015/C 291/05), OJEU C 291/29, available at https://eur-lex.europa.eu/legal-content/EN/TXT/?uri=uriserv:OJ.C_.2015.291.01.0029.01.ENG&toc=OJ:C:2015:291:TOC, para. 1.1

9 September 2010 on Better Lawmaking, the European Parliament "warns against abandoning necessary legislation in favour of self-regulation or co-regulation or any other non-legislative measure [and] believes that the consequences of such choices should be subject to careful examination in each case, in accordance with Treaty law and the roles of the individual institutions".[670]

The concerns expressed in this respect focus in particular on the lack of effective monitoring mechanisms and sanctions under self- and co-regulatory regimes, which in practice often prove ineffective in achieving the objectives pursued. This is most relevant in the area of self-regulation. It applies especially to completely unmonitored systems which can be seen[671], for example, in the terms and conditions set by platforms for their users, some of which go beyond the existing legal framework.[672] These self-regulatory provisions typically only stipulate sanctions for the users of the services (e.g. blocking of accounts or deletion of content) but not for the platform itself. In addition, there is often a lack of transparency in the decision-making process that leads to action or sanctions. Therefore there is a need for a counterweight on behalf of public interests.

Systems in which independent bodies are involved in monitoring (and in some cases drawing up of) codes of conduct, for example in the form of self-regulatory bodies, are somewhat more transparent and effective. Whether these bodies are equipped with sanctioning powers (also in the form of, e.g., public disapproval) depends on the respective arrangement. As a rule several industry stakeholders normally create such arrangements for a certain regulatory area, so that violations can be associated with a negative reputational impact, at least within the industry but also in the wider public opinion. It should also be mentioned that guidelines or directives issued by self-regulatory bodies can become indirectly binding by being

---

670 Resolution (P7_TA(2010)0311), para. 46 and 47, available at http://www.europa rl.europa.eu/sides/getDoc.do?pubRef=-//EP//TEXT+TA+P7-TA-2010-0311+0+DO C+XML+V0//EN.

671 *Finck*, in: LSE Law, Society and Economy Working Papers (15/2017), p. 8; *Dittrich*, Online Platforms and How to Regulate Them, p. 7; cf. on this as well *Koopman/Mitchell/Thierer*, in: The Journal of Business, Entrepreneurship & the Law 8(2), 2015, p. 529, 542 et seq.

672 Cf., e.g., The Community Standards of Facebook, available at https://de-de.faceb ook.com/communitystandards/, where several conditions, for example on hate speech or sexual activities, are regulated; furthermore, for example, the Uber Community Guidelines, available at https://www.uber.com/legal/community-g uidelines/us-can-en/, regulate a seat-belt obligation for drivers which do not exist in every state at the legal level in which Uber offers its services.

consulted or referred to by (mainly national) courts within the framework of the interpretation of uncertain legal terms.[673] Such models operate at an interface between self- and co-regulation.

Much more effective in terms of enforcement, implementation and transparency are co-regulatory systems that involve (mainly national) public oversight bodies or authorities. These may be independent regulators or private bodies charged with public powers through regulatory or administrative acts. Accordingly, the Commission has also clarified in its above-mentioned Communication on Online platforms that *"principles based* self-regulatory/co-regulatory measures, including industry tools for ensuring application of legal requirements and appropriate monitoring mechanisms, can play a role. *Underpinned by appropriate monitoring mechanisms,* they can strike the right balance between predictability, flexibility, efficiency, and the need to develop future-proof solutions"[674]. Without losing the advantages of self-regulation, public interests can also be incorporated into regulation, thus ensuring a more organised approach to implementing the underlying requirements (as has, for example, been described in Chapter 3.3.8.3 for the New Approach). Such a system would then also be backed up by sanctions to allow for effective enforcement tools. Normally, a co-regulatory system's positive effect also rests on involvement of relevant authorities (e.g. the media regulatory authorities in the area of online distribution of media content), as this can lead to a coordination between regulated and co-regulated areas and more public accountability. In addition, these bodies are already equipped with a professional competence that allows them to assess the facts and circumstances associated with regular media regulation.[675]

---

673 In Germany, for example, the advertising guidelines of the Central Association of the German Advertising Industry (*Zentralverband der deutschen Werbewirtschaft*, ZAW) are taken into account by the German courts when interpreting the Law against Unfair Competition (*Gesetz gegen unlauteren Wettbewerb*, UWG) with regard to the question of the lawfulness of advertising; similarly the press code of the German Press Council (*Deutscher Presserat*) is taken into account by the German courts with regard to the interpretation of the concept of due care in journalistic offers.

674 COM/2016/0288 final, supra (fn. 667), p. 5, highlighted by the author.

675 Against this background, it is not surprising that in most European countries the regulators responsible for the audiovisual media have also been entrusted with the performance of tasks in the field of Internet services; cf. AVMS-RADAR, study prepared for the European Commission by the EMR and the University of Luxembourg.

4.2.2.3. Existing Forms of Self- and Co-regulation in the Online Environment

On EU level, the first initiatives for self- and co-regulation initially focused on three areas: technical standardisation, professional rules and social dialogue.[676] However, over time they have been extended to protect consumers, especially in the spheres of business, financial services and industry. They have included, for example, agreements on direct selling and disputes arising from this activity, the development of trust labels for e-commerce, the organisation of cross-border mail-order sales, as well as the reporting of good practice and even certification for professional profiles in the information society, in particular for Internet service providers. These provisions are often accompanied not only by a system for monitoring their implementation but also by simplified rules on consumer disputes, increasing their effectiveness.[677]

As far as the relevant area of the dissemination of online content is concerned, in addition to the initiatives on hate speech and tackling online disinformation presented in detail above (cf. Chapter 2.5), which can be broadly assigned to the field of self-regulation, the provisions of the new AVMSD, which are more of a co-regulatory nature, are of particular interest. Stressing that in order to remove barriers to the free circulation of cross-border services within the Union it is necessary to ensure the effectiveness of self- and co-regulatory measures aiming, in particular, at protecting consumers or public health (Recital 31), the new Art. 4a AVMSD pushes Member States to encourage the use of co-regulation and the fostering of self-regulation through codes of conduct adopted at national level in the fields coordinated by the AVMSD to the extent permitted by their legal systems. Those codes shall be clear, unambiguous and broadly accepted by the main stakeholders in the Member States concerned and shall provide for regular, transparent and independent monitoring and evaluation of the achievement of the objectives aimed at and for effective enforcement including effective and proportionate sanctions. Regarding this, the Commission and the Member States may foster codes of conduct that are developed together with the respective stakeholders. The AVMSD, which regards self-regulation primarily as a means of providing a high level of con-

---

676 Cf. on this European Economic and Social Committee, European Self- and Co-Regulation, available at https://www.eesc.europa.eu/resources/docs/auto_coregu lation_en--2.pdf, pp. 13 et seq.

677 Ibid., p. 15.

sumer protection and considers its use particularly appropriate in relation to new media[678], refers to this solution at several points, in particular regarding the implementation of the provisions on the protection of minors (Art. 6a para. 4 AVMSD), commercial communication (Art. 9 para. 3 and 4 AVMSD) and on video-sharing platforms (Art. 28b para. 2 AVMSD). With regard to the latter, this will probably pose major challenges for legislators and regulators, for which, as far as can be seen, no solutions are yet available.[679] However, while self-regulation might be a complementary method of implementing certain provisions of the AVMSD, the AVMSD focuses more on co-regulation, which could provide the missing legal link with the national legislator (which self-regulation by definition cannot provide) in accordance with the legal traditions of the Member States.[680]

From a national perspective, self- and co-regulation systems have been developed in nearly all EU Member States in one way or another. This is also connected to the fact that the Commission has so far been locating the competency to establish respective rules for the online sector to the Member States.[681] This applies for the media sector anyway[682], where some of the existing self- and co-regulatory systems in Member States cover all media (e.g. self-regulation concerning advertising in the press, broadcasting, etc.), while others are restricted to individual media or new information and communication services.[683] Many of these rules also cover the online sector – whether they were created specifically for this purpose or whether they also apply to the Internet within the framework of the regulation of a specific subject area (for example codes of conduct for the press that could also be "binding" for bloggers). However, although there are similari-

---

678 Cf. Recital 13 AVMSD.
679 In the mentioned report on Self- and Co-regulation in the transposition of the revised AVMSD, prepared for the European Audiovisual Observatory (*Cappello (ed.)*, Self- and Co-regulation in the new AVMSD, IRIS Special 2019-2), the EMR asked the country reporters in particular to describe the situation in the field of protection of minors, advertising and VSPs. While all of the selected countries had systems of self- and co-regulation in place regarding the first two areas, there were no rules or systems regarding VSPs.
680 Cf. Recital 14 AVMSD.
681 Cf. already Chapter 2.5.2.
682 *Furnémont/Smokvina*, European co-regulation practices in the media, comparative analysis and recommendations with a focus on the situation in Serbia.
683 Cf. *Cappello (ed.)*, Self- and Co-regulation in the new AVMSD, IRIS Special 2019-2; cf. already Council Conclusions of 27 September 1999 on the role of self-regulation in the light of the development of new media services, OJ L 283, 6.11.1999, p. 3.

ties[684], there are also significant differences between the ways in which different self-regulation systems are organised and complement or contribute to legislative acts, thus reflecting Europe's democratic, regional and cultural diversity.[685] This is linked not only to the different regulatory traditions of the Member States but also to the conditions in each State, in particular whether there is a differentiated legal framework in certain areas or not. Self- and co-regulatory systems adopted on the basis of Art. 4a AVMSD in the areas mentioned in the Directive may[686], however, converge and at least create similar conditions for the players in the respective Member States.

4.2.2.4. Possible Forms and Conditions of Co-regulation on EU Level

With regard to questions about possible forms of self- and co-regulation in the online sector, it should first be noted that in certain areas, such as the fight against hate speech, there are already instruments at EU level which have shown some first positive, though very limited effects.[687] In this area it may be a question of constantly improving and expanding the existing agreements and, if their effectiveness does not improve, moving the best practices found into a more binding form of co-regulation. Moreover, it is essential that efforts be made to ensure that more and other stakeholders participate in these initiatives. While previous signatories of codes of conduct, such as *Google*, *Facebook* and *Microsoft*, are certainly the key represen-

---

684 In particular regarding, for example, the field of advertising; cf. *Cappello (ed.)*, Self- and Co-regulation in the new AVMSD, IRIS Special 2019-2.

685 Already: Council Conclusions of 27 September 1999, supra (fn. 683); *Marsden*, European Law, Regulatory Governance and Legitimacy in Cyberspace, pp. 67–70.

686 Art. 4a para. 2 underlines that Member States shall remain free to require media service providers under their jurisdiction to comply with more detailed or stricter rules in compliance with this directive and Union law, including where their national independent regulatory authorities or bodies conclude that any code of conduct or parts thereof have proven not to be sufficiently effective. Furthermore, Recital 14 states that encouraging Member States to implement self- and co-regulation measures should neither oblige Member States to set up self- or co-regulation regimes, or both, nor disrupt or jeopardise current co-regulation initiatives which are already in place in Member States and which are functioning effectively.

687 Cf. the initiatives on tackling online disinformation and hate speech portrayed at Chapters 2.5.2 and 2.5.3.

tatives of that industry in the fight against, e.g., hate speech online, there are a number of other providers that need to be brought into the spotlight. In view of its "negotiating power" as a supranational body with numerous powers even vis-à-vis big players, the Commission could certainly be the right initiator here. Finally, the current self-regulatory measures often lack means that would effectively help to measure, evaluate and audit the actions which the industry stakeholders have committed to. For example, they are at the moment unable to harmonise reporting and takedown mechanisms or shed light on the decision-making processes of both automated algorithmic and human content review systems.[688]

However, beyond minimum standards and mere commitments to the fight against illegal and discriminatory content, i.e. when it comes to concrete obligations that pursue concrete objectives of public interest, self-regulation reaches its limits. Co-regulation, on the other hand, can be an effective instrument if it respects the existing legal framework (in the sense of a useful supplementation, not an alternative or replacement) and leaves the competence for defining public interests at the state level. Furthermore, it needs to meet certain criteria[689]:

- transparency and publicity,
- representativeness of the parties concerned,
- prior consultation of the parties directly concerned,
- added value for the general interest,
- non-applicability when the definition of fundamental rights is at stake or in situations where the rules must be applied uniformly in all the Member States,
- judicial control,
- monitoring of the degree and success of their implementation, using objective criteria and reliable indicators defined in advance and specified according to sectors and objectives,
- checks and follow-up of their implementation by preventive measures or sanctions, in order to ensure their effectiveness,
- provision of a system of fines or other penalties,

---

688 *Quintel/Ullrich*, Self-Regulation of Fundamental Rights? The EU Code of Conduct on Hate Speech, Related Initiatives and Beyond, pp. 11–13.

689 See on these criteria: Opinion of the European Economic and Social Committee on Self-regulation and co-regulation in the Community legislative framework, supra (fn. 669), para. 1.7.

- possibility of periodic review in the light of changing situations, legislation and the aspirations of their signatories,
- clear identification of financing sources.

Again, this list is to a certain extent an idealised picture of what a co-regulatory system should look like. Altogether, instruments of self- and co-regulation may be useful, and in particular co-regulation, mainly due to the involvement of industry stakeholders, but there are areas where this reaches its limits. Providers whose business models are based precisely on the distribution of illegal offers (e.g. piracy portals, certain types of pornography and depictions of violence as well as terrorist propaganda), which flourish regularly on the Internet, will normally avoid the regulatory dialogue between legislator and industry that is characteristic of self- and co-regulation. For them, the necessity of a firm legal basis and its effective enforceability remains. Certain co-regulatory solutions may be able to capture these actors if they, e.g., provide for the possibility of sanctions or certification requirements.

4.2.3. The Principle of Proportionality

The general principle of proportionality is one of the fundamental principles of Union law and is reflected both at the level of competences (under Art. 5 para. 4 TEU, the measures taken by the Union may not go beyond what is necessary to achieve the objectives of the Treaties in terms of content or form) and at the level of material law within the framework of the assessment of the justification regarding fundamental rights and freedoms. This applies in particular if possible regulations, such as here, affect the freedom to provide services or the freedom of establishment. The general principle of proportionality is only briefly mentioned here, as it has already been explained in detail in the framework of fundamental rights (cf. above Chapter 2.1).

In addition to respecting specific requirements for restrictions on fundamental rights and freedoms, not only EU acts but also the measures and laws of Member States – even when acting in the exercise of their own exclusive powers – must be appropriate and necessary to achieve an objective of general interest legitimately pursued by the regulation in question. In addition, the burdens imposed must be proportionate to the objectives pursued. If there are several suitable measures to choose from, the least burdensome must be chosen. The principle of proportionality thus generally serves as a guideline for the balancing of conflicting legal interests and therefore calls for the conflicting interests of media service providers in the integration of their content and of users in transparency to be weighed, on the one hand, against the interests of the platforms and other stakeholders in their freedom to conduct their business and, on the other, against that of users in the self-determined use of platforms and devices.

At this point, the interests protected by fundamental rights that are particularly relevant in connection with the dissemination of online content (cf. Chapter 2.1.) are to be emphasised once again. Content that impairs human dignity cannot be balanced against other interests such as freedom of expression, so that particularly strong regulation is possible. The protection of minors is subject to a similarly high interest (but open to balancing with other interests), since it is both a public interest and a state task. Content that violates personal rights or interests protected by copyright may, under certain circumstances, conflict with freedom of expression or freedom of the media, which has led to special restrictions, e.g. in copyright law. In its strategy for a Digital Single Market for Europe, the Commission also stressed the importance of avoiding the deletion of legal content when applying measures to block illegal content.[690] In this regard it is crucial to leave the assessment of whether content is illegal or legal to qualified institutions. The interests of the platforms worthy of protection, which result in particular from the freedom to conduct a business and the right to property, must also be taken into consideration. Regulation may not be so far-reaching that business models protected by fundamental rights can no longer be exercised. In this respect, it may be essential to involve industry in the evaluation of this situation. However, a large part of this sometimes complex evaluation involving a wide range of stakeholders' interests will be based on consultation procedures already carried out and on the work of interest groups involving industry that has already been done.[691]

---

690 COM(2015) 192 final, supra (fn. 18), para. 3.2.2.
691 Cf. on this the consultation procedures mentioned in Chapters 2.4 and 2.5 regarding in particular the reform of the AVMSD and the DMS Directive as well as the High Level Groups on fighting illegal content, hate speech and disinformation.

4.3. Possible Avenues

4.3.1. General Considerations

There are different ways forward in order to respond to the issues identified in this study with the regulatory framework for the online dissemination of content. The existing legislative acts on EU level applicable to this context could be reformed during the mandate of the new Von der Leyen Commission. Completely new legislative acts could be proposed which either come on top of the existing or replace some of these. An alternative to these legislative steps is a reinforced application by competent authorities of the existing framework, and be it "only" to further display problems in cross-border constellations. Further, in the direction of what has been done in recent years, the inclusion of the online industry in developing, defining and applying self-regulatory standards could be steeped up.

If the path of revision of existing legislative acts or creations of new ones would be chosen, there are different ways that this could take. On the one hand, for legal certainty the measures could at least codify the jurisprudence of the CJEU as it applies to the sector and was presented in this study. In doing so, identified gaps that have not yet been addressed by the Court, or at least not in a conclusive manner, could be closed. For example, although the definition of ISS providers has been clarified to an extent by the CJEU, the emergence of new online platform business models, namely in the so-called sharing economy, continue to challenge the boundaries of the application of the ECD. The intermediary service providers rely heavily on the liability privileges as defined in Art. 12–15 ECD, although it has been shown that the premise of wide-reaching protections for passive hosts as long as they do not have any actual knowledge of illegal content or activity has been rightly questioned and subjected to new interpretations by courts. The new interactive content management platforms which build heavily on the exploitation of user data and network effects are at the centre of this business model but in no way of a unified shape. This is why the ongoing general categorisation of "hosting providers" needs to be overcome in light of these platforms.

In addition, from a substantive perspective of law, the difficulties in applying a ruleset designed two decades ago for a completely different Internet environment have become obvious. The actors have changed and the role of platforms in dissemination of online content has become dominant. This necessitates a reconsideration of the way they are addressed by the relevant law. In order to avoid a further fragmentation of the rules ap-

plicable to different types of online service providers and having to introduce new categories of service providers depending on the further development of the online sector, the EU should strive to replace the existing
cross-sectorial approach in form of the ECD by a new horizontally applicable act concerning all types of "information society services" (while departing from this definition where necessary). When doing so, it is especially
important to see whether within a horizontally applicable framework
there might have to be specific subcategories. For example, content disseminators play a different role or have a different significance for society than
purely commercially oriented e-commerce platforms and therefore need to
be regulated in a way that their role as multiplier of the freedom of expression of their users is taken into consideration as much as the potential for
serious and permanent harm in case of illegal content due to its fast and
wide spreading.

A more simple approach to "renovating" the legislative framework
would be to revise the ECD in a way that at least the clarification of categories of providers is achieved and scope exemptions concerning the liability privileges or procedures for better enforcement in case of actual liability of a platform provider are introduced. Because the value-based and
fundamental-rights-driven framework for online content dissemination necessitates the protection of rights of users, foremost of minors, as has been
shown by this study, inactivity of regulatory authorities in response to difficulties in enforcement, to an unclear scope of the applicable law or possibly to a lack of formally assigned competence alone is not an option. If it is
necessary, one possibility in the reform of the ECD would also be to clarify
in which scenarios an exceptional derogation from the country-of-origin
principle is really possible and how the cooperation between regulatory
authorities of the two or more Member States concerned can be enhanced.

4.3.2. Adjusting Country-of-Origin and Market Location Principle

This study has dealt extensively with the country-of-origin principle as set
out in the AVMSD (Chapter 2.4.2.2.2) and the ECD (Chapter 3.2). The
principle is also known in other areas of EU law.[692] It states, in general,
that a service provider that falls under the jurisdiction of one EU Member

---

692 For an overview, especially for non-media- or information-society-oriented services, cf. *Sørensen*, in: Nordic & European Company Law, LSN Research Paper
Series No. 16-32, pp. 2 et seq. The principle is also known by similar expressions

State can rely on complying with the legal framework of (only) that specific state in order to be authorised to deliver its services (i.e. in our context to disseminate content) across all EU Member States. In this regard, the concept follows the idea of the fundamental freedom to provide services as laid down in the TFEU, which obliges Member States not to interfere with the free movement within the single market except in case of justified restrictions. These restrictions have to be based on an overriding public interest and have to be proportionate. They are also possible concerning the freedom to provide services and therefore have also found their way into secondary EU legislation in the context of services and building on this country-of-origin principle. The study has shown that the principle is regulated differently in the EU legal acts, which holds true in particular regarding the possible derogations by the Member States. For example, after its revision in 2018, the AVMSD is no longer based on the ECD in its wording regarding the measures Member States can take against VoD services, although in the previous version the derogation for these types of online services was aligned exactly to the ECD provisions.

The country-of-origin principle was contrasted in the study with the market location principle contained in the GDPR (Chapter 2.4.3.3). This principle follows the approach that service providers must comply with the rules of the state to whose population they direct their offers. Differently than the country-of-origin principle in the AVMSD or ECD, the market location principle in the GDPR also has a kind of extraterritorial reach in that it makes possible under certain circumstances that EU-based supervisory authorities can address providers (in that case controllers or processors) with a seat outside of the EU as long as there is a connecting factor.

There is an obvious advantage of the country-of-origin principle which is why it has been fundamental in contributing to the establishment of cross-border (originally) television and (then) audiovisual media services in the EU: there is legal clarity once the jurisdiction is assigned and there is an economic incentive to then use cross-border dissemination as it comes at no additional "regulatory" cost. Possible disadvantages have always been voiced with the danger that there can be a phenomenon of "forum shopping" or, consequently, a "race to bottom" concerning the regulatory framework for those areas that are not covered by harmonised law or are

---

such as "principle of home state control", "home country authorisation", "seat state principle", etc. Cf. also *Cole*, The Country of Origin Principle, p. 118.

transposed in different ways in the Member States.[693] Since the basic condition of the country-of-origin principle is that service providers only have to ensure compliance with the law of the country from which they distribute their services and can then freely offer their services in other EU Member States, they can base their choice of establishment by making an overall assessment of the most preferential framework conditions. Often these may be found where companies are affected by fewer restrictions than in other places. This can also be the case, for example, for economic advantages such as reduced VAT rates, but more importantly in legal terms in case of, e.g., nationally nuanced interpretations of the liability privileges under the ECD.[694] This is an advantage for providers in view of the fact that corporate interests can be safeguarded. The term "forum shopping", however, refers more to the disadvantages associated with it for others, in particular consumers, competitors on the market, Member States and public interests as a whole. Consumers cannot rely on compliance by providers with the same rules as those they know from their home country. Competitors from other Member States may be disadvantaged by having to comply with stricter rules, especially when competing in the same or similar markets on the Internet. Public interests, which may vary from one Member State to another, such as the protection of minors, can also be affected. Finally, Member States may lose their attractiveness as countries of establishment for businesses if they adopt stricter rules than other EU Member States. This, in turn, can lead to the aforementioned race to the bottom, where Member States may be inclined to establish a regulatory environment (within the respective harmonisation framework) that is as free

---

693 Cf. in detail *Harrison/Woods*, European Broadcasting Law and Policy, pp. 8 et seq.: "Jurisdiction, forum shopping and the 'race to the bottom'"; as well as *Cappello (ed.)*, Media law enforcement without frontiers, IRIS Special 2018-2; *Cole*, AVMSD Jurisdiction Criteria after the 2018 Reform.

694 In the summaries of the replies to the public consultation launched by the Green Paper "Preparing for a Fully Converged Audiovisual World: Growth, Creation and Values" (available at https://ec.europa.eu/digital-single-market/en/news/publication-summaries-green-paper-replies, p. 3), the Commission noted that "[s]ome respondents among Member States authorities and Regulatory Authorities express the view that US companies can better adapt to the fragmented market conditions because they can choose their country of establishment according to the applicable law, e.g. regarding reduced VAT rates, the liability privileges for hosting providers set out in the ECD, the heterogeneous implementation of the AVMSD, in particular concerning the provisions on the promotion of European works."

of restrictions as possible, mainly on the basis of economic and structural considerations.

Possible problems with the country-of-origin principle – as well as with derogations from it – can concern the enforcement for the rules. Regulatory authorities cannot easily intervene against EU providers even if they are of the opinion that these do not only not comply with domestic national rules (which is legal and a consequence of the country-of-origin principle) but also not with the rules of the home state or standards deriving from EU law. The authorities charged with the enforcement are in such cases dependent on the intervention or at least the cooperation of the competent supervisory authority in the country of establishment or, in the current design of the country-of-origin principle, must follow complicated procedures if they want to take measures themselves. The prerequisite for a successful country-of-origin principle is therefore that the authorities of the country of establishment have a sufficient interest and ability to enforce the law.[695] This becomes problematic when an offer from one state is obviously and perhaps even exclusively addressed to an audience in another state. In this case, the (generally competent) regulatory authorities of the home state might not have the same interest in effective enforcement than if it is a service addressing the domestic audience, because there might be, e.g., a language discrepancy. In the AVMSD, for example, this problem is addressed by the prohibition of circumvention. But the procedure to apply a "fictious" establishment approach to a foreign provider is still complicated and uncertain in its outcome as it has so far never been used successfully.

The market location principle addresses these disadvantages by linking them to the market and target audience for the respective service. However, this approach has other disadvantages. First of all, a "pure" market location principle is difficult to reconcile with the idea of the free movement of services in the EU, especially in light of the creation of a single market. If suppliers always have to fear being monitored by foreign regulators based on foreign rules and being confronted with measures, this may disincentivise the cross-border offering. The degree of interference for service providers also depends on the degree of harmonisation on EU level, in particular the (minimum) standards set by EU secondary law.[696] In addition, the marketplace principle leads to establishing a competence of several regulators in parallel, which in turn makes it necessary to install procedural

---

695 *Walk*, Das Herkunftslandprinzip der E-Commerce-Richtlinie, p. 38.
696 Cf. on this already Chapter 4.1.4.2.

safeguards against certain services ending up without regulatory grasp or being confronted with diverging approaches, by introducing coordination measures.

The respective advantages and disadvantages, however, depend decisively on the specific design of the market location or country-of-origin principle. It is remarkable in this context that also the GDPR is not based on a full market location principle but takes up aspects of the country-of-origin principle. This concerns specifically the provisions on jurisdiction in cross-border cases and the requirement of a connecting factor in a Member State in order to trigger GDPR application for that state or supervisory authority. The service provider will be assigned a lead supervisory authority on the basis of jurisdiction criteria, which will then cooperate at a higher level with supervisory authorities from other Member States. These cooperation and consistency mechanisms in the GDPR are considerably more differentiated, but in a way they can be seen as a more detailed codification of the idea that is already contained in the exceptional deviation procedures (departing from the country-of-origin principle in specific cases) of AVMSD and ECD. Thus, the country-of-origin principle is not a fixed construct that is unchangeable but only (and at the same time fundamentally) the starting point. It can therefore be designed according to the needs of the digital age in particular, provided that this is compatible with the freedom to provide services. In particular, certain aspects of the marketplace principle could be adopted which combine the advantages of both principles in a similar way that the GDPR does it the other way round by mainly being based on the market location principle.

Furthermore, there is also a need for procedural improvements with regard to possible derogations from the country-of-origin principle. This concerns necessary clarifications, which must be made in order to remove the uncertainty of Member States and their national supervisory authorities to make use of the possibility of derogation. It is especially necessary to ensure the effectiveness and simplification of the procedures. Such procedural improvements also concern the institutional design and cooperation of competent authorities which will be dealt within the following section. In both respects, a reference to the nature of the content, as already indicated in the new AVMSD rules[697], could be a reasonable way forward.[698]

---

697 Art. 3 para. 2 and 3 AVMSD differ, for example, regarding infringements of Art. 6a para. 1 and Art. 6 para. 1 lit. b) AVMSD; cf. Chapter 2.4.2.2.2.

698 In this regards cf. also *de Streel/Buiten/Streintz*, Liability of online hosting platforms, pp. 52 et seq., but in the context of liability rules.

Incitement to terrorism, child sexual abuse or content infringing human dignity requires more effective and faster enforcement mechanisms than other content, which is an outcome of the fundamental-rights- and value-based orientation of the EU, as has been shown above (Chapters 2.1.3 and 2.3.1). A possible avenue could be to create corridors in which deviations from the country-of-origin principle are possible for authorities on a fast track mechanism, e.g. when they concern these fundamental values such as human dignity violations or when they only have a limited impact. In the context of thinking about a revision of these elements, procedural clarifications should also be made as to the dealing with non-EU-originating content.

4.3.3. Institutional Setup and Cooperation in Enforcement

Concerning the institutional setup in enforcement of the rules against providers that disseminate content online, there are two main challenges: one concerns the setup of competent authorities and their "equipment" with adequate supervision and enforcement powers and capabilities, the other, in light of the tension between market location and country-of-origin principle and due to the cross-border nature of online content dissemination, relates to the cooperation structures and mechanisms on EU level between the national regulatory authorities.

For illegal content that qualifies as breaching criminal law prohibitions, there is a competency for national law enforcement agencies – and for certain types of such content also cooperative structures on EU level –, but the supervision of online content dissemination providers necessitates an additional layer because of the limited possibility for law enforcement agencies to take care for the online sector and the sensitivity of dealing with fundamental-rights-relevant content expressions. Therefore, there needs to be a clear assignment of competencies to such regulatory authorities that are in charge of monitoring and supervising online service providers. Independent regulators that have experience with balancing the freedom of expression of content providers and the enforcement of overarching public interests are likely best placed to take over this role. Accordingly, in most EU Member States regulators that traditionally dealt with audiovisual content in the linear dissemination of content have already been given the additional competence for the online dissemination. These bodies should have clearly assigned tasks. This is especially important when it comes to meaningful co-regulation that does not merely rely on self-regulation of the industry. In that case their role, e.g., in the development of common standards as well as the monitoring of compliance with these should be laid down in the law clearly.

Such regulators should also be equipped with sanctioning powers, as this is an important possibility to enhance compliance with rules by providers in order for them to avoid being confronted with the respective measures of the authority. Moreover, in order to make cross-border monitoring efficient there needs to be some form of institutionalised cooperation between national regulatory authorities in the EU. In such a forum, "community standards" of these bodies could be developed concerning an agreement on what is to be regarded as illegal and harmful and what type of action should regularly be taken by the national competent authority. The exact form of this cooperation needs to consider the specifics of the content-related supervision work (as has been shown above in the context of the discussion around the GDPR institutional setup for cooperation) and ensure an increase in efficiency compared to the situation today. The work of ERGA so far, in which national regulators exchange best standards and discuss possible improvements in procedures, seems to make this structure to be the right starting point for such considerations.

4.3.4. Improving Conditions for Enforcement

Regarding the improvement of enforcement and to counter the dissemination of illegal online content, the study has presented several different approaches to how platform providers are pushed into a more responsible position. This applies in particular to the framework of support, coordination and supplementary measures (Chapter 2.5) as well as to the self- and co-regulation level. Especially details from the Communication on Tackling Illegal Content Online[699] and the Recommendation on Tackling Illegal Content Online[700] can be taken into consideration at this point, which are also contained in other existing approaches.[701] The way in which platform providers can be made more accountable for illegal content is divid-

---

699 Communication from the Commission, Tackling Illegal Content Online, COM/2017/0555 final, supra (fn. 394).

700 Commission Recommendation (EU) 2018/334 of 1 March 2018 on measures to effectively tackle illegal content online, C/2018/1177, supra (fn. 395).

701 Cf. in detail Chapter 2.5.2.

ed into four main areas in particular: transparency, proactive measures, reactive measures and cooperation.

Transparency obligations regularly concern the obligation of platform providers to design their guidelines in such a way that it becomes clear and understandable when and which type of content is considered illegal and what happens to content identified in this way. This type of measure also increases awareness in dealing with digital content and the media competence of users. In addition, regulators and other government agencies also get a better overview of the measures taken by the platforms. Furthermore, transparency obligations also concern information from platform providers on how illegal content was actually handled and what measures were taken until now, presented in the form of periodic reporting obligations. Such reports are provided for in the Code of conduct on countering illegal hate speech online[702], where the reports of the addressees are incorporated into an evaluation report of the Commission, which also provides an overview of current trends and problems.

Proactive measures that could potentially conflict with the current liability rules of the ECD mainly concern the establishment of systems to detect illegal content and prevent such content from being disseminated. Such measures have the advantage that illegal content can be stopped before it is even disseminated, which otherwise leads to a rapid spread online. Therefore, preventing initial placing on the Internet can help very effectively avoiding the infringement of third-party rights. These measures are, however, only very cautiously advocated, as they come into tension with the freedom of expression of the concerned users guaranteed by fundamental rights. Therefore, they are regularly accompanied at least by appeal systems and concern clearly identifiable illegal content. Potential risks remain, however, especially when the uploading control of content is left to algorithms, which is the only viable way in large-scale platform usage scenarios. In the field of copyright law, such measures are not directly provided for by the new DSM Directive, but they were originally contained in the Commission's proposal.[703] As a reaction to the controversy around that, the Commission noted in its Recommendation on Tackling Illegal Content Online that proactive measures could involve the use of automated means for the detection of illegal content only where appropriate and proportionate and subject to effective and appropriate safeguards (e.g. hu-

---

702 Cf. in detail Chapter 2.5.2.
703 Cf. in detail Chapter 2.4.4.2.

man oversight and verifications).[704] Furthermore, there should be measures to guarantee the safety of such technical systems.

Reactive measures describe measures that platform providers can take in response to the concrete or general presence of illegal content on their platforms. This includes in particular the establishment of effective reporting and complaint systems for illegal content and the associated subsequent handling of the content (deletion, blocking, limitation, etc.). It may also cover reporting obligations to other bodies, such as law enforcement authorities, and own labelling obligations. The latter also addresses the issue of cooperation, which can take place in many different levels (between Member States, regulators, providers, third parties) in the sector of online dissemination of content. However, in the context of improving law enforcement, the main focus is on cooperation between hosting service providers and Member States and on the cooperation between hosting service providers and so-called "trusted flaggers".

Cooperation between hosting service providers and Member States is of particular importance, as the involvement of the industry is key in particular in the digital cross-border environment.[705] There need to be points of contact for matters relating to illegal content online between Member States and platform providers to provide an effective cooperation.[706] This applies not only to the general establishment of contact with the providers but also to the specific individual case if illegal content is found on the platform. In this case, the competent regulatory authorities must be able to take effective and proportionate measures, for the implementation of which they regularly have to rely on the cooperation of the platform providers. In this context, the Commission has argued in favour of fast-track procedures to process notices submitted by competent authorities.

Another approach of cooperation is the cooperation between hosting services providers and trusted flaggers. The Recommendation of the Commission defines these as individuals or entities which are considered by a hosting service provider to have particular expertise and responsibilities for the purposes of tackling illegal content online and states that this form of cooperation should be encouraged, in particular by establishing fast-track procedures to process notices submitted by trusted flaggers.[707] Further-

---

704 Commission Recommendation (EU) 2018/334, supra (fn. 395), points 18, 20.
705 Cf. in detail Chapter 4.2.2.
706 Commission Recommendation (EU) 2018/334, supra (fn. 395), Recital 5.
707 Commission Recommendation (EU) 2018/334, supra (fn. 395), point 4 lit. g) and point 25.

more, according to the Recommendation, hosting service providers should be encouraged to publish clear and objective conditions for determining which individuals or entities they consider as trusted flaggers, and those conditions should aim to ensure that the individuals or entities concerned have the necessary expertise and carry out their activities as trusted flaggers in a diligent and objective manner, based on respect for the values on which the EU is founded. The expertise required here to qualify as a trusted flagger takes into account the consideration that reporting or even deleting content can significantly interfere with the content creators' fundamental rights to freedom of expression.

To leave this assessment initially to the platform providers alone, as is the case, for example, in Germany with the Network Enforcement Act[708], seems also problematic considering the fundamental rights setting and the fact that these activities are in principal tasks to be performed by the states. Therefore, trusted flagging should be provided by competent and above all independent institutions which bring the interests of the public and the users into line. These could be self-regulatory bodies staffed by independent experts. However, the disadvantages of self-regulation or regulated self-regulation have already been described (cf. Chapter 4.2.2.2). These findings also apply to the abovementioned stronger inclusion of the regulated industry in the performance of countering illegal content, as their contributions are dependent on factors that are not always open to monitoring and holding accountable. For the flagging process, it should be the regulatory authorities that are mainly responsible for this task, because they have both the necessary independence and the technical and professional competence to achieve the goals.

4.4. Looking Ahead

The study aimed at presenting the current applicability of the EU legislative framework to platforms that are involved in online dissemination of content. Based on the identification of gaps and deficiencies in enforcement of legal standards in this area, the need for a change, or at least shift, of the legislative basis was shown. It needs to be underlined in the concluding look ahead that any amendment to the framework, and any replacement of existing or creation of new legislative acts, should be based on the fundamental rights and values set that characterise the European

---

708 Network Enforcement Act, supra (fn. 361). Cf. on this already Chapter 2.4.4.2.

Union – not only because it is an obligation to ensure that these rights are protected efficiently and that the Member States are giving a framework within which their competent authorities can ensure the upholding of applicable standards while respecting freedoms on the single market, but also because content dissemination touches an area which is sensitive in itself from a fundamental rights perspective (most notably freedom of expression) and because of its role in contributing to opinion-forming processes in our democracies.

The European Union has recently set standards with the GDPR that have a reach beyond the borders of its Member States. Finding an adequate balance between not limiting the use of the communication freedoms in the online context in a too restrictive manner and at the same time coming to a necessary and satisfactory answer to the large amount of illegal or harmful content dissemination that takes places all the time is a challenge. If it is successfully achieved, standards could again serve as models that go beyond the EU and in that way at the same time potentially also further ameliorate the situation in the EU if foreign providers are confronted with other responsibility expectations from their home Member States.

Solutions and approaches developed in this reform process as well as certain elements in existing instruments that concern online dissemination might in future turn out to be applicable for other areas of technology regulation. This might be the case for newly established transparency requirements – including enforcement of standards in the context of this transparency – that could be applied when discussing the possible regulation of artificial intelligence and machine learning technology. Another outcome of the present reform discussion should be a clearer identification of the assimilation of the importance of different roles in the online content dissemination between providers with editorial responsibility and those that apply control over the organisation and means of dissemination of that content. The current discussions and the changes to the understanding of information society services already in the past years is reflective of the situation that the role of intermediaries and platforms has changed in a significant way over the past years. When reforming the framework, an inconsistent division of responsibility and liability depending on what type of content is concerned or which legislative act is applicable should ideally be avoided. A clearer and more up-to-date definition of the scope of application of these acts by reconsidering the criteria to apply to the different providers is an important step.

As a final point there should be one other conclusion underlined that was discussed above: even if nothing is changed or only changed after a long period of discussion, which is to be expected due to the legislative procedures at EU level, national regulatory agencies entrusted with the monitoring of content dissemination should also act in reaction to illegal or problematic online dissemination of content even though it has a cross-border dimension.

5. Bibliography

All URLs mentioned in this study were last accessed on 10.12.2019.

Albath, L.; Giesel, M.: Das Herkunftslandprinzip in der Dienstleistungsrichtlinie – eine Kodifizierung der Rechtsprechung?, in: Europäische Zeitschrift für Wirtschaftsrecht (EuZW) 2, 2006, pp. 38–42.
Cited: *Albath/Giesel*, in: EuZW 2, 2006, p. 38, p.

Angelopoulos, C.: European Intermediary Liability in Copyright. A Tort-Based Analysis, 2017, Wolters Kluwer.
Cited: *Angelopoulos*, European Intermediary Liability in Copyright. A Tort-Based Analysis.

Baistrocchi, P.: Liability of Intermediary Service Providers in the EU Directive on Electronic Commerce, in: Santa Clara High Technology Law Journal 19(1), 2003, pp. 111–130.
Cited: *Baistrocchi*, in: Santa Clara High Technology Law Journal 19(1), 2003, p. 111, p.

Banks, J.: Regulating Hate Speech Online, in: International Review of Law, Computers & Technology 24(3), 2010, pp. 233–239.
Cited: *Banks*, in: International Review of Law, Computers & Technology 24(3), 2010, p. 233, p.

Barata, J.: New EU Proposal on the Prevention of Terrorist Content Online – An Important Mutation of the E-Commerce Intermediaries' Regime, white paper available at http://cyberlaw.stanford.edu/publications/new-eu-proposal-preventi on-terrorist-content-online-important-mutation-e-commerce.
Cited: *Barata*, New EU Proposal on the Prevention of Terrorist Content Online – An Important Mutation of the E-Commerce Intermediaries' Regime.

Belavusau, U.: Fighting Hate Speech Through EU Law, in: Amsterdam Law Forum 4(1), 2012, pp. 20–35.
Cited: *Belavusau*, in: Amsterdam Law Forum 4(1), 2012, p. 20, p.

Belli, L.; Sappa, C.: The Intermediary Conundrum: Cyber-Regulators, Cyber-Police or Both?, in: JIPITEC 8, 2017, pp. 183–198.
Cited: *Belli/Sappa*, in: JIPITEC 8, 2017, p. 183, p.

Bertolini, E.; Franceschelli, V.; Pollicino, O.: Analysis of ISP Regulation under Italian Law, in: Dinwoodie, G. B. (ed.), Secondary liability of internet service providers, 2017, Springer.
Cited: *Bertolini/Franceschelli/Pollicino*, Analysis of ISP Regulation under Italian Law.

Büllesbach, A. (ed.): Concise European IT Law, 2nd ed., 2010, Kluwer Law International.
Cited: *Büllesbach (ed.)*, Concise European IT Law.

Burk, D. L.: Toward an Epistemology of ISP Secondary Liability, in: Philosophy & Technology 24(4), 2011, pp. 437–454.
Cited: *Burk*, in: Philosophy & Technology 24(4), 2011, p. 437, p.

Busch, C.: Towards a 'New Approach' for the Platform Ecosystem: A European Standard for Fairness in Platform-to-Business Relations, in: Journal of European Consumer and Market Law 6(6), 2017, pp. 227–228.
Cited: *Busch*, in: Journal of European Consumer and Market Law 6(6), 2017, p. 227, p.

Calliess, C.: Der Schlüsselbegriff der „ausschließlichen" Zuständigkeit im Subsidiaritätsprinzip des Art. 3b II EGV, in: Europäische Zeitschrift für Wirtschaftsrecht (EuZW) 1995, pp. 693–700.
Cited: *Calliess*, in: EuZW 1995, p. 693, p.

Calliess, C.; Ruffert, M.: EUV/AEUV, Das Verfassungsrecht der Europäischen Union mit Europäischer Grundrechtecharta, 5th ed., 2016, Beck.
Cited: *author* in: Callies/Ruffert, Art. para.

Classen, C. D.: Die Grundfreiheiten im Spannungsfeld von europäischer Marktfreiheit und mitgliedstaatlichen Gestaltungskompetenzen, in: Zeitschrift für Europarecht (EuR) 39(3), 2004, pp. 416–438.
Cited: *Classen*, in: EuR 39(3), 2004, p. 416, p.

Cappello, M. (ed.): The protection of minors in a converged media environment, IRIS plus, European Audiovisual Observatory, Strasbourg, 2015, available at https://rm.coe.int/1680783486.
Cited: *Capello (ed.)*, The protection of minors in a converged media environment, IRIS plus 2015-1.

Cappello, M. (ed.): Journalism and media privilege, IRIS Special, European Audiovisual Observatory, Strasbourg, 2017, available at https://rm.coe.int/journalism-and-media-privilege-pdf/1680787381.
Cited: *Cappello (ed.)*, Journalism and media privilege, IRIS Special 2017-2.

Cappello, M. (ed.): Media law enforcement without frontiers, IRIS Special, European Audiovisual Observatory, Strasbourg, 2018, available at https://rm.coe.int/media-law-enforcement-without-frontiers/1680907efe.
Cited: *Cappello (ed.)*, Media law enforcement without frontiers, IRIS Special 2018-2.

Cappello, M. (ed.): The independence of media regulatory authorities in Europe, IRIS Special, European Audiovisual Observatory, Strasbourg, 2019, available at https://rm.coe.int/the-independence-of-media-regulatory-authorities-in-europe/168097e504.
Cited: *Cappello (ed.)*, The independence of media regulatory authorities in Europe, IRIS Special, IRIS Special 2019-1.

Cappello, M. (ed.): Self- and Co-regulation in the new AVMSD, IRIS Special, European Audiovisual Observatory, Strasbourg, 2019, available at https://rm.coe.int/iris-special-2019-2-self-and-co-regulation-in-the-new-avmsd/1680992dc2.
Cited: *Cappello (ed.)*, Self- and Co-regulation in the new AVMSD, IRIS Special 2019-2.

Castendyk, O.; Dommering, E.; Scheuer, A.: European Media Law, 2008, Kluwer Law International BV.
Cited: *author* in: Castendyk/Dommering/Scheuer, European Media Law.

Cohen, J.: The Regulatory State in the Information Age, in: Theoretical Inquiries in Law 17(2), 2016, pp. 369–414.
Cited: *Cohen*, in: Theoretical Inquiries in Law 17(2), 2016, p. 369, p.

Cole, M. D.: The Country of Origin Principle – From State Sovereignty under Public International Law to Inclusion in the Audiovisual Media Services Directive of the European Union, in: Meng, W.; Ress, G.; Stein, T. (eds.), Europäische Integration und Globalisierung – Festschrift zum 60-jährigen Bestehen des Europa-Instituts, 2011.
Cited: *Cole*, The Country of Origin Principle.

Cole, M. D.: The AVMSD Jurisdiction Criteria concerning Audiovisual Media Service Providers after the 2018 Reform, 2018, available at https://emr-sb.de/study-a vmsd-jurisdiction-criteria/.
Cited: *Cole*, AVMSD Jurisdiction Criteria after the 2018 Reform.

Cole, M. D.: Guiding Principles in establishing the Guidelines for Implementation of Article 13 (6) AVMSD – Criteria for exempting certain providers from obligations concerning European Works, 2019, available at https://emr-sb.de/wp-conte nt/uploads/2019/05/Study-AVMSD-guidelines-Art-13.pdf.
Cited: *Cole*, Guiding Principles in establishing the Guidelines for Implementation of Article 13 (6) AVMSD.

Cole, M. D., with contributions by Etteldorf C. and Henrich, J.: Die Neuregelung des Artikel 7b Richtlinie 2010/13/EU (AVMD-RL) – Spielraum und zu beachtende Vorgaben bei der mitgliedstaatlichen Umsetzung der Änderungs-Richtlinie (EU) 2018/1808, 2019, available at https://emr-sb.de/wp-content/uploads/201 9/12/emr-gutachten_neuregelung-des-artikel-7b-avmd_11.2019.pdf.
Cited: *Cole*, Die Neuregelung des Artikel 7b Richtlinie 2010/13/EU (AVMD-RL).

Cole, M. D.; Etteldorf, C.: Von „Fernsehen ohne Grenzen" zu Video-sharing-Plattformen, Hate Speech und Overlays – die Anpassung der EU-Richtlinie über audiovisuelle Mediendienste an das digitale Zeitalter, in: Medienhandbuch Österreich 2019, pp. 56–65.
Cited: *Cole/Etteldorf*, Medienhandbuch Österreich 2019, p. 56, p.

Cole, M. D.; Fink, U.; Keber, T.: Europäisches und Internationales Medienrecht, 2008, C. F. Müller.
Cited: *author* in: Cole/Fink/Keber, Europäisches Medienrecht.

Cole, M. D.; Haus, F. C.: Dienstleistungsfreiheit brutto oder netto? Probleme der europäischen Sprachenvielfalt am Beispiel der EG-Fernsehrichtlinie – EuGH, Slg. 1999, I-7599, in: Juristische Schulung (JuS) 5/2001, pp. 435–439.
Cited: *Cole/Haus*, in: JuS 5/2001, p. 435, p.

de Gregorio, G.: The e-Commerce Directive and GDPR: Towards Convergence of Legal Regimes in the Algorithmic Society?, in: Robert Schuman Centre for Advanced Studies Research Paper No. RSCAS 2019/36.
Cited: *de Gregorio*, The e-Commerce Directive and GDPR: Towards Convergence of Legal Regimes in the Algorithmic Society?

de Streel, A.; Buiten, M.; Peitz, M.: Liability of online hosting platforms: should exceptionalism end?, 2018, Brussels: CERRE, available at https://www.cerre.eu/site s/cerre/files/180912_CERRE_LiabilityPlatforms_Final_0.pdf.
Cited: *de Streel/Buiten/Streintz*, Liability of online hosting platforms.

Dittrich, P.: Social Networks and Populism in the EU – Four Things You Should Know, Policy Paper no. 192, Jaques Delors Institut Berlin, 2017, available at https://www.delorsinstitut.de/2015/wp-content/uploads/2017/04/20170419_Soci alNetworksandPopulism-Dittrich.pdf.
Cited: *Dittrich*, Social Networks and Populism in the EU – Four Things You Should Know.

Dittrich, P.: Online Platforms and How to Regulate Them, Policy Paper no. 227, Jaques Delors Institut Berlin, 2018.
Cited: *Dittrich*, Online Platforms and How to Regulate Them.

Dörr, D., with contributions by Cole, M. D.: Big Brother und die Menschenwürde, 2000, Peter Lang.
Cited: *Dörr/Cole*, Big Brother und die Menschenwürde.

Dörr, D.; Cole, M. D.: Menschenwürde als Grenze der Programmfreiheit, in: Kommunikation und Recht (K&R) 8/2000, pp. 369–378.
Cited: *Dörr/Cole*, in K&R 8/2000, p. 369, p.

Dröge, C.: Positive Verpflichtungen der Staaten in der Europäischen Menschenrechtskonvention, 2003, Springer.
Cited: *Dröge*, Positive Verpflichtungen der Staaten in der Europäischen Menschenrechtskonvention.

Dumortier, J.; Kosta, E.: ePrivacy Directive: assessment of transposition, effectiveness and compatibility with proposed Data Protection Regulation, study prepared for the European Commission DG Communications Networks, Content & Technology, 2015, available at https://ec.europa.eu/digital-single-market/en/n ews/eprivacy-directive-assessment-transposition-effectiveness-and-compatibility-p roposed-data.
Cited: *Dumortier/Kosta*, ePrivacy Directive: assessment of transposition, effectiveness and compatibility with proposed Data Protection Regulation.

Dutt, R.; Deb, A.; Ferrara, E.: "Senator, We Sell Ads": Analysis of the 2016 Russian Facebook Ads Campaign, International Conference on Intelligent Information Technologies, pp. 151–168, available at https://arxiv.org/pdf/1809.10158.pdf.
Cited: *Dutt/Deb/Ferrara*, "Senator, We Sell Ads": Analysis of the 2016 Russian Facebook Ads Campaign.

Edwards, L.: The fall & rise of intermediary liability online, in: Edwards, L.; Waelde, Ch. (eds.), Law and the Internet, (Hart Publishing) 3rd ed., 2009, Bloomsbury.
Cited: *Edwards*, The fall & rise of intermediary liability.

Edwards, L.; Veale, M.: Slave to the Algorithm? Why a 'Right to Explanation' Is Probably Not the Remedy You Are Looking For, in: Duke Law & Technology Review 16(1), 2017/18, pp. 18–84.
Cited: *Edwards/Veale*, in: Duke Law & Technology Review 16(1), 2017/18, p. 18, p.

Ehmann, E.; Selmayr, M.: Datenschutz-Grundverordnung: DS-GVO, 2nd ed., 2018, Beck.
Cited: *author* in: Ehmann/Selmayr, Art. para.

Ensthaler, J.; Weidert, S.: Urheberrecht und Internet, 3rd ed., 2017, Deutscher Fachverlag.
Cited: *author* in: Ensthaler/Weidert.

Etteldorf, C.: EDPB on the Interplay between the ePrivacy Directive and the GDPR, in: European Data Protection Law Review (EDPL) 5(2), 2019, pp. 224–231.
Cited: *Etteldorf*, in: EDPL 5(2), 2019, p. 224, p.

European Commission: Defining a framework for the monitoring of advertising rules under the Audiovisual Media Services Directive, study prepared for the European Commission by Ramboll Management Consulting and the Institute of European Media Law, available at https://ec.europa.eu/digital-single-market/en/news/audiovisual-and-media-services-directive-avmsd-study-advertising-rules.
Cited: Defining a framework for the monitoring of advertising rules under the Audiovisual Media Services Directive, study prepared for the European Commission by Ramboll Management Consulting and the Institute of European Media Law.

European Commission: AVMS-RADAR: AudioVisual Media Services – Regulatory Authorities' Independence and Efficiency Review, Update on recent changes and developments in Member States and Candidate Countries that are relevant for the analysis of independence and efficient functioning of audiovisual media services regulatory bodies (SMART 2013/0083), study prepared for the Commission DG CNECT by the EMR and the University of Luxembourg, available at https://op.europa.eu/de/publication-detail/-/publication/b6e4a837-8775-11e5-b8b7-01aa75ed71a1/language-de.
Cited: AVMS-RADAR, study prepared for the European Commission by the EMR and the University of Luxembourg.

European Regulators Group for Audiovisual Media (ERGA): Report on material jurisdiction in a converged environment, 18 December 2015, available at https://www.die-medienanstalten.de/fileadmin/user_upload/die_medienanstalten/Ueber_uns/Positionen/Europa/Bericht_der_ERGA_zum_materiellen_Anwendungsbereich_der_AVMD-Richtlinie.pdf.
Cited: *ERGA*, Report on material jurisdiction in a converged environment.

European Regulators Group for Audiovisual Media (ERGA): Report on the independence of NRAs, 15 December 2015, available at http://erga-online.eu/wp-content/uploads/2016/10/report_indep_nra_2015.pdf.
Cited: *ERGA*, Report on the independence of NRAs.

European Regulators Group for Audiovisual Media (ERGA): Report on the protection of minors in a converged environment, 27 November 2015, available at http://erga-online.eu/wp-content/uploads/2016/10/report_minors_2015.pdf.
Cited: *ERGA*, Report on the protection of minors in a converged environment.

European Regulators Group for Audiovisual Media (ERGA): Report on territorial jurisdiction in a converged environment, 17 May 2016, available at http://erga-online.eu/wp-content/uploads/2016/10/report_territ_2016.pdf.
Cited: *ERGA*, Report on territorial jurisdiction in a converged environment.

European Regulators Group for Audiovisual Media (ERGA): Report on Protection of Minors in the Audiovisual Media Services: Trends & Practices, 19 April 2017, available at http://erga-online.eu/wp-content/uploads/2016/10/ERGA-PoM-Report-2017-wordpress.pdf.
Cited: *ERGA*, Report on Protection of Minors in the Audiovisual Media Services: Trends & Practices.

European Regulators Group for Audiovisual Media (ERGA): Report of the activities carried out to assist the European Commission in the intermediate monitoring of the Code of practice on disinformation, June 2019, available at http://erga-online.eu/wp-content/uploads/2019/06/ERGA-2019-06_Report-intermediate-monitoring-Code-of-Practice-on-disinformation.pdf.
Cited: *ERGA*, Report of the activities carried out to assist the European Commission in the intermediate monitoring of the Code of practice on disinformation.

Everling, U.: Durch die Grundrechtecharta zurück zu Solange, in: Europäische Zeitschrift für Wirtschaftsrecht (EuZW) 8/2003, p. 225.
Cited: *Everling*, in: EuZW 8/2003, p. 225.

Finck, M.: Digital co-regulation: designing a supranational legal framework for the platform economy, in: LSE Law, Society and Economy Working Papers (15/2017).
Cited: *Finck*, in: LSE Law, Society and Economy Working Papers (15/2017).

Freeman, J.: Consumer Legislation and E-Commerce Challenges, in: Italian Antitrust Review 2(1), 2015, pp. 75–82.
Cited: *Freeman*, in: Italian Antitrust Review 2(1), 2015; p. 75, p.

Frenz, W.: Handbuch Europarecht, 2nd ed., 2012, Springer.
Cited: *Frenz*: Handbuch Europarecht.

Freytag, S.: Digital Millennium Copyright Act und europäisches Urheberrecht für die Informationsgesellschaft, in: Multimedia und Recht (MMR) 4/1999, pp. 207–212.
Cited: *Freytag*, MMR 4/2019, p. 207, p.

Friedmann, D.: Sinking the safe harbour with the legal certainty of strict liability in sight, in: Journal of Intellectual Property Law and Practice 9(2), 2014, pp. 148–155.
Cited: *Friedmann*, in Journal of Intellectual Property Law and Practice 9(2), 2014, p. 148, p.

Furnémont, J.; Smokvina, T. K.: European co-regulation practices in the media, comparative analysis and recommendations with a focus on the situation in Serbia, study commissioned by the Council of Europe at the request of Serbia's national regulatory authority, available at https://rm.coe.int/european-co-regulatio n-practices-in-the-media/16808c9c74.
Cited: *Furnémont/Smokvina*, European co-regulation practices in the media, comparative analysis and recommendations with a focus on the situation in Serbia.

Frosio, G.: Reforming Intermediary Liability in the Platform Economy: A European Digital Single Market Strategy, in: Northwestern University Law Review 112, 2017, pp. 20–45.
Cited: *Frosio*, in: Northwestern University Law Review 112, 2017, p. 20, p.

Frosio, G.; Mendis, S.: Monitoring and Filtering: European Reform or Global Trend?, in: Centre for International Intellectual Property Studies (CEIPI), Research Paper No. 2019-05, available at https://papers.ssrn.com/sol3/papers.cfm?a bstract_id=3411615.
Cited: *Frosio/Mendis*, Monitoring and Filtering: European Reform or Global Trend?

Grabenwarter, C.: Die Charta der Grundrechte für die Europäische Union, in: Deutsches Verwaltungsblatt (DVBl) 2001, pp. 1–13.
Cited: *Grabenwarter*, in: DVBl. 2001, p. 1, p.

Hans, S.; Ukrow, J.; Knapp, D.; Cole, M. D.: (Neue) Geschäftsmodelle der Mediaagenturen, EMR/Script, vol. 4, available at https://emr-sb.de/wp-content/uploads/2018/04/EMR-SCRIPT-Band-4.pdf.
Cited: *Hans/Ukrow/Knapp/Cole*, Neue Geschäftsmodelle der Mediaagenturen.

Harrison, J.; Woods, L.: European Broadcasting Law and Policy, 2007, Cambridge University Press.
Cited: *Harrison/Woods*, European Broadcasting Law and Policy.

Hartstein, R.; Ring. W.; Kreile, J.; Dörr, D.; Stettner, R.; Cole, M. D.; Wagner, E. E. (eds.): Rundfunkstaatsvertrag Jugendmedienschutz-Staatsvertrag, Handkommentar, 81th ed., 2019, C. F. Müller.
Cited: *author* in: HK-RStV.

Hatzopoulos, V.: The Collaborative Economy and EU Law, (Hart Publishing ed.) 2018, Bloomsbury.
Cited: *Hatzopoulos*, The Collaborative Economy and EU Law.

Helberger, N.; Pierson, J.; Poell, T.: Governing Online Platforms: From Contested to Cooperative Responsibility, in: The Information Society 34(1), 2018, pp. 1–14.
Cited: *Helberger/Pierson/Poell*, in: The Information Society 34(1), 2018, p. 1, p.

Helman, L.; Parchomovsky, G.: The Best Available Technology Standard, in: Columbia Law Review 111(6), 2011, pp. 1194–1243.
Cited: *Helman/Parchomovsky*, in: Columbia Law Review 111(6), 2011, p. 1194, p.

Henrich, J.: Nach der Abstimmung ist (fast) vor der Umsetzung – Ein kurzer Einblick in die Bedeutung der „Upload-Filter" Regelung der Richtlinie über das Urheberrecht im digitalen Binnenmarkt, in: EMR – das aktuelle Stichwort, 2019, available at https://emr-sb.de/wp-content/uploads/2019/04/EMR-Aktuelles-Stichwort-EU-Urheberrechtsreform.pdf.
Cited: *Henrich*, Nach der Abstimmung ist (fast) vor der Umsetzung.

Herold, A.: Country of Origin Principle in the EU Market for Audiovisual Media Services: Friend or Foe?, in: Journal of Consumer Policy 31(1), 2008, pp. 5–24.
Cited: *Herold*, in: Journal of Consumer Policy 31(1), 2008, p. 5, p.

Hofmann, H.: Delegation, Discretion and the Duty of Care in the Case Law of the Court of Justice of the European Union, University of Luxembourg Law Working Paper No. 2018-004, 2018, available at https://ssrn.com/abstract=3169744.
Cited: *Hofmann*, Delegation, Discretion and the Duty of Care in the Case Law of the Court of Justice of the European Union.

Hörnle, J.: Country of Origin Regulation in Cross-Border Media: One Step Beyond the Freedom to Provide Services?, in: International and Comparative Law Quarterly 54(1), 2005, pp. 89–126.
Cited: *Hörnle*, in: International and Comparative Law Quarterly 54(1), 2005, p. 89, p.

Jaeckel, L.: Schutzpflichten im deutschen und europäischen Recht, Eine Untersuchung der deutschen Grundrechte, der Menschenrechte und Grundfreiheiten der EMRK sowie der Grundrechte und Grundfreiheiten der Europäischen Gemeinschaf, 2001, Nomos.
Cited: *Jaeckel*, Schutzpflichten im deutschen und europäischen Recht.

Jaensch, M.: Die unmittelbare Drittwirkung der Grundfreiheiten. Untersuchung der Verpflichtung von Privatpersonen durch Art. 30, 48, 52, 59, 73b EGV, 1997, Nomos.
Cited: *Jaensch*, Die unmittelbare Drittwirkung der Grundfreiheiten.

Nielsen, C. and others: Study on the Economic Impact of the Electronic Commerce Directive, 2007, Copenhagen Economics (DG Internal Market and Services, European Commission 2007)
Cited: *Nielsen and others*, Study on the Economic Impact of the Electronic Commerce Directive.

Keller, D.: The Right Tools: Europe's Intermediary Liability Laws and the EU 2016 General Data Protection Regulation, in: Berkeley Technology Law Journal 33(1), 2018, pp. 287–364.
Cited: *Keller*, in: Berkeley Technology Law Journal 33(1), 2018, p. 287, p.

Kilkelly, U.: The right to respect for private and family life, A guide to the implementation of Article 8 of the European Convention on Human Rights, Human rights handbook No. 1, 2001, available at https://rm.coe.int/168007ff47.
Cited: *Kilkelly*, Human rights handbook No. 1.

Kirtiklis, K.: Manuel Castell's theory of information society as media theory, in: Lingua Posnaniensis 59(1), 2017, pp. 65–77, available at https://www.degruyter.com/downloadpdf/j/linpo.2017.59.issue-1/linpo-2017-0006/linpo-2017-0006.pdf.
Cited: *Kirtiklis*, in: Lingua Posnaniensis 59(1), p. 65, p.

Klatt, M.: Positive Obligations under the European Convention on Human Rights, in: Zeitschrift für ausländisches Öffentliches Recht und Völkerrecht (ZaöRV) 71, 2011, pp. 691–718.
Cited: *Klatt*, in: ZaöRV 71, 2011, p. 69, p.

Koenen, T.: Wirtschaft und Menschenrechte, Staatliche Schutzpflichten auf der Basis regionaler und internationaler Menschenrechtsverträge, 2012, Drucker & Humboldt.
Cited: *Koenen*, Wirtschaft und Menschenrechte.

Kogler, M.: Audiovisuelle Mediendienste-Richtlinie, in: Kommunikation und Recht (K&R) 9/2018, pp. 537–544.
Cited: *Kogler*, in: K&R 9/2018, p. 537, p.

Koopman, C.; Mitchell, M.; Thierer, A.: The Sharing Economy and Consumer Protection Regulation: The Case for Policy Change, in: The Journal of Business, Entrepreneurship & the Law 8(2), 2015, pp. 529–545.
Cited: *Koopman/Mitchell/Thierer*, in: The Journal of Business, Entrepreneurship & the Law 8(2), 2015, p. 529, p.

Korte, S.: Die Geldtransport-Verordnung – Sinnvoller Rechtsakt im falschen Gewand?, in: Gewerbearchiv (GewArch) 6, 2013, pp. 230–235.
Cited: *Korte*, in: GewArch 6, 2013, p. 230, p.

Kuczerawy, A.: EU Proposal for a Directive on Copyright in the Digital Single Market: Compatibility of Article 13 with the EU Intermediary Liability Regime, in: Petkova, B.; Ojanen, T. (eds.), Fundamental Rights Protection Online: The Future Regulation of Intermediaries, 2019 (forthcoming), available at https://ssrn.com/abstract=3309099.
Cited: *Kuczerawy*, EU Proposal for a Directive on Copyright in the Digital Single Market: Compatibility of Article 13 with the EU Intermediary Liability Regime.

Lenski, S.: Öffentliches Kulturrecht. Materielle und immaterielle Kulturwerke zwischen Schutz, Förderung und Wertschöpfung, 2013, Mohr Siebeck.
Cited: *Lenski*, Öffentliches Kulturrecht.

Lievens, E.: Protecting Children in the Digital Era: The Use of Alternative Regulatory Instruments, (International Studies in Human Rights, Vol. 105) 2010, Brill.
Cited: *Lievens*, Protecting Children in the Digital Era: The Use of Alternative Regulatory Instruments.

Lodder, A. R.; Murray, A. D.: EU Regulation of E-Commerce: A Commentary, (Elgar Commentaries series) 2017, Edward Elgar.
Cited: *Lodder/Murray*, EU Regulation of E-Commerce: A Commentary.

Löffler, M.: Presserecht, vol. 6, 2015, Beck.
Cited: *Löffler*, Presserecht, §, para.

Ludwigs, M.: Dezentralisierung der Europäischen Beihilfenkontrolle: Ein Dilemma für den Beihilfeempfänger?, in: Europäische Zeitschrift für Wirtschaftsrecht (EuZW) 19/2004, p. 577.
Cited: *Ludwigs*, in: EuZW 19/2004), p. 577.

Marsden, C.: Internet Co-Regulation: European Law, Regulatory Governance and Legitimacy in Cyberspace, 2011, Cambridge University Press.
Cited: *Marsden*, European Law, Regulatory Governance and Legitimacy in Cyberspace.

Martens, B.: An Economic Policy Perspective on Online Platforms, in: Institute for Prospective Technological Studies (ed.), Digital Economy Working Paper 2016/05, 2016, available at https://ec.europa.eu/jrc/sites/jrcsh/files/JRC101501.pdf.
Cited: *Martens*, An Economic Policy Perspective on Online Platforms.

McCrudden, C.: Human Dignity and Judicial Interpretation of Human Rights, in: European Journal of International Law (EJIL) 19(4), 2008, pp. 655–724.
Cited: *McCrudden*, in: EJIL 19(4), 2008, p. 655, p.

Meyer-Ladewig, J.; Nettesheim, M.; von Raumer, S. (eds.): EMRK Europäische Menschenrechtskonvention, Handkommentar, vol. 4, 2017, Nomos.
Cited: *author* in: Meyer-Ladewig/Nettesheim/von Raumer, Art., para.

Moore, M.; Tambini, D. (eds.): Digital Dominance – The Power of Google, Amazon, Facebook, and Apple, 2018, Oxford University Press.
Cited: *Moore/Tambini (eds.)*, Digital Dominance – The Power of Google, Amazon, Facebook, and Apple.

Naughton, J.: Platform Power and Responsibility in the Attention Economy, in: Moore, M.; Tambini, D. (eds.), Digital Dominance – The Power of Google, Amazon, Facebook, and Apple, 2018, Oxford University Press, pp. 371–395.
Cited: *Naughton*, Platform Power and Responsibility in the Attention Economy.

Nikoltchev, S. (ed.): Protection of Minors and Audiovisual Content On-Demand, European Audiovisual Observatory, IRIS plus, Strasbourg 2012, available at https://rm.coe.int/1680783db7.
Cited: *Nikoltchev (ed.)*, Protection of Minors and Audiovisual Content On-Demand, IRIS plus 2012.

Nolte, G.; Wimmers, J.: Wer stört? Gedanken zur Haftung von Intermediären im Internet – von praktischer Konkordanz, richtigen Anreizen und offenen Fragen, in: Zeitschrift für gewerblichen Rechtsschutz und Urheberrecht (GRUR) 16(1), 2014, pp. 16–27.
Cited: *Nolte/Wimmers*, in: GRUR 16(1), 2014, p. 16, p.

Nordemann, J. B.: Liability of Online Service Providers for Copyrighted Content – Regulatory Action Needed?, In-Depth Analysis for the IMCO Committee, 2018.
Cited: *Nordemann*, Liability of Online Service Providers for Copyrighted Content.

Ohiagu, O. P.: The Internet: The Medium of the Mass Media, in: Kiabara Journal of Humanities 16(2), 2011, pp. 225–232.
Cited: *Ohiagu*, in: Kiabara Journal of Humanities 16(2), 2011, p. 225, p.

Ory, S.: Datenschutz und Datensicherheit in Medienunternehmen, in: UFITA 82(1), 2018, pp. 131–169.
Cited: *Ory*, UFITA 82(1), 2018, p. 131, p.

Pechstein, M.; Nowak, C.; Häde, U.: Frankfurter Kommentar zu EUV, GRC und AEUV, 2017, Mohr Siebeck.
Cited: *author* in: Pechstein/Nowak/Häde, Art., para.

Penski, U.; Elsner, R.: Siegen, Eigentumsgewährleistung und Berufsfreiheit als Gemeinschaftsgrundrechte in der Rechtsprechung des Europäischen Gerichtshofs, in: Zeitschrift für Öffentliches Recht und Verwaltungswissenschaften (DöV) 7/2001, pp. 265–274.
Cited: *Penski/Elsner*, in: DöV 7/2001, p. 265, p.

Perrin, W.; Woods, L.: Reducing Harm in Social Media through a Duty of Care, Carnegie UK Trust, 8 May 2018, available at https://www.carnegieuktrust.org.uk /blog/reducing-harm-social-media-duty-care.
Cited: *Perrin/Woods*, Reducing Harm in Social Media through a Duty of Care.

Peukert, W.: Der Schutz des Eigentums nach Art. 1 des Ersten Zusatzprotokolls zur Europäischen Menschenrechtskonvention, in: Europäische Grundrechte-Zeitschrift (EuGRZ) 1981, pp. 97 et seq.
Cited: *Peukert*, in: EuGRZ 1981, p. 97, p.

Quintel, T.; Ullrich, C.: Self-Regulation of Fundamental Rights? The EU Code of Conduct on Hate Speech, Related Initiatives and Beyond, in: Petkova, B.; Ojanen, T. (eds.), Fundamental Rights Protection Online: The Future Regulation Of Intermediaries, 2019, Edward Elgar (forthcoming), available at https://ssrn.co m/abstract=3298719.
Cited: *Quintel/Ullrich*, Self-Regulation of Fundamental Rights? The EU Code of Conduct on Hate Speech, Related Initiatives and Beyond.

Ress, G.: Supranationaler Menschenrechtsschutz und der Wandel der Staatlichkeit, in: Zeitschrift für ausländisches Öffentliches Recht und Völkerrecht (ZaöRV) 64, 2004, pp. 621–639.
Cited: *Ress*, in: ZaöRV 64, 2004, p. 621, p.

Rhee, R. J.: The Tort Foundation of Duty of Care and Business Judgment, in: Notre Dame Law Review 88(3), 2013, pp. 1138–1198.
Cited: *Rhee*, in: Notre Dame Law Review 88(3), 2013, p. 1138, p.

Rosati, E.: The CJEU Pirate Bay judgement and its impact on the liability of online platforms, in: European Intellectual Property Review 39(12), 2017, pp. 737–748.
Cited: *Rosati*, in: European Intellectual Property Review 39(12), 2017, p. 737, p.

Rowland, D.; Kohl, U.; Charlesworth, A.: Information Technology Law, 4th ed., 2012, Routledge.
Cited: *Rowland/Kohl/Charlesworth*, Information Technology Law.

Sartor, G.: Providers Liability: From the eCommerce Directive to the future, in-depth analysis for the IMCO Committee, 2017, available at http://www.europarl .europa.eu/RegData/etudes/IDAN/2017/614179/IPOL_IDA(2017)614179_EN.pd f.
Cited: *Sartor*, Providers Liability: From the eCommerce Directive to the future.

Savin, A.: Electronic Services with a Non-Electronic Component and Their Regulation in EU Law, in: Journal of Internet Law 23(3), 2019, pp. 1–27.
Cited: *Savin*, in: Journal of Internet Law 23(3), 2019, p. 1, p.

Savin, A.: EU Internet Law, (Elgar European Law series) 2nd ed., 2017, Edward Elgar.
Cited: *Savin*, EU Internet Law.

Schantz, P.: Die Datenschutz-Grundverordnung – Beginn einer neuen Zeitrechnung im Datenschutzrecht, in: Neue Juristische Wochenschrift (NJW) 26(69), 2016, pp. 1841–1847.
Cited: *Schantz*, in: NJW 26(69), 2016, p. 1841, p.

Schepel, H.: Constitutionalising the Market, Marketising the Constitution, and to Tell the Difference: On the Horizontal Application of the Free Movement Provisions in EU Law, in: European Law Journal (ELJ) 18(2), 2012, pp. 177–200.
Cited: *Schepel*, in ELJ 18(2), 2012, p. 177, p.

Schmidt-Kessel, M.; Erler, K.; Grimm, A.; Kramme, M.: Die Richtlinienvorschläge der Kommission zu digitalen Inhalten und Online-Handel – Teil 1, in: Zeitschrift für das Privatrecht der Europäischen Union (ZPEU) 13(1), 2016, pp. 2–8.
Cited: *Schmidt-Kessel/Erler/Grimm/Kramme*, in: ZPEU 13(1), 2016, p. 2, p.

Schulz, W.: „Menschenwürde" im Konzept der Regulierung digitaler Gewaltdarstellungen, in: Medien & Kommunikationswissenschaft (M&K) 48(3), 2000, pp. 354–370.
Cited: *Schulz*, in: M&K 48(3), 2000, p. 354, p.

Schulz, W.; Held, T.: Regulated Self-regulation as a Form of Modern Government: An Analysis of Case Studies from Media and Telecommunications Law, 2004, John Libbey.
Cited: *Schulz/Held*, Regulated Self-regulation as a Form of Modern Government.

Schwarz, C.: Web search engines, in: Journal of the American Society for Information Science 49(11), 1998, pp. 973–982.
Cited: *Schwarz*, in: Journal of the American Society for Information Science 49(11), 1998, p. 973, p.

Senden, L. A. J.; Kica, E.; Hiemstra, M.; Klinger, M.: Mapping Self- and Co-regulation. Approaches in the EU Context, Explorative Study for the European Commission, DG Connect, 2015, available at https://www.eesc.europa.eu/en/documents/mapping-self-and-co-regulation-approaches-eu-context.
Cited: *Senden et al.*, Mapping Self- and Co-regulation. Approaches in the EU Context.

Senftleben, M.; Angelopoulos, C.; Frosio, G.; Moscon, V.; Peguera, M.; Rognstad, O.: The Recommendation on Measures to Safeguard Fundamental Rights and the Open Internet in the Framework of the EU Copyright Reform, in: European Intellectual Property Review 40(3) 2018, pp. 149–163, available at https://research.vu.nl/ws/portalfiles/portal/56655974.
Cited: *Senftleben et al.*, in: European Intellectual Property Review 40(3), 2018, p. 149, p.

Seufert, W. (ed.): Media Economics revisited: (Wie) Verändert das Internet die Ökonomie der Medien?, 2018, Nomos.
Cited: *Seufert (ed.)*, Media Economics revisited: (Wie) Verändert das Internet die Ökonomie der Medien?

Sjurts, I. (ed.): Gabler Lexikon Medienwirtschaft. 2011, Gabler.
Cited: *Sjurts* (ed.), Gabler Lexikon Medienwirtschaft.

Sørensen, K. E.: The Country-of-Origin Principle and Balancing Jurisdiction Between Home Member States and Host Member State, in: Nordic & European Company Law, LSN Research Paper Series No. 16-32.
Cited: *Sørensen*, in: Nordic & European Company Law, LSN Research Paper Series No. 16-32.

Soppe, M.: Datenverarbeitungen zu journalistischen Zwecken – das datenschutzrechtliche Medienprivileg in der Verlagspraxis, in: Zeitschrift für Urheber- und Medienrecht (ZUM) 63(6), 2019, pp. 467–472.
Cited: *Soppe*, in: ZUM 63(6), 2019, p. 467, p.

Steindorff-Classen: Europäischer Kinderrechtsschutz nach dem EU-Reformvertrag von Lissabon, in: Zeitschrift für Europarecht (EuR) 46(1), 2011, pp. 19–38.
Cited: *Steindorff-Classen*, in: EuR 46(1), 2011, p. 19, p.

Stern, K.; Sachs, M.: Europäische Grundrechte-Charta: GRCh, 2016, Beck.
Cited: *author* in: Stern/Sachs, Art., para.

Stöger, K.: Gedanken zur Institutionellen Autonomie der Mitgliedstaaten am Beispiel der neuen Energieregulierungsbehörden, in: Zeitschrift für öffentliches Recht (ZöR) 65(2), 2010, pp. 247–267.
Cited: *Stöger*, in: ZöR 65(2), 2010, p. 247, p.

Streintz, R.: EUV/AEUV, Vertrag über die Europäische Union, Vertrag über die Arbeitsweise der Europäischen Union, Charta der Grundrechte der Europäischen Union, 3rd ed., 2018, Beck.
Cited: *author* in: Streintz, Art., para.

Streintz, R., Michl, W., Die Drittwirkung des europäischen Datenschutzgrundrechts (Art. 8 GRCh) im deutschen Privatrecht, in: Europäische Zeitschrift für Wirtschaftsrecht (EuZW), 10, 2011, pp. 384-387.
Cited: *Streintz/Michl*, EuZW 2011, 384, p

Sydow, G.: Europäische Datenschutzgrundverordnung, Handkommentar, 2nd ed., 2018, Nomos.
Cited: *author* in: Sydow, Art., para.

Taddeo, M.; Floridi, L.: The Debate on the Moral Responsibilities of Online Service Providers, in: Science and Engineering Ethics 22(6), 2016, pp. 1575–1603.
Cited: *Taddeo/Floridi*, in: Science and Engineering Ethics 22(6), 2016, p. 1575, p.

Technopolis Group: Ex-post evaluation of the application of the market surveillance provisions of Regulation (EC) No 765/2008, available at https://op.europa.eu/en/publication-detail/-/publication/473872dd-12cc-11e8-9253-01aa75ed71a1/language-en.
Cited: *Technopolis Group*, Ex-post evaluation of the application of the market surveillance provisions of Regulation (EC) No 765/2008.

Ullrich, C.: A risk-based approach towards infringement prevention on the internet: Adopting the antimoney laundering framework to online platforms, in: International Journal of Law and Information Technology 26(3), 2018, pp. 226–251.
Cited: *Ullrich*, in: International Journal of Law and Information Technology 26(3), 2018, p. 226, p.

Ullrich, C.: New Approach meets new economy: Enforcing EU product safety in e-commerce, in: Maastricht Journal of European and Comparative Law 26(4), 2019, pp. 558–584.
Cited: *Ullrich*, in: Maastricht Journal of European and Comparative Law 26(4), 2019, p. 558, p.

Ukrow, J.: Jenseits der Grenze – Rechtspopulismus in Polen und Ungarn, in: vorgänge No. 224, 4/2018, pp. 57–75. Cited: *Ukrow*, in: vorgänge No. 224, 4/2018, p. 57, p.

Ukrow, J.: Por-No Go im audiovisuellen Binnenmarkt? Jugendmedienschutz im Level-Playing-Field und die geplante Abkehr vom absoluten Pornographieverbot im Fernsehen, EMR, 2017, available at https://emr-sb.de/wp-content/uploads/2017/10/EMR-AVMD-Impulse-1710-01-Jugendschutz.pdf.
Cited: *Ukrow*, Por-No Go im audiovisuellen Binnenmarkt?

Ukrow, J., with contributions by Cole, M. and Broy, D.: Zur Zuständigkeit der Landesmedienanstalten/KJM für ausländische Anbieter – Eine rechtswissenschaftliche Untersuchung unter besonderer Berücksichtigung völker-, europa- und rechtsvergleichender Aspekte, 2017 (legal study not yet published).
Cited: *Ukrow*, Zuständigkeit der Landesmedienanstalten/KJM für ausländische Anbieter.

Ukrow, J.; Cole, M. D., with contributions by Etteldorf, C. and Henrich, J.: Aktive Sicherung lokaler und regionaler Vielfalt. Rechtliche Möglichkeiten und Grenzen der Förderung inhaltlicher Qualität in Presse-, Rundfunk- und Online-Angeboten, (Schriftenreihe der Thüringer Landesmedienanstalt, vol. 25) 2019, Vistas.
Cited: *Ukrow/Cole*, Aktive Sicherung lokaler und regionaler Vielfalt.

Ukrow, J.; Etteldorf, C.: „Fake News" als Rechtsproblem, EMR/Script, vol. 5, available at https://emr-sb.de/wp-content/uploads/2018/04/EMR-SCRIPT-Band-5_Fake-News-als-Rechtsproblem.pdf.
Cited: *Ukrow/Etteldorf*, „Fake News" als Rechtsproblem.

Valcke, P.; Kuczerawy, A.; Ombelet, P.: Did the Romans Get it Right? What Delfi, Google, eBay, and UPC TeleKabel Wien Have in Common, in: Floridi, L.; Taddeo, M. (eds.), The Responsibilities of Online Service Providers, 2016, Springer.
Cited: *Valcke/Kuczerawy/Ombelet*, Did the Romans Get it Right? What Delfi, Google, eBay, and UPC TeleKabel Wien Have in Common.

van Eecke, P.; Truyens, M.: EU study on the Legal Analysis of a Single Market for the Information Society, New Rules for a New Age?, SMART 2007/0037, 2009, available at https://ec.europa.eu/digital-single-market/en/news/legal-analysis-sing le-market-information-society-smart-20070037.
Cited: *van Eecke/Truyens*, Legal analysis of a Single Market for the Information Society.

van Gestel, R.; Micklitz, H. W.: European Integration through Standardization: How Judicial Review Is Breaking down the Club House of Private Standardization Bodies, in: Common Market Law Review 50(1), 2013, pp. 145–182.
Cited: van *Gestel/Micklitz*, in: Common Market Law Review 50(1), 2013, p. 145, p.

van Hoboken, J.; Zuiderveen Borgesius, F.: Scoping Electronic Communication Privacy Rules: Data, Services and Values, in: JIPITEC 6(3), 2015, pp. 198–210.
Cited: *van Hoboken/Zuiderveen Borgesius*, in: JIPITEC 6(3), 2015, p. 198, p.

van Hoboken, J.; Quintas, J. P.; Poort, J.: Hosting intermediary services and illegal content, an analysis of the scope or article 14 ECD in light of developments in the online service landscape, study prepared for the European Commission by the Institute for Information Law (IViR), SMART 2018/0033, 2018.
Cited: *van Hoboken/Quintas/Poort*, Hosting intermediary services and illegal content.

Verbiest, T.; Spindler, G.; Riccio, G. M.: Study on the Liability of Internet Intermediaries, Markt/2006/09/E, 2007.
Cited: *Verbiest/Spindler/Riccio*, Study on the Liability of Internet Intermediaries.

von Rimscha, B.; Siegert, G.: Medienökonomie. Eine problemorientierte Einführung, 2015, Springer.
Cited: *von Rimscha/Siegert*, Medienökonomie.

von Schwichow, L.: Die Menschenwürde in der EMRK, 2016, Mohr Siebeck.
Cited: *von Schwichow*. Die Menschenwürde in der EMRK.

Vedder, C.; Heintschel von Heinegg, W.: Europäisches Unionsrecht, vol. 2, 2018, Nomos.
Cited: *author* in: Vedder/Heintschel von Heinegg, Art., para.

Wagner, B.: Global Free Expression – Governing the Boundaries of Internet Content, 2016, Springer.
Cited: *Wagner*, Global Free Expression – Governing the Boundaries of Internet Content.

Waisman, A.; Hevia, M.: Theoretical Foundations of Search Engine Liability, in: International Review of Industrial Property and Copyright Law 42(7), 2011, pp. 785–803.
Cited: *Waisman/Hevia*, in: International Review of Industrial Property and Copyright Law 42(7), 2011, p. 785, p.

Waldheim, S. J.: Dienstleistungsfreiheit und Herkunftslandprinzip. Prinzipielle Möglichkeiten und primärrechtliche Grenzen der Liberalisierung eines integrierten europäischen Binnenmarktes für Dienstleistungen, 2008, Cuvillier.
Cited: *Waldheim*, Dienstleistungsfreiheit und Herkunftslandprinzip.

Walk, F.: Das Herkunftsprinzip der E-Commerce-Richtlinie: Art. 3 der Richtlinie 2000/31/EG und seine Umsetzung im deutschen Recht, 2002, Herbert Utz.
Cited: *Walk*, Das Herkunftslandprinzip der E-Commerce-Richtlinie.

Wolff, A. H.; Brink, S.: Beck'scher Online-Kommentar Datenschutzrecht, 19th ed., 2019, Beck.
Cited: *author* in: Wolff/Brink, Art., para.

Woods, L.: Duty of care, in: InterMEDIA 46(4), 2018/19, pp. 17–21.
Cited: *Woods*, in: InterMEDIA 46(4), 2018/19, p. 17, p.

Zuboff, S.: The Age of Surveillance Capitalism: The Fight for a Human Future at the New Frontier of Power, 2019, Profile Books.
Cited: *Zuboff*, The Age of Surveillance Capitalism: The Fight for a Human Future at the New Frontier of Power.